Choral Speaking
and the
Verse Choir

Choral Speaking and the Verse Choir

E. Kingsley Povenmire

Graphics by Dale Burnett Mann

South Brunswick and New York:
A. S. Barnes and Company
London: Thomas Yoseloff Ltd

© 1975 by A. S. Barnes and Co.

A. S. Barnes and Co., Inc.
Cranbury, New Jersey 08512

Thomas Yoseloff Ltd
108 New Bond Street
London W1Y OQX, England

Library of Congress Cataloging in Publication Data

Povenmire, E   Kingsley.
　　Choral speaking and the verse choir.
　　Bibliography: p.
　　1. Choral speaking. I. Title.
PN4193.C5P6　　808.5'5　　73-116
ISBN 0-498-01191-7

This effort is gratefully dedicated
to my wife, our two sons,
and to all my students and other co-workers

Contents

Foreword

From Hebrew and Egyptian and Greek rites of ancient times to the chorus that performs annually in the classical plays at Epidaurus during our own time, history has recorded man's enjoyment of speaking aloud in unison. But even those whose experience with choral speaking is limited to saying the Pledge of Allegiance know that the difficulties of being intelligible, to say nothing of being artistic, are formidable. Perhaps that is the reason some teachers of oral interpretation avoid choral work. They recognize that a group must function with the unity of a single reader, communicating all of the elements of a literary work of art successfully to an audience as a viable oral experience. Since the difficulty of achieving a satisfactory performance with a single interpreter is great, the implications for reaching the same level with many readers performing together are obvious. Fortunately, as with many problems in art, when proper understanding is coupled with logical procedures, the difficulties are more apparent than real. As Professor Wallace Bacon of the Department of Interpretation at Northwestern University states, "... a good speech choir, fully rehearsed, in agreement on meanings, attitudes, and implications, moving in unison with the flow of the structure of a work of literature, can be a highly expressive instrument."

It is a matter for rejoicing to those who know and admire his work, that after devoting twenty-five years of his distinguished professional life to choral speaking, Professor E. Kingsley Povenmire has distilled his knowledge and experience with this form of interpretation into a book which promises to be a definitive work. It is a practical handbook of clear-cut procedures and materials that can fill with confidence those teachers who can see the possibilities of choral techniques but are hesitant to try them. The book is also a sound presentation of the semantics, history, philosophy, and aesthetics of choral speaking for experienced teachers who wish to probe more deeply into these aspects of the medium. The work is an anthology for those who need materials especially selected for effective choral presentation, graded for age interest, and skillfully arranged for various voice timbres. Its range includes chapters on voice and diction as they relate to choral speaking, the recreational aspects, and even the relationship of the art to religion. It contains the only full survey of choral speaking activities in American educational institutions.

Most of all, for those of us who feel a bond of deep personal friendship and respect for "King," as we know him, this book is a synthesis of his wisdom, humor, charm, compassion, and integrity. If these adjectives sound effusive, one has only to question the more than 5,000 students who participated in his choirs and verse-choir directing classes, or the many more thousands who were privileged to participate in the innumerable school assemblies, festivals, workshops, recitals, and seminars he

held so indefatigably and with such splendid results.
Some of them, such as Cleavon Little, have gone on to
brilliant acting careers, others have formed their own
verse choirs of high performance standards, still more
have utilized what they learned from him to enrich their
personal lives with a fuller literary appreciation; all of
them have been indelibly marked by contact with a man
passionately eager to share his zest for savoring life at its
most meaningful levels through literature. In short, this
book is the reflection of an extraordinary man, and is a
significant event in the field of choral speaking.

Dr. William J. Adams
Professor of Speech Communication
San Diego State University

Acknowledgments

I wish to thank the following publishers and individuals for permission to reprint their works:

Richard Armour, Professor of English and Dean of the Faculty Emeritus, Scripps College, Claremont, California, for "I Loved You, California."

L. M. Boyd, Syndicated Writer, for the Boris Pasternak story.

Capitol Association of Retarded Children Newsletter for "Lines from a Home for Mentally Retarded Children" by C. Lynn Nelson.

Elizabeth Dresser, a secondary school teacher who is aware that the wonder and fascination of childhood continues through all ages, for "Baby Horned Toad," "Singing Bushes," "Wind Talk," "Invasion," and "Sky Child."

Fish, a Religious Campus Paper, for "Why, God, Why?"

Mrs. Clarence Anderson for "The Squaw Dance" by Lew Sarett.

Harcourt Brace Jovanovich, Inc., for "Chicago" by Carl Sandburg.

Holt, Rinehart and Winston, Inc., for "The Gift Outright" by Robert Frost.

Holt, Rinehart and Winston, Inc., for "The Odyssey of Runyon Jones" by Norman Corwin.

MacMillan Company for "Sea Fever" and "Cargoes" by John Masefield.

Norman Holmes Pearson, copyright owner, for "Socratic" by Hilda Doolittle.

Random House, Inc. / Alfred A. Knopf, Inc., for "The Negro Speaks of Rivers" by Langston Hughes. Copyright 1926 by Alfred A. Knopf, Inc., and renewed 1954 by Langston Hughes. Reprinted from *Selected Poems*, by Langston Hughes by permission of Alfred A. Knopf, Inc.

Rose Dragon Press for "Ballad of Glory Departed," "Sing then," and "Double Rainbow" by Rachel Harris Campbell.

Mr. John F. Smith, for the Annotated Bibliography of Forty Poems Relating to Four Periods in American History.

Mrs. Sadie Lou Tieri, author of "Non-Controversial-—Peanut Butter."

Every one of the several thousand students and friends who have worked with me over the years in choral speaking in various parts of the country have built themselves into this book. So, if I may follow the example of the venerable Jimmy Durante in saying "goodnight" to Mrs. Calabash, I will broadcast to each and every one of you a sincere "Thank you—wherever you are!"

More recently there are all my students who have participated in the many "circas" of San Diego State Verse

Choirs, the community verse choirs, and the many teachers-in-service who have carried on the work in their classes and schools. Their interest, inspiration, questions and creativity have brought about the results that may make this book helpful to others.

I am further indebted to the members of the Drama Department at San Diego State University for their encouragement and technical advice. These colleagues and friends are: Professor Don Powell (Chairman), Dr. Paul L. Pfaff, Professor Hunton D. Sellman, Dr. Kjell Amble, Dr. C. E. Stephenson, Dr. Gordon S. Howard, Dr. Michael L. Harvey, Dr. Mack Owen, Ms. Alicia Annas, Dr. Merrill J. Leslie, and Mrs. Frances Hill. Their technical advice and helpful criticism have constantly distilled the best of each program to bring about gradual improvement. Similarly, the members of the technical staff, headed by Mr. William Hetkner, contributed their imaginative and willing skills in staging and recording our programs on many important occasions.

Other professors at San Diego State University who have given of their expertise are: Dr. Ivan N. McColom, Dr. Alan C. Nichols, Dr. Claude F. Shouse, Sr., Dr. John R. Theobald and Dr. William J. Adams.

Professors Kenneth K. Jones and Robert E. Lee opened the fine facilities of our University studios and added their own expert help in the production of our records, tapes, and films.

The local radio and television stations, KFMB and KOGO, have welcomed our choirs repeatedly on their programs to our great advantage, giving us broad community coverage and the benefit of the personal encouragement and expertise of their staff members.

How do I adequately thank Professor Albert Johnson,

formerly of the University of Redlands, and his wife, Bertha, for many years of friendship that provided understanding and encouragement to continue to experiment in this field?—Or the Coreys, Orlin and Irene, who have so generously shared their vast knowledge and enthusiasm with me?

Mr. Kenneth L. Farrell, from his position as Chairman of the Music Department and Director of the fine Thomas Downey High School Band of Modesto, California, gave valuable advice on the merging of the two arts of music and choral speaking.

Two California writers have helped immeasurably. One is Norman Corwin, formerly of Universal and Fox Studios, who made two of his warm-hearted radio scripts available to our choir and who visited us to add his personal interest and advice. The other is the prolific writer Richard Armour, Dean of the Faculty, Emeritus, of Scripps College, Claremont, California, who generously made it possible for us to include his delightful "I Loved You, California," which gave a spirited lift to the patriotic series of poems for high schools.

Five of the former students who have added their ideas and enthusiasm are: Mr. Clayton Liggett, Chairman of the Fine Arts Department and Director of the Drama Choros at San Dieguito High School; Mr. James R. Peace, who wrote his M.A. thesis on "The Use of the Verse Choir in High School" and developed an imaginative verse choir at El Cajon Valley High School for a dozen years until his abilities moved him into the principalship of that school; Mr. Arthur Dan Willson, who performs miracles with Junior High students and nonreaders; Mr. Bruce Bikson, who is now developing this work through interschool festivals, and Mr. Walter Cochran, who has written a guide for verse choirs for teachers in the San Diego Unified School District. (And I shall never forget his 10-year-old son, Scott, who collected exactly one ton of newspapers for our drive to buy robes! He was later a valued member of our college choir.)

But perhaps it is the audience members who have contributed the most to this book; the adults who understood deeply and felt warmly, the younger people who unleashed their spirited acceptance, and the *children* whose bright eyes and open hearts complete the circle of human response and prove its on-going miraculous nature.

And finally, to Mrs. Dorothy Vanderhyde, a typist and proofreader par excellence, and to my thousands-of-ways-helpful and forbearing wife, Goldie and sons, "King" and "Rich"—thank you.

Introduction

One evening Boris Pasternak was reading aloud from his works to a huge crowd in an enormous auditorium when, in the middle of a long poem, he accidentally dropped the paper from which he was reading. As he bent to pick it up, a voice from the audience called out the next phrase. Then another voice sang out another phrase—and soon hundreds of voices were rolling in unison. Pasternak, the papers in his hands and his hands at his sides, stood quite still while the entire hall reverberated with his lyrics, in a tide of tribute. [1]

What an overwhelming, soul-deep satisfaction for Pasternak, and it was matched by the exhilerating experience for those hundreds in the audience who joined in this spontaneous chorus. What elation they must have known as each one felt himself carried along, contributing his voice and spirit to the mounting wave of sound and emotion that became the living poem, now completing its cycle to the heart of its creator.

That is choral speaking, the uninhibited joining with others in responding to a piece of literature using the

---

[1] Reported by L. M. Boyd, Syndicate Writer, in *Readers' Digest,* "Personal Glimpses," July, 1971.

speaking voice, trained or untrained, as the instrument—so the experience is open to everyone.

This is not to say that training and rehearsal are not necessary for the richest values to be realized, for indeed they are. While Pasternak's audience spoke in spontaneous unison, a cherished quality in itself, we will hopefully see how the use of other techniques and procedures can bring about a fuller and more varied expression and still retain, even enhance, the vitality of this speech art, which may be called choric speech, choral speaking, verse speaking, verse choir, or many other names.

It takes human response to bring a poem to life; an individual to revel in its beauty as he reads it silently or recalls it from memory, an oral interpreter to present it as a solo, a singer or singers to transform it into the lyric of a song—or a speaking chorus to join voices together to experience the nuances of thought and feeling with which the author has endowed it.

Although each experience fulfills its worthy purpose, the speaking chorus seems to serve the poem most adroitly. It uses the most natural instrument; is capable of a surprisingly wide range of variation; is least likely to be unduly influenced by the formalities of art; and, because it involves many people responding freely, is most likely to find and express the central values envisioned by the author.

Choral speaking is a medium of tremendous potential to excite, exercise, and fulfill the latent ability of all participants to express themselves on several levels of human experience and with varying degrees of artistic achievement as they lose themselves in the depths of the author's work.

That is what this book is really about, the ultimate effect of poetry on the *people* who deal with it: the *author* who creates, the *director* who conceives and structures the interpretation and the *choir members* who bring it to life for the *listeners* who respond.

The materials have been gathering for some three decades of teaching and working with students and others in verse choirs. The suggestions are given in the hope that they may help the many who will use this vital speech art in any of the situations suggested herein, or in those that you may face in your own personal or professional experience.

A word must be said about personal pronouns. The "we" is not the editorial sort. Since choral speaking is above all else a plural experience, "we" refers to everyone involved, for everyone *is* involved and contributes to all that goes on. This includes what I hope will be many thousands of "you."

May we allow the "he" to also include "she" instead of repeating the awkward "and/or"? Similarly "she" sometimes includes "he," especially when referring to teachers.

As for "I"; sometimes I couldn't dodge using I so I just said "I."

For the purpose of clarity may we agree on these two brief definitions:

Choral speaking includes any group speaking together simultaneously, with unity of thought or feeling.

The verse choir designates an organized speaking group using the disciplines of the speech arts to advantage.

The Index should guide you to fuller treatments in the text of other new or nebulous terms. The Bibliography will carry you deeper into any phase of the subject you may wish to follow.

Many other things come crowding to mind but the time has come for the book to speak for itself. I do want it to be helpful to you.

Choral Speaking
and the
Verse Choir

Part One

Definitions, History, and Values

1

What Is Choral Speaking — and the Verse Choir?

A verse choir is nothing, I guess,
　　But a whole lot of people who want to more or less
　　　Talk together—like this:
We have light voices, medium and dark voices, too,
　　We talk all together, or sometimes just a few;
　　　And we'll say a something now if we thought that you
Would like to hear some things to remem-m-m-ber.

This simple ditty may carry more than meets the ear, for it means that the verse choir involves many people who speak together in a way that is sometimes larger than life and at others soft as eiderdown. They are organized to gain variety of expression and they feel a calling to serve whoever will listen to literature that is worth remembering. This seems an altogether worthy proposition.

On a recent tour of the country I found great diversity in organization, techniques of delivery, and purpose in choral groups. And this diversity is prominently displayed in the many groups that have developed in the San Diego area, ranging in size from seven to 200, in age from pre-school to senior citizens, in preparation time from one session to daily classes, and in purpose from recreation through education to spiritual inspiration, with many stops in between. It is truly all things to all people.

There is even no uniformity in the name, for choric speech, choral speaking, group speaking, speech chorus, verse choir, verse-speaking choir, etc., are used interchangeably. There are distinctions that can be clearly made, however, between the groups that fall under the general heading of *choral speaking* and those that can be called *verse choir*. Since the broad term choral speaking encompasses all forms of group speaking it of necessity includes the verse choir, but there are essential differences between the two. First, the groups using choral speaking usually do so as an incidental or secondary function which helps them accomplish their primary purpose, while the primary purpose of the verse choir is to interpret literature. This renders choral speaking general and often unrehearsed while the verse choir is particular and well ordered.

Choral Speaking

Choral speaking in the broader sense would include: a school assembly pledging allegiance to the flag; a congregation praying, reading or speaking aloud together; a street crowd shouting its agreement or rejection in unison; an opera audience shouting *Bravo!*, a football team

yelling *Go!* as it breaks from the huddle, or that half of
the crowd which supports it shouting encouragement on
an exciting play and the other half playing the same role
for the opposing team. All these are unrehearsed and
undirected, and their primary purposes are, in order; to
declare loyalty, to worship, to proclaim their partisan-
ship, to praise a singer, to gain dynamic unity for the
next play, and to vocally support the team of their
choice.

On the other hand the verse choir is dedicated to the
primary purpose of interpreting a poem or prose passage so that an audience can better understand it and
experience a richer emotional response to it. So it must
be carefully organized and rehearsed for this particular
purpose.

We find a further comparison of the two in ancient
Greece in the large Dionysian chorus which annually
celebrated the harvest festival by uninhibited and
nonunison shouting and singing. In doing so, they ap-
proached the state of ecstasy in their worship of
Dionysus, the god of the harvest.[1] This is best described
as choral speaking, being undisciplined.

The verse choir is more nearly like the smaller chorus
of 11 to 15 members which was later employed by the
poet-playwrights to perform in a disciplined way, each
member learning his lines and contributing his part in
unison or antiphonally in a well-rehearsed highly coordinated way.

To bring this analogy into the present we could say
that the one-half of the football crowd wildly cheering
its team resembles the large Dionysian chorus, while the
well-disciplined theatre chorus is represented, in this re-

---

1 *Sheldon Cheney, The Theatre: 3000 Years of Drama, Acting and Stagecraft* (New
York: Longman's, Green & Co., 1929), pp. 32-35.

spect at least, by the cheering section since it is precisely trained and directed by the cheerleaders. In fact, we so often made this analogy that a student asked, "If a cheering section resembles a verse choir why shouldn't the verse choir perform as a cheering section?" So we did, and the resulting cheer was taped and broadcast for the stadium crowds. If this seems to stretch the function of an art too thin let it also be said that it brings the art into a vital relationship to a life situation.

The Verse Choir

We cannot dodge the responsibility to form a working definition that will serve as a guideline to organize any given group into a *verse choir*. So we offer this: *A verse choir is a group of people experiencing a poem together, expressing their thoughts and feelings largely and freely for the purpose of communicating with each other and an audience, being led by a director and adapting themselves to the disciplines of the art of group oral interpretation.*

The essential difference between choral speaking and the verse choir is found in the function of just one person, the director, whose responsibility it is to bring the members of the group to such a mastery of technique that they experience freedom in expressing their chosen literature. He may or may not actually conduct the choir in performance but his influence has brought its members to this level of complex unity. This does not mean that all verse choirs must be formal, stand-up groups, for many directors find imaginative and exciting variations in groupings, movement, and performance techniques.[2]

---

[2] Please see chapters 3 and 5 for more of these variations.

The Drama Choros

The *drama choros* is a striking example of this expanded outgrowth. Indeed, it has developed so far from the traditional "choir" concept as to become an art form in itself. The first drama choros originated at Macalester College in St. Paul, Minnesota, and is more fully described in chapter three. Its director, Professor Mary Gwen Owen, has implemented so many ideas so dynamically that her work stands as a model to inspire others, to explore their own resources.

Mr. Clayton Liggett, who was thus inspired by Professor Owen, has shown great resourcefulness in developing the San Dieguito High School drama choros. He explains:

> Most groups such as ours are called verse choirs or verse theatre groups or something of that nature. I have purposely rejected the word *verse* as being too limiting since we read not only poems but prose and just about anything that is worthwhile in message or artistry. *Drama* seems to open all avenues and of course *choros* is Greek: a dance in a ring, a chorus, which "sets the stage" for our varied groupings and choreography.

Both of these drama choroses use "black books" in performance, making possible such a wide repertoire —but after the first few minutes the audience forgets them and after several performances the students rarely need to refer to them. They know the material "before they know it."

The Readers Theatre

The *readers theatre* is another art form with a close affinity to the verse choir though it cannot be said to have

grown out of that fountainhead. It developed independently from play-reading groups which found pleasure
and enrichment from assigning characters to individuals
for a one-time reading. From this simple beginning its
attractiveness for an audience was soon recognized and
various devices and techniques to heighten the dramatic
effect of the piece were employed, but always within the
bounds of oral interpretation, not acting, and with the
script usually in hand. One such device is a stool with a
swivel top that allowed the reader to turn toward the
audience only when he was "in the scene"; another was
to change groupings with transition movements from
one to another according to the dictates of the dramatic
action. Other more complex techniques grew out of the
creativity of those who worked with this intriguing
theatre art form.

Some readers theatre groups make such extensive use
of group speaking that their affinity to the verse choir is
clearly established. Professor Eugene C. Bahn of Wayne
State University gives us a clear example of this "mutual
aid" relationship in his production of "The Eumenides,"
using his verse-speaking choir class as a stationary group
standing full front to the audience. As the play unfolds
we are aware of smaller groups; the traditional chorus,
the fiery furies, smaller related groups, individuals, and
sometimes the entire cast join in unison. This powerful
production literally shakes an audience.

We must conclude that choral speaking and the verse
choir have many forms and faces which cannot be confined in a single definition. They gain refinement and
pertinence when applied and adapted to the needs and
purposes of various groups, but retaining in each case a
vital entity and function. Chapter two will attempt to
show how this adaptability has served the people of five
periods in history.

2

Highlights in the History of Choral Speaking and the Verse Choir

A quick look at what choral speaking has been and how it has served peoples of other times will help us to understand what it has become.

We need, indeed, to go back farther than the oft-quoted first source, the Greek chorus, to find the true beginning of choral speaking, for it is the primitive peoples who gave birth to this speech art. So we will divide its lifeline into five periods; the *Primitive, Ancient, Medieval, Rediscovery* and *Present-Future.*

Primitive Peoples and the Beginnings of Choral Speaking

Choral Speaking is no new experiment waiting to be tried but a millennia-old natural phenomenon of human behavior which enabled pre-literary people to communicate their thoughts and feelings, such as the elation of victory, supplication for rain, or the mourning for lost ones. It also served such practical needs as maintaining the cadence of the trail or the dynamic rhythm of rowing as each oarsman timed his stroke precisely with the others to gain the magic of maximum power. And it helped them to bring a band of warriors to a state of self-hypnosis and hyperactivity as their rhythmic incantations were accompanied by wild dances.

Fortunately, we can actually hear these sounds in the voices of the contemporary primitive peoples of Africa, South America, and other areas where native culture has been allowed to flourish in its unchanged state. There are some vestiges to be found in the ceremonies of our own North American Indians. Carefully researched and produced motion pictures and televised special documentaries can also bring these authentic sounds to us.

Perhaps the most important contribution of this earliest use of choral speaking was in *proving its authenticity* by demonstrating that it was an effective means of communication and expression. Another is that it gave us the *basic elements* from which later efforts have distilled more refined and complex forms.

The Ancients Refined Choral Speaking

The Golden Age of Greece, which gave us such a rich heritage in all the arts, evolved the most highly developed form of choral speaking to be found in the ancient world. The Greek chorus, as it was used by Aeschylus, Sophocles, and Euripides, was so closely knit into the fabric of their plays that it was an integral part of the total production. Instead of confining and limiting it as an art, this close relation with the other elements of the play gave it a well-defined stature as a vital means of communication, serving at once the author, the actors, and the audience.

It served the author by being a *sounding board* for his lyric passages designed to establish mood and relieve emotional tension, by *describing action* which was best held off-stage and by *commenting on and even explaining* the development of the play as it progressed.

It served the actor by becoming a *partner in his dialogue;* by consoling, sympathizing, and advising as the chorus of women does in the play *Electra,* for example. It also served the actor by *reacting to him* and giving a larger dimension to his thought and emotion, becoming in a sense a miniscule audience which gave him the benefit and warmth of an immediate response and in turn provided the huge audience with a *pattern for its own response.*

This service to the audience was no small thing, for if the theatre of Dionysus in Athens held 17,000 and the one at Epidaurus 35,000 it is obvious that such a catalyst was needed, especially by those in the top rows and on the sides. In empathizing with the actor, the audience, in hearing and seeing the chorus' response, could better say, "Yes, that's the way I feel." It further served the audience in the practical matter of *enlarging the sound* to a comfortably audible level and by *providing moments for reflective* thinking during the times when the chorus was performing alone and communicating directly with the audience. In Aeschylus' first play, *The Suppliants,* the chorus claimed the stage more than half the time.[1]

All these functions were enhanced by the illustrative choreography of the chorus as its members moved

---

[1] Sheldon Cheyney, *The Theatre, 3000 Years of Drama, Acting and Stagecraft* (New York: Longman's, Green & Co., 1929), p. 51.

rhythmically and meaningfully in various groupings according to the essence of the play.

So the contribution of the fifth century B.C. Greek chorus was to *refine and develop the art of group speaking,* combining it with movement and integrating it into the total theatre performance. The theatre at once became the host for this speech art and was served by its peculiar function as a "representative of the people." It also firmly established a long *theatre-chorus relationship* which persisted through the Roman theatre of Seneca's time to the present, with a long wait in the wings during the middle ages.

The Medieval Period

The so-called Barbarians who sacked Rome and ended the Greco-Roman cultural era were certainly people of a different culture, fraught with violence and a preoccupation with the necessities of wresting a crude living from a wildernesslike environment and with maintaining a nervous balance with neighboring warlike tribes who were similarly preoccupied. This left no time nor inclination for the theatre and its chorus.

The Gregorian Chant and Choral Speaking

Fortunately a new host, the Christian Church, found a use for choral speaking and through its majestic Gregorian chants carried the art through this critical period to the Renaissance. Pope Gregory firmly established the chant as an integral part of the worship service by, first, forbidding any part of the mass except the Gospels to be sung as a solo, and, second, by developing the "Schola Cantorum," or school for singing. Indeed, his influence

was so great that his "Antiphonary of St. Gregory" became the authoritative standard for the true chant.[2]

But what do these chants have to do with choral
speaking? They *began* with choral speaking! In speaking
together the prayers and worshipful liturgy, the monks,
in their efforts to gain clear and meaningful pronunciation of words and to project these words to the entire
congregation, found themselves repeating the same
voice inflections, rhythms and phrasing each time. These
elements of group speaking became the bases for the
simple intonations and melodies of the chants, known
also as plain songs, which provided so effective a channel for the thoughts and emotions of the clergy.

More importantly, not only the clergy but also the
members of the congregations found personal participation in the singing and movement of this part of the
mass, for even though they could not understand the
Latin phrases they could share in the universal language
of music and spoken intonations and the dynamics of
group expression.

So again we find that choral speaking, now evolved
into the chant, is a natural human experience, deeply related to the highest aspiration of the people. This and
similar chants are serving as an integral part of the worship services not only of Catholic and Anglican but also
other Protestant churches, Jewish synagogues and other
religions today.

Medieval Church Drama and Choral Speaking

The mystery, miracle, and morality plays used small
casts on small wagon stages and although some of them

[2] Edward Dickinson, *Music in the History of the Western Church* (New York:
Charles Scribner & Sons, 1902), pp. 96-97.

expanded their casts and productions to the steps of the cathedrals, we cannot establish that they used choral speaking.

It is reasonable to assume, however, that in the Valenciennes Passion Play, a prime example of church drama on a grand scale in the Middle Ages, a kind of simultaneous improvised speech was used by such groups as the bands of shrieking imps emerging from Hellmouth, and the screams and wailings of the tormented souls they captured.

Similarly the Lucerne Passion Play, a two-day performance covering the entire Bible, must have had such large groups as the children of Israel, Elijah's followers, and the crucifixion crowds at Jerusalem speaking together in some semi-organized manner. While these might be considered choral speaking of a sort they cannot be compared with the polished art of the Greek chorus.

This tremendous spectacle, begun in 1583, played its 56 acts from sunrise to sunset on two successive days before 7,000 townspeople and "pilgrims" from the countryside who crowded the scaffolds, windows and rooftops surrounding the large town square. Surely such a production under these conditions required group speaking on a large scale.

We do have contemporary evidence of medieval use of choral speaking from the Oberammergau Passion Play, begun in 1633 by the townspeople as their act of gratitude to God for sparing from the plague their village of Gau over the Ammer River. It was in the hands of each generation of townspeople, such as the famous woodcarver Anton Lang who played Christus, that the speaking and singing choruses have been carried to us as part of the genuine medieval form and spirit of this epic play. Millions of visitors have made the pilgrimage to this remote village in the Bavarian Alps since it began its five-year production cycle. This was later changed to ten and it has resumed its ten-year sequence after being interrupted during World War II.

The Rediscovery Begins with the Renaissance

The Renaissance gives us meager and spotty evidences of the use of choral speaking and these were only soggy reminders of the vitality of the choruses as used by the Greeks. One such was Stephen Jodelle's warmed-over Senecan tragedy *Cleopatre Captive.*[3] Other renaissance revivals of classical plays also suffered from a too-strict adherence to form and too-little understanding of the spirit that brought about the original.

The emergence of opera at this time has sometimes been coupled with these revivals of the Greek chorus. This is based on the erroneous theory that the Greeks sang their odes. In fact, their choral speech achieved a kind of "spoken musicality," which was characterized by elongated vowels and continuing consonant sounds enhanced by dominant rhythm and varied intonations. These resulted from the beautiful poetic writing and from the necessity of projecting to the vast audiences rather than deliberately singing the lines of the play.

Spotty and soggy as these revivals are they did serve to begin the rediscovery of this ancient art and won it a place in the culture of the western world.

---

[3] Cheyney, *The Theatre.* Cheney states that this play was written in 1552, and was "very rhetorical and trailing such classical remnants as ghost and chorus."

Choral Speaking in the Oriental Theatre
Contemporary with the Renaissance

Beginning in the fourteenth century, the Noh theatre of Japan gives us an example of a chorus of six to ten men that was a part of an extremely meaningful theatre experience, being deeply rooted in the religious and literary traditions of the people. A similar chorus has been and now is a part of the other two types of Japanese theatre: the Kabuki, which serves a broader audience than the Noh, and the Bunkaru, or puppet theatre. All three of these are still vitally serving the people of Japan by breathing life into their traditions and all three still use the chorus as a vital part of their performances.

Choral Speaking in Shakespeare's Macbeth

The thread of choral speaking continued in the theatre of the Western World when Shakespeare used his three witches to converse with Macbeth to prophesy his rise to power and to urge him on to further dark deeds. True, they interspersed their group speaking with individual lines but their speaking together such phrases as:

Double, double, toil and trouble;
Fire burn and cauldron bubble.

and other longer passages were clear and fresh uses of choral speaking, even by so small a number.

The Early Nineteenth Century

It was natural, two centuries later, for the German poet-dramatist Friedrich von Schiller to experiment with the chorus, for he diligently explored every facet of theatrical production and dramatic technique available to make his melodramatic and poetry-enhanced plays exciting. So, in his *Bride of Messina* he used the army of each of the contending brothers as opposing choruses that supported and magnified their quarrel. While this "heavy artillery" aspect of two stentorian-voiced groups thundering at each other across the stage may seem overpowering to us now, it was a new and imaginative use of choral speaking in the theatre of Schiller's time.

Choral Speaking Arrives in the Twentieth Century

We now jump from these few scattered examples to the most notable deliberate use of the chorus in the theatre in the early 1930s when T. S. Eliot formed his townspeople into an effectively articulate chorus in his major tragedy, *Murder in the Cathedral*.[4] This was followed by *Dark of the Moon, Fiddler on the Roof,* and Meredith Wilson's *Music Man*—other modern plays that effectively used choral speaking when natural group expression was called for in their action. These, along with lesser-known plays written expressly for choral speaking and the revivals of classic Greek plays, reestablished this long marriage of theatre and chorus.

Choral Speaking Stands by Itself
as the Verse-Speaking Choir

The intrinsic value of choral speaking was not rediscovered until 1922 and then it was as a separate art, independent of the theatre and called a *verse-speaking choir.* The term grew out of the Verse-Speaking Festival, an

---

[4] This play was given its American premiere on the stage of Yale University Theatre with Professor Constance Welch directing the chorus.

annual event held in Glasgow, Scotland, in which oral interpreters vied with each other for excellence in poetry reading.

In 1921, John Masefield, the then Poet Laureate of England and enthusiastic sponsor of the festival, was so impressed with the work of Miss Marjorie Gullan's individual readers that he encouraged her to return the next year with the girls speaking as a group. This they did, nine of them were called the "Glasgow Nightingales," and performed in such a way as to delight all hearers and to plant the seed that revitalized an ancient art and set it on a new course.

Even though the first material used by Miss Gullan was a chorus from a Greek play, it was presented without benefit of staging or dramatic action, gaining its power and beauty sheerly from the orchestration of the nine speaking voices under the direction of this inspired teacher.

Miss Gullan soon found other, more pertinent, material to match the new trend, stating that, ". . . the old Scottish ballads, with their haunting refrains and their vivid dialogue, gave just the inspiration needed for Scottish choric speakers."[5] So we find that choral speaking has returned to its function of being an exercise of people speaking material that is indigenous to their culture in a spirited and exciting way. In this respect it relates even more directly to the *utterances of the primitive tribes* that gave it birth than to the *more formalized theatre choruses or chants of the church services* that carried it up to our time. While both the theatre and the Church, as well as schools and colleges, will use this art in the future, it is now an entity in itself, capable of capturing an audience,

[5] Marjorie Gullan, *Choral Speaking* (London: Methuen & Co. Ltd., 1931). This book is also available from Boston: Expression Co., 1931.

holding it entranced, and bringing to its participants a worthy experience in its own right.

The Verse Choir in America

The verse choir arrived in America after having been embraced by the education systems of the British Isles, Glasgow being the first city to add it to its school curriculum in 1922, immediately after its introduction into the Glasgow Verse-Speaking Festival. It crossed the channel to France and Germany and spread through other European countries, gaining acceptance as an entertaining art as well as a helpful educational adjunct.

There had been some scattered efforts in choral speaking in America before Miss Gullan's two visits in the late 20s and early 30s, but it was she who gave the movement tremendous impetus by taking time to organize groups of educators and focus their interest on the more disciplined and rewarding Verse-Speaking Choir, or Verse Choir as it has become known. To some she gave single lecture-demonstrations and to others she conducted extended courses in which she freely shared her knowledge, sensitivity, and techniques.

As graduate students, several of us were privileged to be present one evening in New Haven, Connecticut, when, on her second trip, she transformed over a hundred tired teachers into a unified chorus of speakers completely revived in spirit and refreshed in mind and body; a neat trick, for it was Friday! She did this by leading us in speaking English ballads and American poems together in a manner which magnified the meaning and highlighted the spirit of each number. On further reflection we realized we were being freed not only from present inhibitions but also from long-held concepts of how poetry should be read and expressed; concepts encumbered with the exaggerated sounds of elocution, the formalized postures and gestures of Delsarte, the too-strict emphasis on meter and rhyme patterns, and the semi-pious manner that often had accompanied the oral expression of poetry. These barnacles were scraped off in one fell swoop and were replaced by the wave of joy and exhilaration that she engendered. While she did this in a seemingly effortless manner we know that the "effortless" quality of any art is bought with dedication to its principles and techniques.

Thus introduced into our schools, the verse choir spread throughout the country, though it took its deepest roots in the midwest. It was a strangely flexible vehicle for it served the varying needs of primary and elementary children as well as those in the junior and senior high schools, reaching its most serious and highly developed fruition at the college level.

Some educators saw it as the panacea for all speech needs and loaded it up with more expectations than it could satisfy. For instance, when Frank, an intense young man, discovered that he no longer stuttered after a semester with the Norwood High School Verse Choir, it was hoped that all stutterers could be successfully treated in this way. It was soon learned that particular techniques tailored to specific needs, especially in speech pathology, were needed to insure improvement. It is true, however, that the rhythmic flow of words inherent in the verse choir is of great help to stutterers.

Educators have now learned that the verse choir does in truth serve to *improve more different speech and reading faults than any other one speech technique.* For one thing, it functions as an enjoyable group exercise that makes arduous individual effort more pleasurable. Marked im-

provement has also been noted in articulation and pronunciation. Voice production becomes more "solid" as
minor faults fade away and students begin to enjoy
"doing something" with inflections and rhythms to express heretofore hidden meanings and feelings. They
even learn to listen better, which results in improved
scholarship—and personalities. Confidence and poise,
interest and comprehension also improve and reflect in
their work in other classes, raising the general level of
the school.

No wonder the new vehicle is attractive to educators.
It is a veritable cornucopia of learning and growing
stimuli on many fronts—and all at once! Many high
schools throughout the country make room for it, adding to its broad use in junior high schools, and in
intermediate and primary grades.

The best is yet to come, for it is at the college level
that the potential of the verse choir is most fully
realized. Here the thrust is threefold: to teach the technique to teachers and other leaders, to use it with other
campus organizations such as the theatre, and to develop independent performance groups. These last-
named groups present programs of great variety and
gain recognition for the art in the same category as
theatre and forensics, singing and instrumental groups,
athletics, and other organizations representing the various campuses.

On a sabbatical study tour of the country my wife and
I gained first-hand information when we visited 46
campuses where the vigor of this activity was demonstrated. Chapter 3 will report on the particular details of
the work being done at that time on 35 of these campuses, but the following general findings will attest to
the imagination and enthusiasm we found.

To begin, the *names given to the groups* showed a wide variety: "Wordmasters," "Speech Choir," "Designers in Sound," "Dramatones," "Drama Choros," "Rhythmic Choir," "Verse-Speaking Choir," "Verse Choir," "Choric Speech Quartet," "Genesis Company," "The Jongleurs," "Concordia Speakers," and many others. There was also an extraordinarily *wide, wide range in the materials* used, from the most difficult and unlikely to very simple poetry, prose and drama. There was a willingness to try the thing that was most meaningful to the group, whether it was well-known, new, short, long, serious, humorous, complex, or simple. The dominant criterion for choosing a selection was whether it was intellectually challenging and inspiring, considering the age or grade level for which it was intended.

There was great diversity in *size of the groups,* ranging from a quartet to choirs of 11 to 52. One composite choir was organized from 230 high school students attending a speech festival. They all had learned the same poems before coming.

Diversity in organization was evident. Some adopted the stand-up form in the manner of a singing choir, but many found this too confining and broke into smaller groups and singles allowing for much movement and change of focus. Some used a small cast pantomiming the poem or story in front of the standing group. Other choirs were used in plays, milling around as townspeople or as Indian maidens. A creative dramatics company blended choral speaking subtly into their dramatized story.

Two Greek plays were served very effectively: *Electra* by a beautifully coordinated chorus of 11 and *The Eumenides* by a choir of 28, standing full front to the audience in readers theatre fashion, gaining dramatic intensity primarily through changes in the speaking voices.

The *directors were as varied as the choirs* in points of manner, techniques, and position in relation to the group. Some stood in front of the choir and conducted in varying degrees and kinds of movement while others sat in the audience, relying on the training gained in rehearsal and on the leaders in the choir who gave unobtrusive cues.

Recruiting choir members was usually done in three ways: Some were quite *selective,* using tryouts and previous performance to discover people most likely to contribute the voice quality and abilities needed to build a balanced choir. This method usually resulted in a small group. Others *accepted all comers* and adapted the organization of larger choirs to the voices and abilities of the people who came. The third method was to *transform a given class* or assembly into a choir, resulting in groups ranging in size from 16 to 600! (We have taken a Spring-Sing audience of 4,000 on a "Lion Hunt" that was hardly a polished performance but truly a unified choral speaking experience.)

Finally the 92 instances of choral speaking being used as a part of other courses and activities is *strong evidence of its ability to motivate and support other disciplines,* including teacher-education, theatre, oral interpretation, readers theatre, voice and diction, literature, music, dance, etc.

This service function is gratifying to all who are involved, but it should be pointed out that this partial use of choral speaking *foreshortens our opportunity to explore all its facets* as an art form and educational medium. To adequately exploit its full potential, it rightly deserves and needs the full-course time and corresponding credit value that many institutions now give it.

We should remember that this tour covered only a small percentage of the four-year institutions which responded, also leaving out all junior colleges and special institutions of higher learning where choral speaking may be used.[6] It also deals with one point in time and makes no note of the schools that have since discontinued or added the activity.

Lest we who love this work are lulled into believing it is universally accepted and successful, I must quote one answer to our survey question, "Do you now have a choral-speaking group on your campus?"—the answer "No, and we do not intend to have one." Another answer to this question was, "We did until six years ago—discontinued because it was too exhaustive for our directors."

[6] In addition to the various educational institutions, the verse choir has found other hosts in this country, such as churches, recreation departments, clubs, special-interest organizations, the military—and even prisons. These will be discussed in later chapters.

3

Choral Speaking in American Colleges and Universities

In the six months from February through July, 1964, my wife and I visited or contacted 46 four-year colleges and universities that offered choral speaking, traveling 18,000 miles in 38 states. Preparing for the trip we surveyed the 981 four-year institutions listed in the College Blue Book, believing they would represent the *most advanced theory and practice,* and were not disappointed. From the generous response of 618 schools, we found that 146 offered choral speaking in some form and to some degree, 53 having either a course and/or performing group and the other 93 using it as a part of another course or activity. The choirs were effectively used to bring "town and gown" together and for extensive promotional tours, two through Europe to South Africa. One senior high school was so outstanding we "had" to include it as its standards were equal to many of the colleges.

One survey cannot hope to cover all the work being done in this field. Nor can one tour and report adequately treat all the fine things being done by each campus visited. (We neglected the west coast and snow kept us out of the entire northwest.) So in the interest of clarity and space we have condensed the report in two ways; first by *selecting 35 representative schools* from the 46 visited; and second, by *attempting to lift out the key features* of each institution that best depict its particular contribution and to offer these as hard evidence of the depth and scope of the work being done.

You may be encouraged, as we were, in knowing that so many people are succeeding in so many ways. Perhaps their ideas, materials, approaches, and experiences may help answer your questions, or better still, set off new thinking in new directions to bring this versatile movement to bear on the problems and opportunities that come to us all. The present does belong to us—and we can influence the future.

These first eight institutions should interest teachers of all levels who wish to use choral speaking to motivate and "lubricate" classroom learning. We begin with an expert with younger children.

Wisconsin University, Madison, Wisconsin: Primary and Intermediate Grades

Miss Carrie Rasmussen's continued success with the verse choir as a teacher in the Madison Public Schools has resulted in her becoming an authority on its use in the primary and intermediate grades. Her extension and summer session courses at Wisconsin and Northwestern

Universities and her books *Let's Enjoy Poetry* for grades 1, 2, 3 and for grades 4, 5, 6 have been of great help to teachers.

She has added to these two new books, *Let's Say Poetry Together and Have Fun* with accompanying records, one for primary and the other for intermediate grades. You should have them, if only to hear how her second graders feel about "The Old Gray Goose is Dead."

She does not use the light, medium, and dark voice distinctions in the elementary grades but gains variety by boy-girl and small-group divisions. She is not concerned about an audience since "our own self improvement is enough," though sometimes "when we do a good one we call in another group to inspire them, and us, too." She especially likes the works of Dr. Seuss and Vachel Lindsay.

Miss Rasmussen has studied with Marjorie Gullan both at Columbia and Wisconsin Universities. As one good author to another, she recommends Louise Abney's series of books for each of the first six grades.

Time and place did not work together for us to visit Miss Abney but in a long-distance phone conversation to this inspiring person and author, who had also studied with Marjorie Gullan, we learned that there was "a vigorous interest" in verse speaking in the mid-west as evidenced by the many invitations she has from speech conventions, language arts and church conferences for lecture-demonstrations on the subject.

Montclair State College, Upper Montclair, New Jersey: Little Time—Big Results

We were impressed with the grasp of verse-choir techniques Miss Ellen Kauffman's 28 students had gained in only three of the five weeks allotted to this work in a three-unit course, "Methods of Teaching the Speech Arts." The momentum gained from meeting the class four times a week was an advantage.

They had considered the nature, values, dangers, role of the director, arranging the group, selection and analysis of materials, and arranging materials for the various types of group interpretation. They had applied these considerations to the problems of working with young children, intermediates, and junior high school, and were now involved with the senior high school and adult level, using themselves as a laboratory choir. (Today the world—tomorrow the planets!)

On the day we visited, four students took ten minutes each to select a group from the class, brief them on analysis and interpretation, and rehearse the poem, after which Miss Kauffman gave a cogent criticism of the director's work—with good comments from the class. This appears hurried on paper but each director achieved significant results, due largely to the oft-repeated injunction to "be concise." They emphasized "color" words as a device to unify the poem and highlight its theme.

Queens College, the City University of New York,
Flushing, New York: **Variety in Arrangement and Movement**

The major emphasis in Dr. Dorothy Rambo's two-unit course in "Choral Speaking" seemed to be giving her students experiences in detailed and interesting arrangements of the poetry they interpreted. To this she added significant use of stage groupings as well as actions and pantomime to give a visual dimension to the interpretation. For instance, in e. e. cummings' "Chancon Innocente" she had individuals jumping rope, playing jacks, and engaging in other children's springtime activities in front of the two major groups, men and women, who shared the vocal interpretation. Soloists within these groups were adroitly used to lift out single words for surprising effects. The action was well integrated with the rise and fall in intensity of the poem.

Within Edwin Markham's "The Man With the Hoe," Dr. Rambo worked for a big, unified impact by forming the entire group into an inverted triangle that remained constant throughout the number. The same formation was used for Archibald Macleish's "Ars Poetica."

In the traditional "Get Up and Bar the Door," the wife, husband, and two men enacted the drama in front of the chorus, which in this case became the narrator. In another traditional poem, "Leave Her, Johnny, Leave Her," the choir was divided only into two major groups, men and women who expressed the lines in concerted actions as they gave them orally.

And finally, Conrad Aiken's difficult "Morning Song from 'Senlin' " was opened up and made clearer by the use of a male soloist offset by a men's and women's group. These three units guided us through the poem in a kind of dialogue, with no actions.

I have given this much detail to show the great variety of Dr. Rambo's direction, all of which was based on careful analysis and discussion of the material to involve the members of the group and give them the reasons for the enlarged expression.

District of Columbia Teachers' College, Washington, D. C.:
  "Have Fun with the poem——and it will break open!"

Our return trip to this predominantly black school proved worth the second effort when we visited Mrs. J.D. Fletcher's class in "Choral Speaking and Creative

Dramatics," a logical and good combination. The first half of the course develops methods for elementary teachers in these two fields and the second emphasizes the analysis and rehearsal of materials on the secondary level.

Mrs. Fletcher is a person of unusual imagination, ingenuity and resourcefulness and so brings a fresh approach that even she has difficulty in describing. She says, "We just have fun with the material and then it breaks open." As we observed the "having fun" phase, she established a relaxed environment that encouraged her people to react freely to the material she presented. They said such things as: "It makes me *feel* like—," "I can *see* a—," "I want to *dance* with them—," "The rhythm is the main thing, it *goes*—," and more and more. The verbs in each of these statements show that the students were giving that inner kinetic response often put forward as a worthy goal in interpretation. In the second "breaking open," phase they really went to work discovering why the poem did these things to them and finding the techniques and form which would elicit from an audience the same response when they performed it as a choir. Here is a blueprint for interpreting a poem and adapting it to a choir that works—from its sheer simplicity. *"Have fun with the poem–and it will break open."*

Mrs. Fletcher's students became so facile with this approach that individuals can direct the class in the same manner as four girls did with the poems "The Low Beating of the Tom Toms," by Langston Hughes, Carl Sandburg's "Jazz Fantazia," Don Blanding's "Foreboding," and the traditional "St. Catherine." Their future classes will be alive with the heartbeat and beauty of literature, a far cry from the sterile treatment that more nearly resembled "autopsies," to use Mrs. Fletcher's phrase, that I can still remember from high school days.

Arkansas State Teachers College, Conway, Arkansas: The Values of a Large Choir

It was encouraging to learn that fifty-two students had elected to take the "Verse Choir, Choral Reading" course at this teacher-education institution. Participating with so large a touring group and being a part of all the problems involved in its organization and management would give invaluable experience to each young member who may one day direct such a choir as a part of his teaching contribution. About one-half of the 17 men and 34 women are majoring in elementary education.

Their director and teacher, Miss Leona Scott, says their material covers a wide range of subjects but the one number that is requested most often is "Old Southern Street Cries," which comes from the streets of New Orleans and was written by Agnes Curren Hamm of Mount Mary College.

Texas Women's University, Denton, Texas: The Verse Choir Becomes Other Things

Miss Dorothy Bell's course, "Verse-Speaking Choir" was also geared to educating teachers. It was especially characterized by giving students major responsibility in the production of programs. For instance, a group of graduate students wrote the script, organized, and directed a choir for an impressive Christmas program. Also, the traditional and major Thanksgiving celebration, directed by Miss Bell, was well supported by individual student contributions because it made extensive use of groups in speech, dance, and music. One of her students had introduced verse choir in a summer camp and the resulting momentum resulted in many significant programs. All this portends well for the future.

In addition to this teacher-education activity, and closely related to it as an incentive and culminating experience, the school made a rich contribution with the touring group the Texas Woman's University Verse Choir.

Tennessee Agricultural and Industrial State University, Nashville, Tennessee: Great Literature Deeply Experienced

Dr. Janye C. Williams has developed an unusually fine course in "Choral Speaking" that she uses both in teacher-education and as a performing group. A keenly perceptive person herself, she emphasizes exhaustive analysis of each poem by her students as the basis for its interpretation.

A glance at a few of the authors she uses shows the wide range of subjects, time periods, and points of view represented in the grist she feeds into the mill: Kingsley, Houseman, Rossetti, Longfellow, Masefield, Hughes, Lindsay, Lowell, and several selections from both the Old and New Testaments. Such complete examination of and experience with the thoughts and feelings presented by these men in their works would give each student a well-distilled and lasting impression of their contributions. This vital, engrossing approach to literature will enliven the future classes of Dr. Williams' students.

Findlay College, Findlay, Ohio: First the Verse Choir—then Individual Oral Interpretation

Here was a rich find in a relatively small school. Both Dr. Virgil Logan, Chairman of the Speech Department, and his wife, a Professor in the Education Department, have made extensive study and use of the verse choir in education.

It is significant that Dr. Logan uses choric speech to introduce individual oral interpretation, as a "break-through to give the basic feeling." He further states that an individual may go deeper into the poem while the chorus will find new and different slants, both being worthy outcomes that can be mutually helpful.

As a dramatic demonstration of how to structure a verse choir program, he once took the one "best reader" from each of forty-four junior high schools and pre-sented a program of several major poems after working with them for a halfday. During this time he organized them into voice groups, found the common note of their interpretation, chose soloists, narrators, etc., im-plemented it all with the techniques of choral expression and rehearsed them to performance pitch. Optimum personnel? Perhaps; but what evidence of the common bond provided by good literature when good readers and a fine director join together!

The next six institutions have a religious orientation, which adds a new dimension to their approach.

Marion College, Marion, Indiana: A Speech Quartet with an Extra

We were impressed with what only two men and two women could attain in the "Choric Speech Quartet." When directed by Laura S. Emerson the minimal expec-tations are somewhat higher for so small a group as there is better opportunity for control. Great variety, crisp diction, distinct individual differences, good power in unison passages, subtle nuances, and good balance were all abundantly satisfied.

And these folks had an extra—it was their commonly held religious conviction and faith, so much a part of each that it shone with unassumed naturalness through their demeanor and performance. Passages that might only have been impressive were invested with reverence, an invitation became fraught with urgent concern, pity was raised to compassion, censure was tempered with gentleness and victory became triumphant. I seriously doubt if they could have achieved these same delicate shadings through a purely intellectual and emotional approach without the alchemy of their faith. Nor was its effect limited to their religious numbers, for they seemed markedly free from inhibition in their whole-hearted approach to secular material, especially the humorous poems. "Seek ye first—"

Northwestern College, Orange City, Iowa: One Evening—Two Programs

Dr. Theora England was repeating an extensive annual tour through the eastern half of the United States and Canada when we heard her fine verse choir of 11 men and 15 women, called "The Choral Readers." She feels that 26 is the ideal number as "echoes" sometimes develop with larger groups.

Her students have the same aspect of unity and dedication as the quartet from Marion College. Their vocal work showed vitality, was sharpened by sure diction, and tied together by a strong and continuing rhythm. Their performance was marked by great visual variety, ingeniously contrived by reversible poncholike vestments used for varying effects over white formals and black suits. The colors of blue, green, red, purple, and black were dramatically used for their traditional connotations.

Tight picture groupings were facilitated by small stools of varying heights making possible many and quick changes.

The scriptures and modern religious writers were generously used in the first part of the program but the main theme was carried by a major dialogue that highlighted points in the Bible and related their challenge to the present day. After the service the verse choir entertained in the recreation hall with delightful selections from Nash, Thurber, and others. The total evening was a demonstration of versatile and effective use of an unusually well-trained choral group to bring a well-balanced experience to a given body of listeners. Also, it gave ample reason for Northwestern College's "The Choral Readers" to be on their fifth successful tour.

Clark College, Dubuque, Iowa:
600 Is Not Too Many—Imaginative Outcomes

An hour's interview with sparkling Sister Mary Xavier left little doubt as to why she has met with success in Choral Speaking. Her work is directed primarily toward educating teachers to work with classes ranging from pre-school children through the college level, with well-selected materials for each level. She, too, likes the works of James Weldon Johnson, who has emerged as a favorite of the great majority of the directors we've met.

There seems to be no limit to the applications she sees for choral speaking. To begin, she considers it to be a stepping stone to creative dramatics, suggesting that after a choral experience with "The King's Breakfast," such questions as "What else might the Queen have said," etc., would open up creative thought and action.

Sister Xavier considers the fields of geriatrics, the

mentally disturbed, and the culturally deprived to be lying fallow and ready for this work. She has used the entire student body of 600 with the Gospels of St. Luke and St. John with notable success, but believes the 60 young sisters, Novitiates, give the clearest and deepest response to the scriptures due to their marked spiritual quality and dedication.

She rarely takes time to prepare a program for performance, preferring to multiply her energies and ideas through her students. A striking example of this was the speech chorus composed of servicemen in Korea directed by one of her students who was a Special Services Officer.

Rosary High School, Detroit, Michigan: Inspired Director—Multiple Returns

This was the only high school we visited and what a program in choral speaking they have going! There are two freshman classes of 35 each feeding into the sophomore class of 70, which is their performing group. In addition, their upper division drama work features choral speaking in their plays, an expected result of so much early experience.

We saw the three verse-choir classes in session and were impressed by the enthusiasm, sustained effort, and finesse exhibited in each. The prime reason for this is the unique ability of Sister Rose Terrence to inspire, organize, and direct this work.

A better reflection of her work can be gained from statements gleaned from a student survey that was taken after the first four years of her verse-choir course program. They show the breadth and depth of her contribution to these girls:

"I've learned to work with others and to get along with them"; "I find myself speaking differently, not only in choral speaking, but in all my other classes and at home, too"; "I've learned to memorize much faster"; "I couldn't stand poetry but now I love it"; "I've gained a greater appreciation for all literature"; "Never before did I realize how to play with words"; "I used to be frightened to speak before a class but choral speaking has helped me to get over that"; "Verse speaking is a comforting thing. You're not up there all by yourself"; "The blending of my voice with all others has given it a beauty and appeal it could never have alone"; "I never before dreamed of doing my own writing but since we've studied so many beautiful things I've begun to try"; and finally, "The verse choir members express themselves so well. They say things the way I would like to say them."

Quotes from audience members who heard them are in the same vein, somehow proving the pudding.

Bethel College, McKenzie, Tennessee:
Change Scenes without Scenery

This group of ten "Trinity Players" effectively combined a verse-choir presentation with dramatic interludes at a Sunday morning service in Huntsville, Alabama, as they began their fourth annual tour of the southern states.

Their drama was R. H. Ward's "The Figure on the Cross," based on the last seven words of Jesus. It was directed by B. W. Clifton who used a basic "cross" formation to give the narrative and evaluative portions. The seven interludes, each interpreting its part of the message in a modern setting, were done by different groups of two or three, placed in varying positions in relation to the whole. He made generous use of expressive movement, both by groups and individuals, and achieved a smooth, well-transitioned performance by simply having the rest of the choir "close-in" and focus on the smaller scene, allowing us to suddenly discover it. These effects were greatly aided by the pastel blouses and shirts that fell into the right combinations.

There was no break in the forty-five minute presentation and the group sustained and built interest by great vocal variety and a good sense of rhythm and pace. There was no drag. That they could accomplish this without direction from the floor, without scripts and in the cold morning light seemed to us a major achievement and proved a good marriage of these two speech arts, drama and choral speaking.

Garrett Biblical Institute, Evanston, Illinois: An Adult Christmas Program with Courage and Depth

How often and long have we searched for new and better-than-average Christmas materials. If you, too, share this quest it may be profitable to examine the selections put together by Ph.D. candidate and San Diego State University graduate David Corbin for a worship service, using a verse choir of 12 wives of Garrett theology students.

He began gently with a solo reading of Charles Tazewell's "The Littlest Angel;"[1] moved into the rhythmical "A Christmas Carol Medley," arranged for the choir by Fred Miller; then to Eleanor Slater's short, provocative, "December Twenty-Fourth," introducing the Calvary theme, which was carried to its full power by James Weldon Johnson's "The Crucifixion." This in turn set the stage for the challenging "Carol: New Style," by Stephen Vincent Benét. He then released the tension

---

[1] "The Littlest Angel" also adapts well to full choral arrangement, using banks, individuals, full choir and other variations.

and returned the emphasis to the living Christ with the two short, poignant numbers; "Hope," anonymous, and "The Carpenter of Galilee," by Hilda W. Smith, and used a violin and "interpretive movement" by two of the choir members to close the program with Malotte's "The Lord's Prayer."

This program has a good beginning, a suspenseful progression to a powerful climax and a well-balanced denouement—and the materials lift us beyond the "tinsel" stage of Christmas celebration. It was well joined together by an original narrative.

Mount Mary College, Milwaukee, Wisconsin: "If I Don't Say It—It Won't Be Said!"

A fine example of choral speaking being well blended into a full theatrical production was seen here when this fine girls' college performed Longfellow's "Hiawatha." The director, Mrs. Agnes Curren Hamm is another of the educators in this country who studied with Marjorie Gullan.

She used a chorus of twenty-four girls, mostly freshmen, which was divided into the traditional light, medium, and dark sections. This chorus, fresh and flexible, carried us through the dramatic poem serving in a three-fold capacity as narrator, Indian characters, and in the manner of the Greek chorus. Their full-bodied voice production and clean-cut delivery reflected the excitement of the moment, somber warnings, chiding, deeply felt grief, and the exultation of the lyric lift with which Longfellow ends his poem.

Mrs. Hamm achieved this striking performance by having each individual master all cues, speeches, reactions, pauses, movements—the total response—*as if that one person were the only member of the choir who would give this response.* The same procedure was used by other directors whose choirs performed as a part of a play. To achieve it requires great concentration and effort but it is the best way to free the choir from the fatal drag that can be exerted by even one half-hearted member. Conversely, it is the only sure way to bring to each member, the whole choir, and, thus, the audience all the values inherent in the performance, and it was well demonstrated by the Mount Mary College Verse Choir.

Centenary College, Shreveport, Louisiana:
Finely Honed Art—Emotional Catharsis

I can no longer delay telling you about Centenary College and the Coreys! Their production of *Electra* is a top-most experience in choral speaking blended so well with all the other theatre arts as to be a perfectly cut diamond. This is the first of four schools that dealt with Greek plays, each one making its own helpful contribution to those who work with choral speaking at this level.

This theatre group, the *Jongleurs,* gave a superb example of the traditional use of choral speaking by the ancient theatre when, under the inspired direction of Orlin Corey, they lived through Sophocles' *Electra* so dynamically that they reached out and completely involved the audience—which included several spellbound children.

The chorus of eleven women was so well integrated into the dramatic essence of the play that it seemed to become one character that responded to the action, commented on the turn of events, advised and warned the leading characters, empathized with them so completely that we felt the same emotion.—In fact it served as a sounding board for the audience who would like to do all of these things and were now given the opportunity to experience them vicariously.

Director Corey laid the groundwork for this by exhaustive analysis of the play, which clarified their multiple purpose and deeply involved them emotionally. He then made it easier for them to achieve optimum vocal variety through well-planned vocal groupings, from one single voice to different banks of from two to the entire chorus. These banks changed often to meet the demands of the play, adding surprise and beauty to the total impact. There was also great range of individual voices within the chorus and all gave evidence of good training in voice and diction. In fact they devoted a full hour before each rehearsal and performance to body and voice warm-up exercises. Corey also helped to clarify and heighten the various effects of the chorus by imaginative and meaningful visual pictures or groupings, accomplished by smooth and well-motivated transitions.

We were so impressed with this theatre group that we returned after a 1,200 mile loop to join their bus trip to the St. Luke's Methodist Church in Houston, Texas, to hear the majestic treatment by their verse choir of 28 of "Romans," Paul's Epistle. We agree with the Coreys that this work is too grand and complex for one voice and so calls for the greater power and variety of a chorus. Later we also extended our tour into the summer to visit Pineville, Kentucky, where the Everyman Players, made up largely of Centenary graduates and directed by Corey, entered their sixth season of "The Book of Job," to be followed by their second international tour through Europe to South Africa. Each of these productions seemed to top the preceding one in artistic refinement and dramatic power.

While we are primarily concerned with the sounds of

choral speaking, we would be remiss not to recognize the artistic environment that nurtures it. To begin, Irene Corey's sets and costumes, inspired by the icons on Chartres cathedral and Byzantine stained glass windows, were as courageously right as was the vocal concept of the productions. Also important was the lighting, the sound effects and all other production elements, demonstrating again that the theatre is the meeting place for all the arts, each heightening the effect of the others.

Regarding selection of material it should be further noted that "Electra," "Romans," and "Job" represent great and difficult literature, and the inspired treatment given them by the Coreys and their people bring much credit and enrichment to all who participated in them, including the audience. Little wonder that both the Coreys have received favorable attention from New York critics.

The Coreys have since organized a professional company with a repertoire of eight classics that have made five national and four international tours, which include Canada, Great Britain, Europe, and South Africa. Their two productions done entirely in choral speech, "The Book of Job" and "Roman's," by Saint Paul, head the distinguished list that includes *Electra, The Pilgrim's Progress, Reynard and the Fox, The Tortoise and the Hare, Don Quixote,* and *The Tempest.* Their *The Book of Job* is still continuing its summer seasons at Pine Mountain State Park, Pineville, Kentucky.

Illinois Wesleyan University, Bloomington, Illinois:
Voices Only

Dr. Marie J. Robinson used a readers theatre approach to Sophocles' *Electra,* with a chorus of ten women supporting the principals. This is an extra-curricular group called "Designers in Sound." They make minimal use of stage movement, read from scripts, and are directed from the floor—putting their emphasis on vocal interpretation.

Director Robinson works simply to express the idea and mood inherent in the situations in the play and it was remarkable what a difference her simple injunction to "make it real" made in their delivery.

That so much could be accomplished by the sheer use of the speaking voices and without the support of the other theatre arts prepared us for Wayne State University's Readers Theatre, which is next.

Wayne State University, Detroit, Michigan:
Powerful Readers Theatre

After two experiences with *Electra* we were almost willing to say that the remorseless murderers, Clytemnestra and Aegisthus, had received their just dues and that Orestes should go scot-free—(the theatre has a dangerous power). But we were shocked back to a recognition of the demands of organized society when Orestes was tried by the Furies and Dionysus in Aeschylus' *Eumenides.*

And shocked is the word for there was no escaping the power of Professor Eugene H. Bahn's readers theatre production in which he used the 21 students in his "Verse-Speaking Choir" class. The magnitude of this all-out rehearsal matched the emotions of the play and swept us along with it, even under the conditions of a humid afternoon, a large first-floor classroom, and giant rumblings from street traffic.

These observations noted that day, may help you see how this was achieved:

The complete involvement and all-out projection leaves no doubt of the meaning, makes up for the lack of production elements, sustains momentum and gives cohesion, lifts up sensory responses—"smell the blood"—and removes any hint of embarrassment because of direct contact with the audience.

All speeches were given straight out, not to each other nor to the audience but looking past us. This gave an impersonal aspect that allowed a certain amount of emotional isolation on our part. Seriousness was reflected by the choir members while not speaking, leaving us free to focus on the speaker(s). Scripts were used but we soon forgot them.

There were no group nor gross individual movements but instead excellent use of suggested movement that allowed us to finish it in our minds. Cues came from the script, not the director. All the techniques of voice production and good diction were obvious. Prominent duration of sound suggested the "spoken musicality" considered to have been used in the ancient Greek theatre. The group became "one great voice" with many organ stops. The furies were violent, virulent, and vicious. (We were glad for the daylight.)

Vocal and visual groupings were clearly established and remained fixed throughout, the principals forming a line across the front. There was no theatre lighting, costumes, or sets. Dr. Bahn doesn't accept less from the choir than he sees in the play. He clarifies meaning by apt paraphrasing and repeatedly asks his people to "lift out the key words." The script was well edited, using approximately half of the original.

One blind girl with a lovely big voice used a braille script and was *always* on cue. (My wife kept track.)

All in all, Wayne University demonstrated a most effective use of choral techniques adapted to a readers theatre presentation with no help from other theatre arts.

The Catholic University of America, Washington, D. C.:
A Vital Tradition of Excellence Continues

Choral speaking has long been an integral part in the life of the Drama Department of this fine institution, having been developed by Mrs. (Dr.) Josephine McGarry Callan, who worked for years as a teacher of interpretation and coach on dramatic productions with such directors as Walter Kerr and Alan Schneider. Her work contributed to the Broadway theatre when she directed the choral-speaking passage in Rodgers and Hammerstein's original *Allegro*.

Dr. Callan's high standards are being continued by her former student Edward Cashman, who says that he "follows her methods slavishly, so any success I have is owed to her." His success and her methods are well represented in the choruses of such plays as *Oedipus Rex, The Oresteia, The Bacchae,* and *Murder in the Cathedral*. He is presently responsible for both the choral and stage direction of *The Birds,* which is now being produced by the University's touring company, "The National Players," which has maintained a distinguished reputation for many years.

Mr. Cashman makes a series of suggestions that will be helpful to any who are working with the choruses of Greek or other classical plays, giving us a "peek" into his production book.

The first suggestion is that when there are both a choral and a stage director they must be in accord regarding the interpretation; this interpretation is to be "implanted on the chorus because it is time wasted to get the views of each chorus member concerning the reading of a line. The time is better spent developing choral tone, modulations, nuances and the like."

He makes a surprising discovery that enlarges on what we have termed "spoken musicality" when he says: "It is possible to obtain almost musical results with the speaking chorus. Such musical devices as *harmony* and *counterpoint* have been attempted with amazing results." (This is reminiscent of the "half-sung" or "musical speech" that Orlin Corey achieved in his *Electra* chorus.)

Five more of Mr. Cashman's helpful ideas and techniques are:

1. "In casting choral members, we prefer to use *actors of little experience* rather than actors of great experience to avoid individualistic interpretations—and the problem of forcing "soloists" to be subservient to the group. We aim for a balanced chorus of high, middle and low voices; or light and dark, or even soprano, alto, tenor and bass, to use a musical parallel."

2. "For variety's sake we interpolate some lines for solo voices, for two voices, for all men or all women or for other banks. However, we find it inadvisable to break up a choral passage into all solo lines, since this gives the effect of 'town gossips' rather than a chorus."

3. "We do many cues by counts and others are done as sight or movement cues. In this respect the *chorus must be considered to be one actor,* making it necessary for the stage director, choreographer and choral director to merge their efforts so each is 'saying' the same thing." Mr. Cashman warns that spreading out a chorus can bring agonizing results because "the members must hear and feel one another. It is therefore unwise to have the chorus in more than one

grouping when speaking, except to achieve an antiphonal effect."
4. He finds that the use of full masks causes the sound to reverberate inside and also reduces the volume of the individual voice as well as hindering chorus members from seeing and hearing each other. "So we use half-masks which leave the lower face area free."
5. *"Vocal and physical exercises* are a *must* as a warm-up before chorus rehearsals and performances—our groups spend a minimum of 30 minutes on this."

He closes with an emphasis on "drill, drill, drill and work, work, *work!" to achieve the freedom that only discipline can give.* We thank Mr. Cashman for these insights into the continuing excellence of choral speaking at the Catholic University of America.

Chestnut Hill College, Philadelphia, Pennsylvania: Marjorie Gullan's Four M's

In a long interview with Miriam Davenport Gow I could almost believe that Marjorie Gullan was speaking through the person of her student and long-time friend. Miss Gow is one of the few who have been certified to use the Gullan principles in teaching the verse choir and freely discussed them.

There is of course no nut-shell treatment possible but Miss Gow spoke of the four artistic M's as being the heart of her approach: these being the *meaning of the word,* adding the poet's thought of the instant to the basic meaning; the *music of the word,* being the total sound—especially the vowels; the *movement of the word,* the rhythm, life and spirit; and the *mood of the word,* the emotional overtone,—and that Miss Gullan added to these "a great part of herself." She also spoke of the early days when Poet Laureate John Masefield encouraged Miss Gullan to organize nine young poetry readers into her "Glasgow Nightingales" and, in 1925, twenty-four busy adults into the "London Verse-Speaking Choir," which was in full operation until World War II.

In her years at Chestnut Hill College Miss Gow has built an enviable reputation through her performing choirs and teaching (this came from another source). She believes that if a student has time for only one speech course "it should be the verse choir, for it includes good speech, interpretation, knowledge of human nature, and the development of the personality—and the soul."

Macalester College, Saint Paul, Minnesota:
Vital Ideas Dynamically Presented

This choir stands by itself as a superb example of a modern verse choir. Macalester College provided ideal conditions and Mary Gwen Owen maximized them by developing this most versatile group.

An entirely different aspect of choral speech is represented by the drama chorōs. This group of twenty-eight spontaneous students were like the atoms in a molecule, each one expressing himself *vibrantly in his own way and still being an integral and needed part* of the larger pattern. And *liveliness* is the word to describe their work in voice, thought, group movement, choreography, and individually expressive actions—all of which stems from a headlong and whole-hearted approach to their material.

The chorōs performs on a platform, independent of the production elements of the theatre except for small property and costume items which are added to their basic black-and-white attire. They do poetry, prose, dialogues—whatever they find to match their imagination. They have been a vital part of the Macalester College campus for many years, under the masterful direction of Mrs. Mary Gwen Owen, who states that the choros is built around *ideas.* She challenges her students to think critically and then to create their best response from their common experience. She does not use the light, medium, and dark groupings formally but finds the right individuals and banks to meet the demands of the material.

Significantly, they worked with seeming complete abandon and thoroughly enjoyed their self-expression. They also demonstrated that this *joy is not antagonistic to the disciplined effort* required for any finished product but is its natural reward as well as the spark that motivates the discipline and makes it tolerable. It is closely related to each individual's becoming aware of the essential core of the material and striving to express it, with the others.

Haven't we in education waited long enough for such an "open sesame" to vital learning?

Another prominent factor in the choros' work is the inescapable, though flexible, rhythm into which they lock their interpretation. We are not speaking of meter but of the underlying beat that courses through the life situation being dealt with in each number. Their rhythm varied not only with the subject, from Norman Cousins' "Lonesome Train" to Corey Ford's "The Computer," but was the framework on which they built sparkling flexibility within each number in terms of speed, inflection, phrasing—in fact all the variables in group speaking.

Their rhythm forestalled all the awkward delays and jarring differences that want to occur when the pattern calls for solos and various groups to blend short passages into the whole. They used hand claps and vocal exclamations to accent their rhythm as a composer would use grace or "accidental" notes.

Another art form was poignantly used in Langston Hughes' "Dreams Deferred" when lithe and large-eyed Shelly Mitchell danced close to the heart of the poem. It was a rehearsal and we were the only audience but we were overcome with the emotion she lifted up, in harmony with the voices.

This year the choros has performed for twenty-thousand students and on one tour they did four high-school-assembly programs a day for three days running! In one of these, in a culturally deprived area, the initial disorder bordered on chaos until the students realized what they were hearing. Then they were captured in rapt attention throughout the program; good evidence that choral speaking deals with fundamental human experience that in this case bridged wide cultural canyons. Add to these taxing tours their eight hours of rehearsal every week of the school year. All this voluntary involvement is further proof that young people representing a cross section of a college campus in the present day will respond to the rewards inherent in this work without extraneous enticement, when imaginatively directed.

A drama choros does not come about the first month or year but is the result of decades of building, experimenting, faith and endless hours on the part of a Mary Gwen Owen, as it must be for all who work with choral speaking. But—the rewards!

University of Minnesota, Minneapolis, Minnesota:
When the Meaning Needs More

Professor David Thompson states that there is no course in verse choir as such in his department but that in his "Oral Interpretation" course he encourages groups to try multiple voices "when the meaning swells to need more than one voice to express it," a most succinct statment of the raison d'être for the verse choir.

Augsburg College, Minneapolis, Minnesota:
When Opportunity Knocks

Miss Ailene Cole's first opportunity to use choral speaking came at the request of a music teacher to have a speaking group introduce the numbers of a concert. This close association with music is a frequent, good and mutually beneficial thing.

The next Christmas her verse choir featured its part of the program with such numbers as the wistful "The Maid Servant at the Inn" by Dorothy Parker, Elizabeth Coatsworth's apologetic "After Christmas a Landlord Remembers" and "Prayer for a Young Mother," all excellent selections having a contemporary flavor. While continuing her activity in choral speaking, Miss Cole has found an additional interest in the "Readers Theatre" approach.

University of South Dakota, Vermillion, South Dakota:
Some Plays Are Better

Dr. Wayne S. Knutson is working with the readers theatre technique, having good success with ten graduate students reading *Dark of the Moon* by Howard

Richardson and William Berney. The many group scenes in this play give excellent opportunity for dramatic use of choral speaking, and singing, and amply demonstrate the natural way in which group expression grows out of the life situations so naturally depicted by this folk play.

University of Nebraska, Lincoln, Nebraska:
Can Democracy Work between Director and Choir?

Dr. Maxine Trauernicht's courses in Speech Education at the university are closely related to the University High School program that emphasizes Creative Dramatics, Oral Interpretation, Play Reading, and the Verse Choir.

She offers an answer to the often-asked "good" question of "How to get the choir to decide on the meaning in a democratic way, without dictating and still keeping control of the group?" She is strong for the democratic approach and believes the director can lead the choir members in discovering their own greatest common denominator in relation to the poem. This best collective thought usually rises to the top in well-ordered group discussion. She finds that the more formal machinery of democratic action, the election of officers and voting on "the best way to do the poem," are of little help in this more flexible and creative use of the democratic principle. It demands mutual confidence in the serious intent of everyone concerned.

An all-state high school summer speech program on the University of Nebraska campus culminated in a verse choir of sixty voices giving a final concert for an outdoor audience of eleven hundred.

Midland College, Fremont, Nebraska: **Ask a Busy Man**

That Ivan Davidson, as a one-man theatre department, can offer such a wide range of courses is significant but that he can still find time to organize a non-credit verse choir and take them on a nine-day four-state tour demonstrates their intense interest and the vital public relations value such a group is to the college.

Their materials include all of James Weldon Johnson's "God's Trombones" except two, and selections from the "Psalms," the "Love Chapter," "Songs of Solomon," and Benét's "John Brown's Body."

The choir reads from scripts in performance. This was their second year. Mr. Davidson holds tryouts and selects six men and six women whom he divides into four sections he terms Soprano, Alto, Tenor and, Baritone, although it is a speaking group. The script for "God's Trombones" showed these vocal divisions were used with sensitivity and imagination to produce a multiple representation of that "magnificent voice" that Johnson ascribes to the folk preachers who gave us these sermon-poems. The trombone is the instrument that most nearly approaches its great range, hence the title "God's Trombones."

Georgetown College, Georgetown, Kentucky: Where The Book of Job Began

Mrs. Robert Snyder's "The Wordmasters" is another group made up of volunteers who must try out to qualify. While they mainly attract speech majors and minors, their tryouts are open to the entire campus. There are twenty in the choir this year and their attire is simple black and white.

Mrs. Snyder emphasizes religious numbers in the selection of materials and this past year had striking success with the book of Revelations, an apt choice when one remembers its resounding passages. They also have done T. S. Eliot's *Murder in the Cathedral* as a full theatre production.

It was at Georgetown College that Orlin and Irene Corey first produced *The Book of Job* under the inspiring leadership of Miss Rena Calhoun, now retired.

West Virginia University, Morgantown, West Virginia: Lunch Hour Rehearsals

Whether the volunteer groups have greater vigor than those classes receiving units of credit would be hard to determine, but to add this much effort and time to an already full schedule shows unusual interest both for the students and faculty members involved. Mrs. Beverly Cortes has two such groups here, each meeting for one hour a week and both together for a half of the lunch hour every day when they are preparing for one of their half-dozen engagements each semester.

Their material covers an extremely wide range according to their enthusiasms, which is perhaps the best criteria, as is shown by these poems: *How the Grinch Stole Christmas,* Dr. Seuss; "Home Came the Old Man," folk; "Nature Lover's Creed," Thomas Curtis Clark; "When the Frost is on the Pumpkin," James Whitcomb Riley; Genesis and other books from the Bible; "The Squaw Dance," Lew Sarett, and "Jesus Walked in Galilee," a haunting folk number filled with repetitions that suggest beautiful overtones.

Mrs. Cortes also believes that the verse choir results in

her people having better basic speech skills when they speak individually.

Yale School of Drama, Yale University, New Haven, Connecticut: American Premiere

While this very busy theatre has found it necessary to discontinue the "Verse Choir" course, Professor Constance Welch gave us an interesting sidelight on a problem faced by every theatre director who wishes to use choral speech in a play.

During their rehearsals for the American premiere production of T. S. Eliot's *Murder in the Cathedral*, they discovered that the well-coordinated sound of the chorus, which had been rehearsed as one large group with carefully placed vocal units, was being thrown out of balance when the chorus was divided up to meet the demands of stage pictures and dramatic action. The ultimate outcome was worth the effort of adjusting because the lines of the chorus took on greater authenticity when they were returned to the life situation which had given them birth, the living scene being performed.

This was a reminder that choral speaking is a natural expression of a group of people who have something to say that can be better communicated by their one collective voice.

University of Redlands, Redlands, California: Major Choral Dramas

Albert and Bertha Johnson, that wonderful directing-and-writing team of complementing geniuses, pioneered with the verse choir in the early thirties with their own arrangement of Milton's *Paradise Lost*. For this they used a speaking chorus of some fifty voices, with solo voices doing Adam, Eve, Satan, and other principals. Next came "Acts of Saint Peter" by one of the early men to inspire the verse choir's rebirth in Scotland, Gordon Bottomley. It was written for the speaking chorus as were others of his plays.

Their own play, *World without End,* was a choral drama that was really a new art form in which all the members of the cast emerged from the speakers' and dancers' chorus of thirty to play the various roles that carried the story line. It was published by Walter Baker in 1935, and was toured both on the west coast and abroad. These three were done while they were directing the theatre at Cornell College, Iowa.

While directing at the Glenn Wallachs Festival Theatre at the University of Redlands they wrote a contemporary treatment of the medieval classic, *Everyman.* In this they used a speaking chorus of nine women who carried a substantial part of the exposition, helped to move the action forward, and created ambience for the transitions. It holds the distinction of having had *five simultaneous premieres* in various part of the country. Besides touring the west coast, it has had a large production in West Germany. It is published in *Church Plays and How to Stage Them* by United Church Press.

The major contribution of this creative couple is their ambitious and dynamic use of choral speaking in producing great poetry and dramas, and in creating their own choral dramas.

Northwestern University, Evanston, Illinois:
230 in a High School Verse Choir

Dr. Charlotte Lee's teaching and writing have promoted the fine tradition in oral interpretation this school has maintained over the years. She also has made a major contribution to choral speaking in developing this work in high schools of the state.

Recently in a culminating program for the "Southern Illinois High School Choric Interpretation Festival" she took one day to rehearse 230 students in poems that had been introduced to them by their teachers. Such major poems as Benét's "The Mountain Whipoorwill," Lindsay's "Daniel" and "The Ghost of the Buffaloes," Johnson's "The Creation," and Sandburg's "Chicago" were among the fourteen used.

Currently she is using verse-choir techniques in several speech-education courses and has co-authored a new book with Speech Education Chairman, Dr. Carl Robinson. It is *Speech in Action,* and includes a fine chapter on choral speaking, helpful especially to teachers.

Carriage House Theatre, Baltimore, Maryland: Mental Picture is the Key

If choral speaking is the outgrowth and "multiple cousin" of oral interpretation, then creative dramatics is surely another close relative, adding further dimensions to the other two.

Mrs. Isabel B. Burger, Director of the Children's Theatre Association that meets in this wonderful old carriage house, strikes the note that all three "cousins" have in common by stating that "each idea and feeling should be given as a *mental picture* that can be understood and made a part of the hearer's experience."

After a seminar with this master teacher I emphasized this technique in presenting materials to our college verse choir and found it to be a shortcut through confusing verbiage that quickly and clearly communicated the concept to the entire group and in turn structured a unified presentation to the audience.

Dr. Charlotte Lee makes a similar point for oral interpretation when she emphasizes *analysis and mastery* of the pieces of literature before attempting their expression; and drama director Eugene C. Bahn painted *instant mental pictures,"* in technicolor," to give further reinforcement to the effectiveness of this idea.

Emerson College, Boston, Massachusetts:
Speech Choir Creates Its Own Material

Emerson College is one of the first institutions in America to embrace choral speaking. The work is now being carried forward by Professor June Hamblin Mitchell in her course, "Teaching Methods in Choric Speech" and in the Emerson College Speech Choir. This group of 30 members features a fall and spring performance among others. They have performed their own original work called "Old and New Boston," which makes it a completely creative experience. They show further originality in adapting two spirituals in "Black Nativity" into an effective speech-choir number. This resulted from hearing the Williams Folk Singers.

One of Professor Mitchell's former students, Mr. Vito N. Silvestri, is making effective use of choral speaking to *deepen the understanding and appreciation of literature* in his classes at the State University College in Potsdam, New York.

The City College, New York, New York:
Avoid the "Sing Song" Trap

A two-unit course called "Choral Speaking" focuses its major effort on giving education majors fundamental techniques and so does not operate as a performing group. It is taught by Professor J. B. Harvey, who makes the important point that the *firm use of emphasis, timing, and inflection that respond to the major underlying elements* of the poem, will avoid the "traps" set by undue attention to meter and rhyme that appear more on the surface in the "limerick" style. Even though young children are happily first attracted by the rhythmic lilt of their poetry, they can be spared having this become a too-prominent feature that keeps other values from being expressed. This can be done by using this natural lilt to usher them into the richer and deeper and still natural expression he describes.

San Diego State University, San Diego, California: Large Numbers Are a Boon and a Bane

The verse choir has had an unbroken lifeline here since it was founded in 1926 by Professor Sybil Eliza Jones after she had met and studied with Marjorie Gullan. I have been privileged to work with it since 1946. We offer two courses, "Verse Choir" and "Verse Choir Directing." The two-unit course "Verse Choir" meets three times a week and becomes the San Diego State Verse Choir, which has supplemented its campus activities with two long-play records, an instructional motion picture, television appearances, and annual Verse Choir Festivals held in our theatre for other choirs.

Two of the things we have learned may be helpful to you. The first is a boon. There are real values in making the course easily accessible to the entire campus rather than only to speech and drama majors. This gives the course a *broad base of students with many and varied interests,* calling for the selection of materials challenging to this "intellectual melting pot." This broad case is a good thing, for the necessary search should result in materials more generally appreciated by audiences of different backgrounds without sacrificing quality. It is also good because the choir now "belongs" to the entire campus and community, possibly saving it from being a one-department activity with limited outside recognition or acceptance.

This breadth also counteracts the social sterilization many students feel in the "corner-of-the-campus" aspect of their specialized classes. They say it is "refreshing to meet people of different interests," and "healthy to find a new common bond of interest." We averaged 12 different departments, with athletes being an enthusiastic and loyal segment, taking extra responsibilities and giving strong vocal support. A further good is that many students find the choir to be an *introduction to aesthetic appreciation* that leads them to further enrichment. And last, it is a major thrill to hear the power and precision—and emotional depth—engendered by a large verse choir.

Second, the bane. Such a broad base and easy access results in large numbers with *all the problems of administration and control* taking their tiresome toll from rehearsal time and concentration. So we take a larger number (196 at the end of last semester) a shorter distance down the road of artistic refinement, often sorely missing the nimble subtleties we enjoyed so much in other groups.

We readily recognize the greater cultural enrichment smaller choirs with more highly selected personnel can give to their members and audiences. We also pay homage to the Macalester College Drama Choros, whose 108 voices somehow manage to achieve both sets of values.

The Readers Theatre at San Diego State University,
San Diego, California: Many Directions Well-Taken

Running concurrently with the last ten years of the verse choir, a group of intrepid and gifted speech artists served their school and community under the brilliant leadership of Dr. William J. Adams, who first established himself as an imaginative theatre director. He soon demonstrated a mastery and prodigious knowledge of literature which supported the goal of his readers theatre group to "produce every form of literature from every period and style."

To name only a few of their offerings, they began with Dürrenmatt's *Traps,* and continued with Shaw's *Back to Methuselah,* Salinger's *Catcher in the Rye,* Ferlinghetti's "Coney Island of the Mind," *The World of Carl Sandburg,* and Sophocles' *Oedipus.* Others of the many authors they produced were: Robinson Jeffers, Lord Byron, Edna St. Vincent Millay, T. S. Eliot, and the Brownings.

Their productions ranged from reading from stools with swivel seats, by which they could turn in and out of the scene, to full theatre productions. Choreography, projections, special lighting, and other theatre arts were adroitly used to skillfully present their highly successful programs. Choral speaking was abundantly used in these productions.

In the midst of all this they found time to record a large volume of literature for the blind, a project that became more major with the weeks and months it consumed. They are now embarking on a remedial reading program, which has been carefully planned from an educational base and which will also give inspirational help to those pupils in the public schools whom it will serve under the able administration of Mr. Arthur Dan Wilson, from whose master's thesis it evolved.

Just recounting all these achievements and plans leaves me panting, but Dr. Adams believes that there is also room in his program to revitalize the San Diego State Verse Choir. He is the one most likely, able, and welcome person I know to continue this endeavor.

* * * * * * * *

You may find in the achievements of the groups at these 35 four-year institutions some things that will be pertinent and helpful to you in your work with this exciting and rewarding art. These do represent a broad spectrum of activity in this field and their *divergent characteristics result from the efforts of their directors to accomplish a chosen purpose* under the conditions found on each campus.

4

"Why is a Verse Choir?"

We Are Losing Our Birthright to Larger-than-Ordinary Speech

The simplest reason for choral speaking to be practiced is our need to use our speaking voices with greater power and expressiveness than every-day use affords us. In our present "bottled-up" society our speech is confined largely to one-on-one conversations with friends, family, and salespeople, to speaking into voice recorders, participating in business conferences, and other limited situations.

True, outdoor workers do extend their voices more largely but the sorry fact is that our opportunities to "let off steam" vocally are being drastically reduced. Fewer people live on farms to wake up the countryside with their bellowings as they round up their livestock, or in small towns to call a cordial greeting across Main Street. This used to happen even in larger cities, but the custom is drying up as we become more encased within ourselves. Even our public speakers, ministers, and some teachers talk moderately into a microphone, which relieves them of the necessity, and values, of projecting their voices—and themselves—with the message.

It is primarily the people who make up the crowds at sporting events who feel the exhilaration of "blowing the carbon" out of their lungs and nervous systems. And more and more of us are content to mumble at the television screen as it presents the event in miniature.

A Versatile Communication Medium

The verse choir restores these lost opportunities by providing a natural and enjoyable means of extending our speaking voices to the top of their capacities and experiencing the accompanying physical and psychological releases. The verse choir is also a powerful and effective means of communication capable of great versatility. It presents its message to the *intellect* of the audience by interpretive vocal techniques, to its *emotions* by the magic of simultaneously sharing the emotion of the instant, and by the universal language of *bodily movement,* ranging from illustrative pantomime to dynamically expressive action that accompanies and reinforces the vocal presentation. These three avenues usher the choral-speaking experience into the *cognitive, affective,* and *psycho-motor* realms of education.

Materials of Great Magnitude

The verse choir gives appropriate dimension to the expression of subjects of such great magnitude that one voice cannot sound the depths of their meaning and emotion: such as Lindsay's, "The Congo;" Sandburg's,

"Chicago;" Millay's," The Murder of Lidice;" Johnson's, "The Crucifixion;" Lorca's, "Lament for the Bullfighter;" "The Song of Moses," Job, and many of the Psalms from the Old Testament, and tragic and joyous passages from great plays and literature.

It is somewhat like an Ohio minister who once said to an assembly of young people, "You'll say I'm 'preaching' to you. Well, of course I am! How can one help it when the truth comes welling up from within?"

And so with us, when the vital message has such proportion and power that it comes welling up, crying for adequate expression, how can we help but match it with the maximum and optimum resources of multiple human voices?

"Little" and Subtle Concepts

Conversely, materials that are simple and childlike are invested with greater importance by the resources of a verse choir. A child hearing an enlarged and highlighted presentation of the favorite "The King's Breakfast" will be happy that "all these people" agree with him that Milne's poem is worth so much attention. This feeling will be enhanced when the adults in the audience also accept and enjoy it—as they always do.

And subtleties become more poignant with the "many-voice treatment." Every director working with a verse choir *must* have it express something *as quietly as possible* to discover the strange power of this "contained vocal power." For an example, when a registration mistake presented us with an unusually large choir we thought we should do such strong rhythmical numbers as Kipling's "Danny Deever" and Lindsay's gusty "Daniel" with King Darius' "voice of thunder!" However, most of the audience members who came back after the outdoor performance spoke of the quiet beauty of Frost's "Stopping by Woods on a Snowy Evening," which was done in sensitive and quiet unison by our 143 voices!

Group Reinforcement of "Singular" Values: Young Children to Young Adults

A further reason for doing this "hidden-in-a-closet" type of material is that comfort is given to individuals in knowing that others understand and subscribe to thoughts and feelings that they had heretofore considered personal and singular, and too tender to expose to the cold winds of possible ridicule. This is especially helpful to young children who are just "finding their minds" and discovering aesthetic and refined values.

This reassurance is also helpful at that period when young people begin to "turn in" on themselves and respond mainly to the pressures of their peer group. This reticence begins somewhere around the fifth grade and continues through junior and senior high school varying with individual personalities. The person is freed from his self-imposed confinement only when he can openly express these formerly considered personal, singular values and claim them as a part of his own identity. Then, he can be his "own man" while sharing the life and expression of the group. The verse choir implements both of these needs.

Indeed, this confinement often persists with college men and women whose intellectual sophistication in some cases, and big muscles and rugged environment in others, preclude the expression of such simple and refined aesthetic values. But once freed, they can take one more step toward becoming an adult. I shall never forget how one popular young man "went out on a limb" to defend the values he appreciated in Eugene Field's "Little Boy Blue" and the deep satisfaction he felt when, after we had worked with the poem, the rest of the choir broke down and admitted they really felt the same way about it.

What a fine service it is for the verse choir to perceive and sensitively express these innermost values and thus free the individual to "claim" them, and it provides this service at every stage of his development.

Communication within the Choir

This is only the beginning of intra-choir communication, a sometimes-overlooked value being overshadowed by the choir's performance function. It continues with the exchange of ideas and feelings by individuals in the *relaxed give-and-take discussions* while the choir and the director are exploring to discover the essence of the poem and how best to present it. It involves suggestions of "what the author really meant" or the "overall mood" and deals with decisions as to which sections of the choir and what techniques can give the most adroit expression.

Granting serious consideration, the "right" interpretation representing the greatest common denominator rises to the top very quickly. This of course also happens in other classes but here it has the impetus of *finding a common workable product* to meet the demands of a coming performance.

Those choir members who may still hold a differing opinion will not suffer from lending their firm support to the concept that has gained general support. In fact, while "trying it on for size" they may expand their think-

ing to accept the new idea—or, failing this, may return
to their original opinion under other circumstances. In a
democracy we are often called upon to support the
judgment of the majority while maintaining our own individual integrity.

Emotional Unity

Another kind of communication sometimes happens
as an unsought bonus. It is a "felt" emotional enthusiasm that captures the group as they hear their ideas
being translated into the sounds of their combined
voices, a sort of "I wouldn't have believed it" feeling. This
also works between sections of the choir.

In our choir it often happened that when one section
had finally "gotten a passage right," after having worked
separately on it, the remainder of the choir rewarded
them with spontaneous applause and vocal approval.

This kind of empathy cannot be planned nor deliberately brought about. It is a "happening," a "come-
uppance" and it results in a mutual pride in achievement of the choir as a whole. It also solves many morale
and behavioral problems, some of which will always be
with us.

Choir-to-Audience Communication

All of the above serves to shape the final product offered to the audience, that eager-sleepy, attentive-
restless, receptive-recalcitrant, large-small—but always
challenging and lovable collection of people that completes the author-artist-audience triangle that is common
to most artistic endeavors.

There are two aspects of this relationship that bear

notice: the first is that it is a "people-to-people" experience. An author wishes to have his work appreciated by people—for even though there may be only one reader at a time he hopes there will be many!—and he also hopes that he can strike a common chord with them all. The multiple nature of the choir facilitates the discovery and vivid presentation of this "greatest common denominator," which it now lifts up in such a way that the many-membered audience can recognize and respond to it—and claim it for its own.

The second aspect is the breadth and depth of the material thus made available for this acute kind of acceptance. In addition to making available vital, unique, and enjoyable programs of contemporary material, the verse choir bridges the ages of history and brings and audience into a "we-are-there" relationship with those who first participated in these human experiences.

More important is the depth of the experience, for the verse choir has now transformed the material into a quality that can be assimilated into immediate full-consciousness by the audience. Other art forms do this also, some more completely—such as the theatre, but the verse choir's directness and simplicity is its unique contribution.

There is a further value in the author-artist-audience triangle. It is the feed-back the audience can give to the author. Few are as spectacular as that given to Pasternak, described in our introduction, but when the author is present for a performance he feels a great satisfaction in knowing that his work has run the human gamut and returned to him as a tried and proven product.—It may also give him a key as to how to improve it.

Even in those instances when no audience can be pres-

ent the author-artist part of the triangle is worth the
doing for the satisfactions that come to each.

Excellence is the First Goal—All Else Follows in Proportion

Before we deal with the educational and psychological
values we should recognize that they all "happen" to the
student in direct proportion to the *degree of excellence*
attained by himself and the choir.

This means that doing the job at hand, such as a simple warm-up rhythm, to the best of his ability and the
height of his enthusiasm, will pay the same kind of div-
idend that will return to him from the polished performance of an intricate number—for they both promote pride of achievement, confidence, and the many
other values that follow.

Educational Values

The aforementioned course in "Verse-Choir Directing" has been taught in the Extension Program at San
Diego State University for more than two decades, serving some 600 teachers-in-service ranging from those
who taught primary and intermediate grades through
secondary and college levels. It was our habit to identify
the educational and psychological values they had seen
demonstrated by their students through participation in
choral speaking, thus replacing hopeful theorizing with
observable results. From their answers these two-dozen
values have been distilled, regrouped, and made ready
for your use in answering questions. They appear within
the paragraphs in italicized form.

The most prominent value is *improvement in all speech
skills*. These begin with a relaxed *"tall" posture*, which

makes *central breathing* a natural and easily habitualized process. This in turn is the basis for *"solid" voice production,* free from breathiness and other lazy faults, and facilitates *accurate articulation* and *pronunciation* when combined with effective exercises. At the top of this stairway the door is now open to reap the harvest of meaningful and interesting speech through natural variations in *pitch, power, phrasing,* and *tempo,* those four stops in the human speech "organ" that provide genuine expressibility when used with proper motivation and balance. These will be further developed in Chapter Eight.

These next three values are closely related. The first, the verse choir opens the door to an *appreciation for good literature* through close acquaintance with the concepts and living pulse of the poetry, dramas, and prose selections performed by the choir. This is not a study of literature as such. Hopefully our students will be further attracted to the beauty of form and other aspects of literature and will become as deeply involved in their study in other classes.

The second, it provides a *vital introduction to authors* by first immersing the student in their writings and giving him a feel for the author. This will prepare him to better understand the nature of his subjects and the quality of their treatment. From this point he may want to know more about when and where the author lived, what caused him to write and other biographical material. This is a far cry from a well-remembered assignment, coming as a seeming afterthought at the end of the class period: "Write a biographical sketch of Alfred Lord Tennyson for tomorrow." I have been guilty of using the ploy of holding back the author's name until someone asked, "Who wrote this?" Then we were all on the toboggan.

And the third, the student is now building a *treasure-house of valued memories* gained from this deep involvement with literature and vital association with the people who created it. This will serve to relieve boredom in solitude, vitalize conversation and, better still, become a springboard for new adventures of the mind and spirit, including a needed critical sense.

These next two values fall naturally from the verse-choir approach to literature. The first is an *increased vocabulary,* both in number of new words and in the perception of different and deeper meanings of familiar words. Frost's "dark and deep" has several exciting layers of meaning. The sharpening of *listening abilities* is the other. This occurs not only from paying closer attention to explanations and directions but also from becoming aware of shades of meanings that develop as the interpretation takes shape. Students have admitted surprise and pleasure at these discoveries.

Two more related natural "fall-outs" are the improvement of *oral reading and comprehension* and an increase in ability to *analyze abstract concepts.* Two of our graduate students, Mrs. Gen Mershon and Mrs. Gladys Berner, ran a study with a class of slow readers in the fourth grade. They found that after several weeks of working with poems in choral speaking their people read faster and comprehended more when presented with *new* material.[1]

As for the second, we must remember that abstract concepts are easier for some students to grasp than

---

[1] This is described in the book *Lion Hunt, Anyone?*, by Mrs. Gladys Berner, an engaging account of her experiences as a Navy Wave who returns to college and completes her degree.

others—who may give up after a series of failures. But when the members of a large group focus their attention on discovering these nebulous meanings together, the process becomes a joint and exciting quest, often roughened by disagreement, but the victory is shared by all!

The last two educational values also belong together because they strengthen each other. The first is that this whole process *stimulates the imagination,* causing your people to perceive more than lies on the surface and to follow sparks that fly off into new realms of thinking and experience. Thus Lindsay's "The Congo" becomes an adventure filled with vivid mental images, intriguing people and sounds that scream across the sky. "The Lion Hunt" will serve younger people in the same way.

Once the imagination begins to percolate, it provides an *interest-wedge into other subjects.* Langston Hughes' "The Negro Speaks of Rivers" could pique such questions as: "Where is this Euphrates River?," "What kind of boats were on the Nile and Congo?," and "What was Lincoln's boyhood really like?" Similarly, Edgar Allan Poe's "The Bells" will set off many exploratory reverberations from his silver, golden, brass, and iron varieties with their accompanying experiences.

These and other questions will send your people into geography, history, literature, social studies, music, science, transportation, space studies, minerology, mathematics, and other fields—and with new motivation. The school at large can profit from this leavening force—if and when we get it started.

Not mathematics? Try Carl Sandburg's "Arithmetic" for an opener, and "The Clock and the Calendar" by Miriam Marcus and Naomi Archer for some reflective fun.

Psychological Values

Dr. Ivan N. McCollom, former chairman of the Psychology Department at the San Diego State University, has stated that the expressive arts, such as music, dance, art, drama, and speech provide vital assistance in the treatment of psychological problems—especially because of their outgoing nature. The values in this next series primarily lend themselves to personality development in this way.

The first is quite simple, but the rest depend upon it. It is that the verse choir *takes the student's thought away from himself,* that first step toward self-actualization—and adulthood. I have often been impressed by the acuteness and magnitude of the problems that students carry around that preempt any interest in other things. Once they are pried loose from these, even for a short time, the door is open to the vistas treated above and can result in that invaluable commodity, *enthusiasm!*

This propelling and unifying force is an absolute necessity in any group where people depend upon each other and expect to succeed. U.C.L.A.'s master basketball coach, John Wooden, equates enthusiasm with *eagerness!* And Don Coryell, San Diego State University's former football wizard says, "It ties it all together." Any theatre person is well aware of how much this inner impetus adds to a performance.

The verse choir is an especially apt arena for enthusiasm since it provides an opportunity for *uninhibited emotional expression in a socially acceptable form.* Many students have stated that they felt better after a rehearsal because of released tensions from "giving out instead of taking in."

This can be especially helpful to *troubled students* who

may have some problem for which they haven't yet found the answer, but which can be temporarily relieved by "blowing off steam." Each rehearsal session is begun with relaxing exercises followed by rhythmical vocalizing that usually reaches such generous proportions of sound, and fun, that any extra explosiveness needed by the troubled one can be released without attracting undue attention. Once he has topped this hurdle he may be receptive enough to participate in the orderly expression of emotion as presented by the author and engaged in by the entire choir—an experience that sometimes reaches a high degree of emotional catharsis.

This just may be the *turning point away from giving up,* or "copping out," and toward responsible effort. With the right follow-up another would-be dropout may find that school can be an interesting place. These critical and drastic turning points are often triggered by seemingly small things, hardly recognized at the moment, and they may happen at any time under any circumstance. The point here taken is that the verse choir sets the stage and structures the activity that could implement the positive action, granting the right chain of fortuitous events. Our troubled student, and indeed everyone to a greater or less degree, can now begin to *build an identity* he can live with and with which others around him can live.

The road is now open for him to join the rest of the choir in developing *poise,* that underlying girder that smooths out ordinary problems, attracts friendships and supports the person in times of crisis. Poise has often been mentioned by our students as being a much-appreciated result of their verse-choir experience. This state of being is easy to attain for it develops from simply taking all the responsibilities expected of a contribut-

ing choir member in preparing a program and is enhanced in the performance itself, especially if an audience can crown the effort with appreciation and approval.

As an extra outgrowth, poise makes a person feel secure enough to really relate to others with *genuine tolerance,* not the "I guess you can stand there" variety that
usually comes with a "down-the-nose" look but the kind
that results from a true appraisal and acceptance of the
other person as a working partner. It says instead, "Hey,
we're different—but let's see if we can work together."

All of this takes some doing, for even the cogs of a
gear wheel need to have their sharp corners rounded
off for better articulation. In the choir this happens
when the *over-aggressive person learns to recognize the worth
of others* and the *lonely, sensitive one begins to value his own
worth* as he earns his place in the group. This *mutual recognition* of the contribution of all members and
appreciation of shared experiences build an intra-choir rapport that has been called "morale" or "spirit," but by any
name is invaluable. And it operates with persons of all
ages.

This "mutual good feeling" has the further and extremely important value of developing *teacher-student
rapport* in a relaxed yet controlled atmosphere. The class
becomes aware that the teacher has somehow descended
from the "authoritarian pedestal" to engage as a fellow
human being in all these goings-on and even seems to
be *having fun–with us!* She now becomes a leading co-
worker who, if the good truth were known, is the wise
catalyst, if not chief engineer, of the entire
procedure—but these secrets she may be content to keep
to herself.

The cumulative effect of the total verse choir experience is that it teaches *responsibility and loyalty* to the group's best interests, which are heightened by a *love of participation and sense of achievement* through giving something to the choir and thence to an audience. The final pay-off is that it develops the ability to say *"we" instead of "I"* in referring to the work of the choir.

I have purposely held until last two often-quoted services rendered by the verse choir. The first is to those people who need *speech therapy*. Dr. Alan C. Nichols, Professor of Speech Therapy and Audiology at the San Diego State University, states that "the verse choir serves these individuals only in an incidental and non-direct way, doing no harm but not giving all the help needed." As directors, our responsibility to these people is to recognize their problems and to refer them to specialists who can give them particular and thorough treatment.

He further believes that the director can build confidence in these people with speech defects by *accepting their partial participation as a comfortable experience,* putting no pressure on them to do more than they can manage and seeing to it that they share the exuberance of the group. Sensitive individual rapport and guidance is also needed to protect them from expecting too much when pressures outside the choir destroy this comfortable support by the group.

The importance of this rapport was brought home to me by my failure when a stutterer who spoke smoothly with the college choir took minutes to complete a sentence as I listened after class.

The other service is to that undetermined but suspectedly large minority group, the *non-singers*. To these a verse choir is a godsend for it provides an experience, analogous to a singing choir, which welcomes full-voiced participation through all the techniques of group speaking. A hidden but vitally important part of this experience is the development of a sense of *rhythm* that might otherwise be denied them.

That these people do suffer, quietly and sometimes deeply, was made painfully clear in one instance reported by a mother who was a member of our choir. As her son's sixth-grade class moved onto the stage to sing in a public program the teacher, with a strange smile, patted him on the head and said, "Let's you not sing." He didn't. In dreary fact, he became so generally repressed that it seemed he would never come out from under the blanket of introversion that developed.

Through the good efforts of his mother and some of his friends we managed to get him, now a college sophomore, into the verse choir. In his first semester his reticence faintly cracked open to allow some tentative attempts to keep up with the choir—these efforts became more determined and were sometimes accompanied by a "lifted" countenance—and later he was seen to smile and obviously take real pleasure in participating. It was not until the second semester that he developed an abandon and gusto in giving his "all-out" support to the numbers we were doing. His personality reflected his new-found confidence in the more open way he responded to his friends and the keener interest he seemed to take in things beyond himself.

In rereading these many answers to the question that heads this chapter, "Why Is a Verse Choir?", it appears that I may have "shot a rabbit with a cannon."

I take shelter in the hope that some of these answers *may be pertinent to your problems* and in the fact that all of them, represented by the *italicized words and phrases*, are *supported by observed actual experiences*.

Part Two

How Is a Verse Choir?

5

How to Organize a Verse Choir

The Central Principle

That there is no one best organization pattern for a verse choir is obvious from the many successful choirs in such divergent forms reported in Chapter 3. There is, however, a central consideration that if followed can effectively serve all choirs equally well. That principle is to find the arrangement that *best enables your people to accomplish the chosen purpose* of your particular choir on a given occasion.

Architects tell us that houses designed to be functionally efficient and to fit the needs of the family are also the most aesthetically satisfying. So the organization that best *implements the purpose of the choir* will find itself in the form *most pleasing to the eye* as well as fulfilling its primary function of providing *optimum vocal versatility.*

This latter factor is the most important, for the verse choir represents *one great voice* that must remain similar to its counterpart, the *individual human voice,* preserving all its wide range of varieties while capitalizing on its own unique ability to enlarge on each one of these for greater expressiveness.

Finding the best way to organize a choir so that its multiple voice can best implement a given purpose is the burden of this chapter.

Heterogeneous Group

The first form we will consider was used by a director in the Lincoln Center in New York. He kept the group in one unit, avoiding any divisions at all, wishing as he said to "let the voices 'tinkle' naturally together." This indeed does work with well-poised individuals with well-trained voices who can hold their own within the group at large. With younger and less-trained voices the tendency of such a choir would be to flatten itself out to the median sound, resulting in sodden monotony.

When one is presented with a given group, such as a mob scene in a play or a large crowd for a one-session choral speaking experience, this formation is of course convenient and does give the participants a sense of unified vocal power. Also, you can improvise variety by asking certain groups such as men or women to speak together—but this is haphazard at best and precludes many subtleties.

Boy-Girl Grouping

Miss Carrie Rasmussen advocates this simple division through the elementary grades, and it has many advantages. It capitalizes on natural group loyalties, is convenient to the classroom and makes good use of the natural difference in the quality of boys' and girls' voices. It also can be varied by the use of individuals and of smaller groups of nearly identical voices, called "banks," thus meeting the demands of most of the literature written for children.

Men-Women Grouping

There are limited advantages to this division. True, the two groups speak with generally different characteristics that can be effectively used in antiphonal numbers, especially those written for men-women repartees. It is also convenient for groups already so arranged that may wish to introduce short-spoken passages.

However, the maturing of individual personalities and their resulting voice characteristics presents the choir with great variety within each group and calls for an organization that better utilizes this rich potential.

So the grouping considered next, with all its possible variations, is offered as the most productive basic arrangement for a verse choir. It is based on the natural sound each individual speaking voice produces.

The Sound of a Speaking Voice

The individual speaking voice is a complex instrument, both in its construction and its operation, and each one varies definitely from all others. In fact this individuality is so definite that an electrical "voice print" is *as accurate as a set of fingerprints* for purposes of identification. (Now we are considering only *voice production,* not articulation, pronunciation, nor the skills of connected speech. Please see Chapter 8 for these.)

The sounds these differences make generally fall

under these six characteristics and each voice will find itself somewhere on the sliding scale of each characteris-
tic, as follows:

1. From breathiness to a firm *solid* quality, making
   projection comfortable.
2. From harsh stridency to a *relaxed* sound that is easy to
   listen to.
3. From too-much nasality to *balanced* throat, mouth,
   and nasal *resonance*.
4. From lack of reverberation as in a "dry" voice to rich
   overtones of balanced resonance.
5. From a staccato sound that results from a "stabbing"
   attack of each word or phrase to *balanced duration* that
   gives proportionate value to each sound in the word
   according to its meaning and emphasis. This is called
   "presence" in broadcasting.
6. Voices also differ in being pitched habitually high or
   low, similar to the "tessatura" of a song.

Each voice makes up its own syndrome, or combination,
of these characteristics.

This all seems to complicate rather than simplify our
problem of finding characteristics that are common to
enough voices to make possible some kind of useful
groupings.

Our suggested solution is to consider only the differences in *resonance and pitch,* numbers four and six, and
to expect the work of the verse choir to improve all the
others—which it will.

Groupings Utilizing Light, Medium, and Dark Voice Qualities

This brings us to the *light, medium, and dark* groupings.
Light voices are usually characterized by being high in
pitch and with relatively little resonance. They are especially useful when lilting, bell-like or brilliant sounds are

called for. A *dark* voice is usually low in pitch and is rich in resonant overtones, giving the choir a solid foundation or rumbling power when needed.

These two distinct groups do give us the basis for organizing the choir, for we can now build the two *light* sections from those voices, both men's and women's, that are definitely so characterized. Similarly, the *dark* sections will evolve from those voices that clearly belong together because of their characteristics.

The *medium* sections will then be made up of those voices that are neither distinctly light nor dark. These are perhaps the most useful groups in the choir because they *more easily establish a common bond* with the audience, being unconsciously recognized as "sounding like my voice" by the great majority of people and therefore communicating unobtrusively and naturally. The light and dark sections can then be used for *extreme peaks and depths* of sound to reflect thought emphasis and emotional expression comparable to the wide variety used by any given individual voice for these purposes.

Add to these considerations the fact that all six sections have great potential for variety of pitch, power, phrasing and speed and we can begin to see how many stops this multi-voiced "organ" makes available to us, especially when we add the use of striking solo voices and smaller "banks" of nearly identical voices found in each of the groups.

In a stand-up choir the voice groups would appear as in the following diagram:
each group, unless it was so "tailored" by tryout selection.

This arrangement can be modified in several ways.

This is an ideal situation, however, for a choir would be very fortunate to be so divided with an equal number in

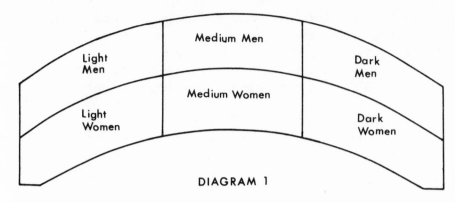

DIAGRAM 1

First by mixing the men's and women's sections together and having only one each of light, medium, and dark sections. This adds an interesting dimension of sound with the blend of the different quality of men's and women's voices in each section, as demonstrated in the chart below:

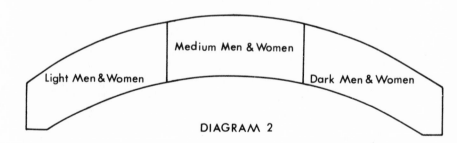

DIAGRAM 2

Comparison with Stringed Instruments

A clearer idea of the sound each voice quality will produce can be gained by comparing them in turn with four stringed musical instruments. *Light women* will resemble the *violin* while *light men,* having a "heavier" quality, will sound more nearly like the *viola. Medium women* will approximate the *viola* while the *cello* will give the nearest approach to the sound of *medium men.* The *cello* will be closest to *dark women* and *dark men* will be best represented by the *big double bass,* or bull fiddle as it is sometimes called. The difference in the two "instruments" represented in each of the sections will produce a pleasant "counterpoint" effect. The choir will be arranged like this:

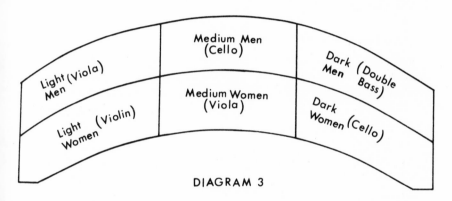

DIAGRAM 3

Children and the Light, Medium, and Dark Arrangement

The question arises: "At what stage of development can this arrangement serve a children's choir better than the boy-girl division?" A personal experience may shed some light. When one of my verse-choir directing students was doing her practice teaching she combined three sixth-grade classes to do Tazewell's "The Littlest Angel" as a verse-choir number. Being surprised to find boys in all three voice groups, I asked Virginia how she had managed to "sell" the boys on joining the two lighter groups. She said, "I just told them they had light or medium voices and there was no problem." They were in fact more comfortable speaking with their natural voice quality and within their pitch range than if they had strained to join their buddies whose voices had developed a darker sound.

While no hard-and-fast rule can be applied, we can be guided by some principles. The first is "performance comfort," or surrounding each individual with people with whom he is most vocally compatible. Another is to use the grouping that best serves the number being performed and the occasion it serves.

Neither of these, however, should cause a social problem for an individual. For instance, we might be "buying trouble" for a large boy with a light voice by insisting that he work in the light group with smaller boys—and girls. Peer pressure can be devastating at certain ages and the subtleties of voice groupings can wait, according to the judgment of a wise teacher or director.

Shall we "take five" to remember that the nurturing of human values is the ultimate goal of the verse choir?

A Choir with a Four-Voice Grouping

Another modification combines the light, medium, dark arrangement with the men-women division and produces a flexible and very usable choir. One immediate value is that it can absorb the "large boy with the light voice" and other unusual individuals without social trauma. It appears on page 113.

Advantages of the Four-Voice Grouping

The first advantage here is that sections (1) and (4) are now clearly and distinctly "lilting, bell-like, and bril-

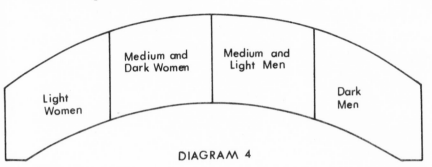

DIAGRAM 4

liant" and steeped in deep "rumbling power" respectively, without any adulteration. This allows for surprising and satisfying "spikes" of sounds at both ends of the vocal spectrum that will enhance the interpretation of the number.

The second is that it retains the enrichment of counterpoint gained by combining the *medium and dark* women in section (2) and the *light and medium* men in section (3).

A third is that it helps to equalize the size of the sections numerically for these relatively few dark women can fill out the medium section and a similar small number of light men will blend into the men's medium section without crowding it out of proportion.

Also, performing with the men's medium section will tend to add resonance and lower the pitch of a man's light voice. This is a good service for it renders his voice more expressive and less conspicuous.

Another advantage is that the two medium sections will provide a place to assimilate an unpleasantly outstanding voice by surrounding him or her with speakers with strong voices who will help neutralize the conspicuous quality and will also tend to improve the one voice in the direction of the more attractive characteristics of their voices. This worked with one unfortunate co-ed whose extremely high and shrill voice stood out like a piccolo in an orchestra.

It is of course better if the student is aware of the procedure and can willingly participate in its improvement value by trying to blend with the other voices. In any case it is better than the "let's you not sing" treatment given to the sixth-grade boy in Chapter 4.

All of the above advantages were experienced in the San Diego State Verse Choir. The "deepening" of men's light voices by including them in the medium section was especially appreciated at the college level. The numerical equalization worked out surprisingly well with our 196 members except in section (2), the *medium women*. In our particular case, we found we had an unusually large number of *dark women's voices* that swelled this section out of proportion—so we capitalized on our blessing and formed them into a *dark women's section* and used them both separately and to enrich the *dark men's section*.

The four-voice formation worked remarkably well for our presentation of Edgar Allan Poe's "The Bells," with crystal-clear light voices opening with:

Hear the sledges with the bells, silver bells.
What a world of merriment their melody foretells—.

The more mellow sound of the medium and dark women reflected the deeper and more-lasting joy of:

Hear the mellow wedding bells, golden bells.
What a world of happiness their harmony foretells—.

The medium men were asked to take any softness out

of their voices and simulate the raucous monotone of the clanging brass bells with the first two lines:

Hear the loud alarum bells, brazen bells,
What a tale of terror now their turbulency tells!

but managed great variety to express the spectacular nuances of excitement as the third section of the poem advanced.

The dark men were superb in beginning the sonorous tones of the last part:

Hear the tolling of the bells, iron bells,
What a world of solemn thought their monody compells—.

The remainder of each section of this masterpiece runs the scale from a mood of quiet reflection to the wild cacaphony of the fire bells to express Poe's unbridled imagination, and gives the choir unlimited opportunity.

This is only one example of the many variations possible in the use of the basic light-medium-dark formation to better serve groups of various sizes and proportions. It is a fact of life that these three voice qualities "will always be with us" so our choice is how and to what extent to use them.

George Bernard Shaw was aware of these natural differences in voices and made good use of their distinctive qualities in casting his plays. In his *Saint Joan*, he asked for his military nobleman to have a "tenor" voice with a light brilliant and "trumpet-like" quality, which would compare to the "light" speaking voice. For his Bishop he suggested a "bass" voice to exude confidence and authority, this corresponds to the "dark" speaking voice. And he wished his Chaplain to have a flexible, practical, work-a-day voice, which he called "baritone," that would give him the "common touch," a good description of the "medium" speaking voice.

Many other playwrights have been cognizant of the contribution voices make in characterization and have written the lines of each character to subtly capitalize on these differences as well as describing them in their casting notes. Eugene O'Neill was unusually sensitive and skilled in this.

Comparison with Singing Voices

While the singing voice represents a special art and therefore produces a sound of a different quality than a speaking voice, there is a helpful, though loose, analogy that may be drawn between the sections of the two kinds of choirs, as follows:

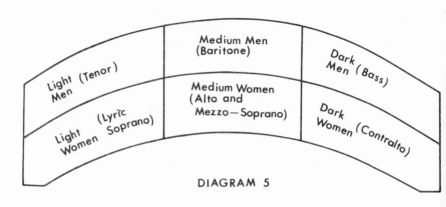

DIAGRAM 5

This cannot be trusted entirely, however, for there is often a wide disparity between the sound of a given individual's singing and speaking voice. Lyric tenors often speak "way down there" as a bass would be expected to do and there are many other instances of this phenomenon.

The above arrangement would be better than a simple men's-women's division if, while executing a song, a singing choir needed to do speaking passages that were fairly complex. It would also render a singing choir immediately well organized to become a verse-speaking choir without changing the position of the personnel.

The Verse Choir Becomes a Group of Orchestrated Voices

By now we should see, by the use of any of these groupings, or a combination of them, that the natural quality of the speaking voice being used at its optimum pitch and in its relaxed condition provides for a verse choir a value similar to that which a given instrument provides to an orchestra. Therefore we are within the realm of general analogy to refer to the verse choir as a group of *orchestrated voices*. This polyphonic quality of the total sound may be distinctly heard when the choir is speaking naturally without any dramatic import, as they will do in being introduced.

Simultaneous Use of Singers, Stringed Instruments, and Speakers

There is a further and even more intriguing way in which informal orchestration may be used with the three sections of the verse choir. It is suggested by the comparison with stringed instruments and singing voices in diagrams 3 and 5 respectively in this chapter.

Each one of the L, M, and D speaking sections may well be combined with great benefit with its corresponding singing voice and stringed instrument to enhance and enrich the total impact of the author's meaning, making use of the spontaneous creative abilities of the three kinds of artists. This blend could be accomplished by using the speakers, singers, and stringed instruments in alternating dominant and supportive roles, giving each medium the freedom to improvise—always remembering to preserve balance for the sake of the total message of the passage.

Such an arrangement would exceed the possibilities of the recitative and other formal uses of speech with musical compositions for it will allow the director to ask in turn for each of the supportive media to improvise a response to the one that is carrying the dominant expression of the passage. These could be *nonverbal spoken sounds* using vowels and continuing consonants, *nonverbal singing sounds* making greater use of pitch and other singing techniques, and *imaginative sounds of the strings* to evoke directly the thoughts and emotions of the passage. All of these could later be refined and given their most expressive proportion with the whole by the director.

An example would be to ask the strings to enlarge on the emotional impact to the phrase "My cup runneth over"—perhaps a wavelike, overflowing sound or a less-literal expression of immense satisfaction. When this subsides, the dark voices could solidly say, "Surely," and be joined by the medium and light voices in completing the passage: "Goodness and mercy will follow me all the days of my life, and I will dwell in the house of the Lord, forever." At the same time the singers can add their nonverbal musical tones and the strings their supportive contributions all though the build until they all three reach the magnificent *"forever!"* And we are not finished, for they can continue in a diminishing series of "forevers" with first the speakers dropping out, then the singers, leaving the strings to spin out the on-going, never-ending concept of timelessness. The entire poem can be treated in a similar fashion, beginning with the musical elements establishing the pastoral scene and then responding to the speakers.

Perhaps the most important factor in the blending of these expressive arts is that it emanates from the free creativity of each of the three. Our verse choir attempted such a blending in the treatment we gave "The Battle-Hymn of the Republic" and "Dixie," found in Chapter 16.

Three Traditional Ways of Using Music with a Verse Choir

The first use of music with a verse choir is to have either singers or instruments as a *simple background* to the speaking choir. When this is done, the main consideration is to be sure that both the music and speakers are carrying the same message and that the music stays "under" the speakers in power.

The second, and most obvious, way of combining the two arts is to use *speaking and musical groups separately,* keeping them independent except for the general nature and import of the program. Their alternate use adds freshness and variety to the program, each strengthening the effect of the other. The same choir could speak and sing alternately, according to the nature of the numbers, to achieve this same effect.

The third is to *combine all three media:* speaking, singing, and instruments, writing them into the composition so that each makes its definite contribution in relation to the others. This is a formalized outgrowth of the improvised use of the three suggested above for the Twenty-third Psalm.

Fred Waring uses this more-sophisticated blending in his treatment of Johnson's "God's Trombones," where his Pennsylvanians are joined by two speakers and an orchestra playing the music of Roy Ringwald. More recent instances of formally joining speaking voices with musical groups, called *aleotoric music,* is discussed in Chapter 13 under the section "Bands Are Saying What They Cannot Play."

The Versatile Formations of the Drama Choros

The drama choros, at both Macalester College and San Dieguito High School, has arrived at a uniquely fluid organization that allowed unlimited variations. It is not necessary for them to form light, medium, and dark sections for they can immediately change into any strategic grouping they wish, implementing their philosophy of performing materials of wide variety and strong idea content.

The facility with which they manage to quickly change into these interweaving groups, small units, individuals, and many other exciting formations without breaking the rhythm of the performance is a smooth operation that escapes one without careful scrutiny. The "secret" is that each formation and change is an immediate reflection of the natural demands of the number being performed, resulting in movement and groupings that inherently express the essence of the material.

Their manner of getting onto the stage quickly and in

a loose formation is worth noting, as it can be used by many choirs.

Using four levels, the floor and a three-step riser, they approach in two parallel lines, one on the floor and one on the second step. Then at a signal, every-other person moves up one level, resulting in "elbow room" for everyone and making all their choreography and intricate formations easily possible. The following diagrams will illustrate this for a choir of thirty-two members, though it can be adapted to larger or smaller groups.

Entering Formation

(This can be done from opposite directions to add snap.)

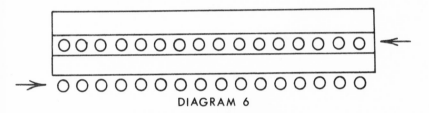

DIAGRAM 6

Basic Speaking Formation

(This facilitates quick changes in position for meaningful and dramatic groupings.)

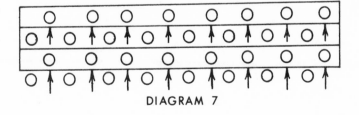

DIAGRAM 7

When we add the types of organization demonstrated in this chapter to the many and varied formations used by the college choirs described in Chapter 3 we can see that no choir needs to be "locked" into a preconceived grouping, but that every verse choir is free to adapt its organization to its personnel, the needs of its material and the occasion for its performance.

6

The Basic Elements of Directing — The Seven Variables

Of the many different aspects of the director's job, the one most demanding and rewarding is that of transporting a chosen piece of literature *from a printed page to the consciousness of a live audience.*

The elements, or tools, he has to work with are all the techniques of group oral interpretation. These have been variously named and differently defined by others but for our purposes we wish to identify them as the *seven variables.* These are: *voice quality, number of voices, bodily movement, pitch, power, phrasing,* and *tempo.*

Voice Quality

There are two aspects of voice quality the director can use. *The first,* discussed at length in the preceding chapter, deals with an individual voice finding itself on the scale of *light, medium, and dark,* considering primarily its pitch range and resonance potential but *recognizing all the other characteristics of production* that make it a voice of individual beauty and distinctive characteristics. We have shown how the director can use each of these groups for their natural basic sound or combinations of them for special effects.

Beyond its natural basic sound each one of the voice groups offers great variety. Just as each singing voice and musical instrument is capable of many variations of sounds in rendering its composition so does the speaking voice, regardless of its grouping, bring great versatility to the task of interpreting the number the verse choir is performing—as shown by the second aspect of voice quality.

The *second aspect* is that effect on the quality of any voice that *results from its reaction to a thought or emotion.* We speak of it as "talking mean," or "you sure do sound chipper this morning"—and sometimes "I can tell by the tone of your voice you don't mean it." This is nothing more nor less than the natural voice inflections and "extra things" we do with our voices to express the subtle shadings of meaning and drastic changes of emotion that we automatically express with our voices as we think or feel them.

It is easy enough to recognize this in an individual who is overcome by the certainty at the end of Edgar Allan Poe's "The Raven" that:

—my soul from out that shadow that lies floating on the floor
Shall be lifted—nevermore!

But how do we get twenty or two hundred people to express the same quality of thought or emotion in response to this hopeless passage—and simultaneously?

The "secret" really is simple. Almost too simple to convince the group that they can do it. It lies in the *credibility* of the experience being expressed. The choir must simply *believe* what they are saying. Instead of asking the choir to say it "as if they knew," convince them that they *do know for certain* that their souls "from out that shadow that lies floating on the floor, shall be lifted—nevermore!" You will all be surprised at how much unanimity will be expressed.

There will be no undue emphasis on the final word, simply a smooth statement giving *proportionate emphasis* to all elements of the sentence and ending with a note of conviction. Minor variations of *individual interpretation* will be merged in the *overpowering central flow* of the meaning.

The same phenomenon happened when eighty-eight emigrants who were studying to receive their Americanization papers were formed into a verse choir to do *The Preamble to the Constitution* as a part of their ceremony. Their opening words, "We the People of the United States!"—rendered with heartfelt pride and conviction by their twenty-nine different native dialects—left no doubt as to the oneness of purpose they intended for this and for the remainder of the preamble—which was a wonder to hear.

It is a miracle of "felt" communication that emanates from a *real experience* and knows no bounds of numbers nor language. Surely it can be used to communicate to a given group of any age the essence of thought or feeling the director wishes the choir to experience.

It will unite a kindergarten group in gay confidence as they finish Vachel Lindsay's "The Turtle" with "— — but he can't catch me!" And it will join a fourth-grade class as they shudder in mock fear as James Whitcomb Riley warns:

And the Gobble-uns'll git you,
Ef you
  Don't
    Watch
    Out!

And it will, and should, cement all ages in a common bond with John Donne's inescapable "No man is an Island entire of itself." It is the "tone of voice," the "stamp of integrity," that the voice carries that needs no other proof of veracity.

At times a longer passage will need a fuller paraphrasing to convey the central core of meaning. An example of this may be found in Chapter 16 in the treatment of the *Twenty-Third Psalm*.

Number of Voices

This second variable simply refers to *adding or subtracting* whole sections, banks, smaller groups, or individuals to increase or diminish the power or richness of the sound to better express the meaning. While this would no doubt be used in conjunction with the increase or diminishing of the power exerted by the voices, we are considering only the matter of numbers in this case.

By using this simple technique a three-section light-medium-dark choir could develop a powerful build and denoument in the King James version of this moving passage from "The Song of Moses" (Exodus 15: 14-16):

(It begins with a frightened single light woman's voice.)

L Solo   "The peoples have heard, they tremble:"
         (The light section now supplies reinforcement as the fear becomes plural.)

L   "Pangs have taken hold on the inhabitants of Philistia."
         (The medium section adds substance to the fear of the chiefs.)

LM   "Then were the chiefs of Edom dismayed:"
         (The entire choir now reverberates the trembling and terror.)

LMD   "The mighty men of Moab, trembling taketh hold upon them:
         All the inhabitants of Canaan are melted away.
         Terror and dread falleth upon them;
         By the greatness of thine arm—"

         (The denoument begins here by taking out the light section.)

MD   "They are still as stone;
         Till thy people pass over, Oh Jehovah,"
         (The denoument now finds its solid base of confidence by the dark section alone.)

D   "Till thy people pass over that thou has purchased."

Although no one of the seven variables is ever used entirely by itself, different combinations can, by careful planning, support each other to gain various subtleties of sound, as we shall see.

Bodily Movement

The examples and descriptions of this variable given in Chapters 3 and 5 show its many exciting possibilities. They include smaller groups doing pantomimes or cameo dramatic scenes within or in front of the choir, individuals taking dramatic action to "spike" or accent a line, using a dance group with the choir, using the choir as a dance group with intricate choreography as they speak, having the two halves of the choir weaving in a contrapuntal manner and even the entire choir moving together—if they do move together, but confusion is just around the corner. You will enjoy creating the unique and exactly right movement to express the exact thought or feeling.

Another consideration of movement has to do with a standing choir, which is seemingly immobile due to its size or formation. Is it possible to speak as "largely" as the members of a verse choir do without "wanting" to move?

Psychologists describe three degrees of movement: *sensitization,* wherein the stimulus excites the muscle and poises it for action; *gesture degree,* in which the muscle begins the action but does not carry it through; and *gross movement,* which is the fully developed action; the full sweep of arms, a leap or run, dramatic action or patterned choreography, some of which we have shown to be possible with the verse choir.

It is this second phase, *gesture degree,* that can invest a standing choir with movement that is *as authentic* as if it were carried to its fullest fruition. When each and every member *begins* the movement that is inspired by the thought his voice is expressing at that instant, he will add an *invaluable note of aliveness and authenticity* to his total impact. This has been called "animation," "getting 'up'," "being with it," and when everyone does it exactly on the beat, it translates a sense of unity into a physical act that locks the entire choir together in *visible as well as auditory precision.*

A further bonus of this unified gesture degree of movement is the signal effect it has on the audience for it will find itself joining in the "abbreviated surge" of movement as a vicarious experience. Some individuals reported that they found themselves completing the full movement in their minds, as an animated mental picture.

To convince a choir, you might have them "try it" both ways and they will find that without this animation they are not only flat-footed but can manage only a "soggy-voiced" treatment of the passage.

"Gesture Degree" Contrasted with "Gesture"

This *gesture degree* must not be confused with the traditional meaning of the word *gesture,* which includes the "bird-wing" and many other stilted movements and postures. Any of these would defeat the dynamic flow described above if used seriously and out of rhythm.

However, we have seen choirs make delightful use of these antiquated vestiges of acting by using them in a comic vein to accent their own ideas and keeping them within the rhythm and spirit of their performance. We prefer to use the term *expressive action* for all serious and well-coordinated movements because they usually involve the whole body as it reflects the thought or feeling, whereas *gesture,* in the traditional sense, more often referred to a hand or arm movement that seemed "tacked on" and unrelated to the rest of the body.

These last four variables, *pitch, power, phrasing, and tempo,* are identical to those used by an individual voice to gain expressive variety, and are listed in this order by most books on the subject. We do nothing different to them when we work in the choir but we do it all together, which gives us some problems along with our advantages.

First off, all four of these variables are dependent

upon two necessities, the first being *clarity of sound*. That is to say each and every member of the choir must make each and every sound basically the same way, within the scope of slight individual differences, to accomplish the simple basic requirement of having the words understood. This is especially important when speed or loudness (or softness) are needed.

The second general necessity common to all four is that of *timing*. There must be no lagging behind the beat, nor can anyone "jump the gun" and anticipate your signal. The reward for this absolute precision will be a feeling of exhilaration that is a part of the "freedom through discipline," a soul-satisfying experience that comes to everyone who truly tries to do his best, and finds himself "in tune and time" with all the others.

Pitch: And now to deal with each one separately:

This refers to the variations of the voice on the musical scale and results from the *number of vibrations per second of the vocal folds*, beginning at 256 at "middle C" and going up or down in pitch as the vibrations increase or decrease. It is usually referred to as *inflection* and it is the most noticeable of these four voice variables, especially when wrongly used.

Children have no problem with pitch. They use it naturally, freely, and to great extremes as their voices ride the waves of their exuberant high spirits and sink to the depths of their major tragedies of lost puppies and broken dolls. This lasts until young people begin to "find" their voices about the time they are seeking to develop an attractive identity, with the result that they are prone to use pitch in an exaggerated way that results in "pretty" speech. This is more related to artificial melody patterns than to the ideas they are expressing.

Two common faults with *adults* of various ages are *monotony,* which reflects a lack-luster or defeated approach, and its opposite, an *extravagant use of pitch.* Some individuals become so carried away by the sound of their voices that the thought is lost in the "vocal pyrotechnics" that fill the air. Both of these, and others in between, usually become habitual speech patterns and "melodies" that express the personality of the individual more clearly than the content of his or her conversation. Though they are all well-intended, they miss the mark of true communication.

We can best serve our people, beginning at the second stage of "finding" their voices, by helping them *regain the natural freedom* that children have so that they may better express the intellectual acumen, sensitivity and sophistication they are rightly working so hard to develop.

How can we as verse choir directors help our people achieve this? Again there is a "secret," and again it is so simple it may be hard to grasp.

It is simply to cause each individual to *think the thought first* and be so influenced by it that when he says it the resulting inflection will express his reaction accurately, naturally, and free from preconceived patterns. The same will work when the thought is accompanied by an emotion, for then he will be adding another dimension (such as fear, joy, anger, pleasure) that will both expand the inflection and cement it all together.

There is a saying, "He whom a dream hath once possessed knows no more of doubting." We are now saying, "He who has been captured, influenced, imbued, 'possessed' by a thought and its feeling is now sure of how to say it!"

He no longer needs to worry whether he should use "rising or falling inflections" nor how much "expression" he should put into it for he now *belongs* to the thought and it will express itself through him naturally and, in a sense, automatically.

You might well ask, "This may work for a single thought but what about a complex series such as in a long poem or prose selection?" The fact is that we speak in *thought groups* that are sometimes as long as sentences or even paragraphs, and often much shorter—even single words or exclamations.

The answer is simply that as long as *your mind stays ahead of your voice* this natural and truly expressive inflection will change as rapidly and often as the thoughts change, regardless of how short or long or complex the passage may be. When this becomes habitual, your inflections will be automatically "tailored" to fit the drastic or subtle changes in your thoughts and emotions.

The clincher on our job as verse-choir directors is *unity;* to get each individual in the choir to respond to the idea and feeling in exactly the same way at the same time. We have shown earlier in this chapter how "felt communication" accomplishes this.

A further technique that may be helpful is offered here. It is for the director to *paraphrase* the desired interpretation that he feels best represents the greatest common denominator of the choir's thought or, until this has been established, the director's perception of the essence of the passage.

A simple example may be found in the first phrase of the *Twenty-Third Psalm,* which is often blandly given as

The Lord is my shepherd, I shall not want.

This really says something and nothing in its singsong tiresomeness.

We have often asked a choir to say to themselves:

"Look, you may put your faith in anything you wish; money, real estate, egotism, satisfaction of the moment,—but as for me, *my* faith is in the *Lord,*" so

The LORD is MY shepherd. (And therefore) I shall not want.

This definite identification and resultant quiet confidence has so often been the *resulting natural inflection* that paraphrasing seems to have established itself as a valid procedure to focus the individuals in a large group on a single interpretation.

It can be used in a simpler way with a word or phrase to give the "set" to the thought, or you may need to use more elaborate paraphrasing and explanation as is shown in Chapter 9 and also in Chapter 16, where the *Twenty-Third Psalm* is more fully treated.

POWER

This refers to the variations of the voice on the dynamic scale and results from the *magnitude of the vibrations of the vocal folds* and is measured in decibels. It is sometimes called "volume," "force," or "loudness," but we prefer the term *power* as it more nearly describes its exact nature and also because it seems to imply a smoother transition as it increases or decreases from various levels of intensity, usually described as "power modulation."

There are several considerations to note in the use of power. The first is that the choir uses it for emphasis much the same way as an individual does, simply making the *emphatic point* or points in the passage by marked *increase in power.* (Emphasis can also be gained by a surprising decrease of power.)

A second is that the thought is usually tied together better when the *power build is related to the elements of the sentence rather than used as a sudden blast,* or "spike." A gratifying example of sheer vocal power increasing over a long passage was discovered when we began working on *The Preamble to the Constitution.* Our discovery that this political document possesses literary grace should not be surprising, for it was a part of what European leaders called, "The greatest human document ever struck off from the minds of men."

The Preamble to the Constitution

(We used the choir as a unit, relying primarily on power modulation to achieve the build. It begins with a frank acknowledgement of identity, quietly and proudly stated.)
"We, the people of the United States,
(And continues with their firm statement of purpose.)
In order to form a more perfect union, establish justice,
(This next relaxes the strain to complete the first nuance.)
Insure domestic tranquility,
(From here on it builds inexorably in power, maintaining the same deliberate tempo and rhythm and giving full value to all the sounds until it reaches its magnificent culmination.)
To promote the general welfare, provide for the common defense
And secure the blessing of liberty for ourselves and our posterity
Do ordain and establish this constitution
For the UNITED STATES OF AMERICA!

This type of unrelenting build has been called "progressive jazz" in musical circles and is an effective means of capturing the attention of hearers and carrying them to a thrilling climax.

Another short patriotic statement lends itself remarkably well to this treatment. Many teachers have asked for help in making it a more vital experience.

The Pledge of Allegiance

(As we worked with this the students discovered that the secret lies in the simple matter of sincerity. This in turn is reflected in the firm and full articulation of the words and phrases to maintain a steady rhythm and to accomplish the power build. Especially is this true with the phrase "Under God," which President Eisenhower added. This is an integral part of the statement that must be given firmly and in rhythm to make its proper contribution to the whole.)
I pledge allegiance to the flag
Of the United States of America,
And to the Republic for which it stands.
One nation, under God, indivisible,
With LIBERTY AND JUSTICE FOR ALL!

This cumulative effect can of course be strengthened by the use of others of the seven variables but in these instances we have depended simply on conserving the vocal power of the entire choir and unleashing it by degrees until its full potential has been realized.

As children are taught in this way to *mean what they say* this pledge will become a vital part of their ongoing experience.

Controlled Power versus "Shouting"

Now that we are developing so much roaring power we should pause to point out the difference between *controlled power* and *shouting*. The first results from *central breathing* that develops its increase of sound through the muscles of the central part of the body, the *diaphragm and abdominal muscles*, leaving the *throat and larynx relaxed* for optimum use. "Shouting" results from trying to develop the force from *shallow breathing* at the upper chest with the result being a *severe tension in the throat that tight-*

ens the larynx and causes a "blasting," almost "bleating," sound that gives the opposite of the powerful effect we are seeking. It is also very hard on the voice and when repeated, such misuse can cause permanent damage, whereas *controlled power* from central breathing can be continued for long periods without undue tiring of the voice. This will be explained more fully in Chapter 8 on Voice and Diction.

Spikes

This does not preclude the effective use of sudden bursts of power, or "spikes," when they are balanced by other elements. We used one to sharpen the effect of the word "menace" in the last stanza of Poe's "The Bells." The sentence is: "In the silence of the night, how we shiver with afright at the melancholy menace of their tone." This is also an example of progressing from a quiet beginning through a short build to the spike and back to a quiet, sustained mood. It all must go smoothly, as if one person were saying it.

Dark Men (quietly) In the silence of the night
Light Women (with "little girl" fear) How we shiver with af-right
Medium Women (joining them with full-bodied fear) At the melancholy
Medium Men (alone, making the most of this one word) MENACE!
Dark Men (returning to the somber mood) Of their tone, for every sound that floats, from the rust within their throats is a groan.

Establishing Mood through Power

This last part of Poe's sentence suggests a subtle use of *sustained power* to establish an underlying mood, this time a dolorous one accompanied by rich evocative sounds from his limitless imagination. This is the opposite of "stabbing" or sounding only the first syllable of a word. It is also more than giving each syllable its proportionate sound. It is dwelling on, "riding," or continuing the sound for its euphonic value to enhance the mood more than the sheer intellectual meaning of the words would do.

This underlying use of *continuing sound* is within the realm of power because of its solid, sustaining quality. It can be loud or soft in intensity and when combined with pitch change can simulate wind and other natural, and supernatural, elements. It effectively represented the approach of Death in Goethe's *Der Erlkönig,* or *The King of the Elves,* and gave gigantic proportions to Darius the Mede's "voice of THUNDER" in Vachel Lindsay's poem "Daniel," even continuing to rumble under the following line.

Phrasing and Rhythm

Phrasing

Phrasing is related to rhythm so closely that it is difficult to determine which to name first in importance. Certainly they should be used in such a way that they do not conflict but rather reinforce each other, blending together to better express the meaning.

This blending can be done in several ways: by *"resting"* for a certain number of beats, maintaining the basic rhythm; by *moving the pauses* from one place to another; by *extending a sound* over several beats, or by *"bending"* the *meter pattern* by borrowing shades of time from one beat or syllable to add to the next. None of these should be allowed to change the author's meaning, but should give

the interpreter freedom to express his sincere response
to that meaning.

For instance, in Eugene Field's phrasing of the line:

And that was the time when our Little Boy Blue,
Kissed them and put them there.

The author has put both verbs together in the same line
as a single act of love. But if the director feels a greater
poignancy in treating each verb as a separate act of love
he might phrase it this way:

And that was the time when our Little Boy Blue
Kissed them,—and put them there."

Similarly, Longfellow does not break his line:

The murmuring pines and the hemlocks.

The author seems to appreciate them both as a part of
his forest primeval. I hold that it does not detract from
this concept but emphasizes the importance of *each* to
phrase it thusly:

The murmuring pines—and the hemlocks.

This slight pause, bending the meter a little, causes the
choir to linger over the beauty of the pines—and then to
suddenly discover the hemlocks and appreciate them as
an added surprise in the beauty of the forest.

Phrasing belongs to the author, who uses it to define
the subtleties of his meaning, but it also should *allow the
choir room* to express itself in relation to that meaning.
And, most importantly, phrasing must remain within the
flow of the predominant rhythm of the poem.

In his book *Making Words Come Alive,* Dr. Cornelius C. Cunningham shows how being sensitive to rhythm clarifies and enriches the interpreter's intellectual understanding and emotional appreciation of the poem. His Chapter VIII, "Surrendering to the Rhythm and Melody," is very explicit and thorough on this point.

Rhythm

The true source of the rhythm of a poem is the *basic beat of the life situation* that inspired the poet. When this is felt as a fluid element, it both enriches and ties together the concepts and their sounds and also aids in bringing the mental picture of the subject of the poem into focus.

For a simple example of this let us imagine walking with Longfellow through his primeval forest and hearing the wind murmuring through the trees, the squirrels skittering, the birds singing and the sound of his own passing as he scattered the leaves. He may have thought, "How wonderful this all is and I must put it down so others may enjoy it as I do." His first phrasing may have been a fluid "This is the forest primeval— —the murmuring pines and the hemlocks," with only three points of emphasis, or "long" syllables, as he may have "felt" the pervading rhythm.

But when he was forced to commit this moving passage into dactylic sextameter, hoping to thereby carry the flow of the words to his readers, it became fixed with "long" (italicized) and "short" (unitalicized) syllables:

"*This* is the *for*est *pri*meval, the *mur*muring *pines* and the *hem*locks." It is now an entirely different thing than he originally intended, if each beat of the meter is meticulously and rigidly adhered to. *But the reader need* *not be so enslaved,* as noted in the earlier treatment of this line, and our second example under *Phrasing and Rhythm.*

So this division of the meter pattern into different combinations of long and short syllables is merely a *mathematical representation* of the poem's basic rhythm. These should implement the smooth flow of the poem and would do so if kept in the proper proportion of emphasis, serving the same function as the time pattern in a well-executed piece of music.

However, too often in the presentation of poetry in our literature classes the meter pattern is emphasized for its own sake, sometimes worshipped as a fetish, forcing the poem to jerk along a bumpy road and lose the load of beauty with which the author has invested it. The sorry fact is that this happens in the late intermediate and early secondary grades when young people should be developing a love for the fruit and juices of the poems but are more often repelled by the dry husks that encase them. It is for this reason that an early introduction to choral speaking and the verse choir is so important.

As an antidote to this we suggest that the director and the choir or class, after becoming interested in its subject, try to "get the feel" of the basic beat of the poem. This can be compared to putting a car in overdrive or a higher gear so that the engine does not have to work as hard to make the car travel at the same speed, still needing to hit on all cylinders which in this case is the minimized and smoothed-out meter pattern.

We were presented with an acid test of this procedure when we prepared "Farewell to the Steam Locomotive" and "Casey Jones" as a fun sequence for some school performances.

We began with some background material that included the facts that Casey Jones lived in Memphis,
Tennessee, where his home is now a national shrine;
that he did die in a head-on collision; that he had three
brothers, all of whom were fine engineers; that his son
invented the "Whipoorwill Whistle" referred to in the
poem; that the term "rounder" meant a railroader or his
friend; a "block board" was similar to a traffic light, and
a "white eye" was the caution signal. Other facts supported the importance of railroads, and the men who
ran them, to the development of the country. This was
intriguing to some of the younger generation who never
had been lulled to sleep by the far-off steam whistle,
doppler effect and all. Recently the Illinois Central Rail-
road ran a passenger train drawn by a steam locomotive
south from Champaign-Urbana and the roads immediately became filled with cars and people who thrilled to the "wonderful new sound" of its throbbing pulse,
its gay rumble, and its moaning steam whistle.

Both numbers represented the action of complex
machinery and therefore depended on faithful adherence to their fundamental beat which we identified in
the following way:

> *Come* all you *roun*ders for I *want* you to *hear*
> The *sto*ry *of* a *brave* en*gin*eer,
> *Ca*sey *Jones* was the *roun*der's *name*
> On a *big* eight-*whee*ler of a *mighty fame*.

We "walked through it" several times to achieve absolute
fidelity to the emphatic beats noted by the "long" syllables. (This is "hitting on all cylinders.") Not all poems
will be so dependent on the emphatic syllables.

We treated the entire poem in this manner before

making it more meaningful and less tiresome by "bending" the meter here and there, borrowing time from one
word and adding it to another, pausing for several beats
(a "rest" in music), and deliberately holding one word
for two full beats (*mo*an-n-*n*-n-n-n) to double its effect.
In addition to these variations, we made use of others of
the seven variables discussed in this chapter. (This is the
"overdrive.")

For instance, we used light, medium, and dark sections for certain passages; soloists for the dialogue between Casey and his Fireman; great changes in pitch,
power, and speed as the action became exciting; and,
though there were two hundred in the choir, we could
hardly restrain ourselves to the "gesture degree" of
movement. Some members of the audience reported that
they could "feel the floor shake," but we figured they
were close relatives of choir members. The full text of
these two numbers is found in Chapter 14.

Few poems will need this much work to "loosen them
up," especially those written with a more flowing
rhythm. The great poets can use a formal rhythm pattern in such a way that the reader can experience great
freedom in its expression. These and poems using less
formal patterns, even free verse or blank verse, and
many prose selections will have rhythm structures that
will offer a smooth approach to their dynamics and will
welcome the choir to their easy and inspired expression.

My esteemed colleague and brilliant reader of poetry,
Dr. John R. Theobald, refers to this as "getting inside
the poem," and sensing its rhythm is the one best key.

Tempo

Tempo refers to the rate of *speed at which a number
progresses. Its best ally is rhythm, which acts as a balance wheel*

or gyroscope relating tempo to the central beat of the poem and reducing the chances for too-sudden or too-severe changes that would have a "scattering" effect on the whole. It also affects each of the other six variables, in differing degrees, so is an extremely important factor as it influences the entire structure of the presentation.

The most obvious dangers in using tempo lie in the two extremes of being too fast or too slow.

Too Fast

The tendency to equate "tempo" with "fast" is a natural one for enthusiasm and liveliness usually result in an increase of speed. One director of a fourth-grade choir says his people feel that if they speak "fast and loud" they are "putting expression into it." In fact in the fourth grade this is not too bad, for the group is now concentrating on the poem instead of themselves and are ready for the director to show them the value of subtleties.

Too much speed in any choir, however, will cause fuzziness or complete destruction of articulation. We have a saying: "You may speak as rapidly as you can be understood—if the poem calls for it." Too much speed may also present more material in one sequence than an audience can assimilate, as if they had eaten more than they can digest.

Too Slow

Going too slowly with a poem is also the child of a natural tendency. It usually results from the director's being too deliberate or cautious and the choir responding in a "dampened" and self-conscious way, taking the edge off the lively passages and giving a somber aspect to the presentation as a whole. This even divests the passages that should go slowly of the dignity and meaning they deserve by depriving them of contrast with the rest of the poem.

"Just Right"

Of course there is no one "just right" tempo, for what we are going to suggest may cause the choir to go faster or slower than might seem feasible at "first-try."

If we may be allowed another "secret," it is to *make the tempo fit the spirit.* This, too, may seem too simple but we have found that when the choir and director are so in tune with the poem's inner spirit, the rate of tempo corresponds *almost automatically* to this central essence. And why shouldn't it for we are now in tune with the poet's first response to "the murmuring pines and the hemlocks."

When we say "almost" automatically it is to accept the reality that nothing is that easy. Rather, this sensitivity to the spirit of the poem will act as a guide to the director in finding the exactly right tempo to express its various changes of thought and nuances of feeling. The value of this approach is that it puts this perception first, in a position to influence the resulting overt expression, just as we did with all the other variables.

* * * * * * * *

Since this concludes the seven variables, or tools the director has at his disposal, we need to make two observations:

The first is that *they are interdependent* and are always used in combination—often all together. At the risk of taking ourselves too seriously we can say that as words give a poem *form,* a proportionate use of these seven variables will give it *life*.

The second is to reiterate the principle that all that you do must follow and *result from the perception of the author's concepts* and is never imposed upon the poem as a foreign element. This will save you and your choir from using elaborate preconceived devices that may be spectacular and interesting in their own right but stand a good chance of missing their primary purpose of interpreting the spirit and substance of the poem.

7

How to Direct:
Principles and Procedures

Who Can Direct?

Even though the verse choir is a group experience,
there is one central person who is responsible for all that
happens: from conceiving the idea, igniting the group,
and managing all the practical matters to the finished
product.

At the "first-try" level you need have little or no training nor experience, for, once the rhythmic beat is established and the spirit of the poem begins to percolate, the
group will follow sincere leadership to a vigorous if un-
polished performance.

Those who have taken this first step include a kinder-
gartner who wanted to "lead the next one," a high
school girl, who asked her class "to do" her favorite
poem, a camper who had a "swell idea for tonight's
campfire," a leader of a church group, and a club pro-

gram chairman who wanted something "we can all do together," and an adult girl scout leader who was "given
the job, so I did it."

Those who wanted to learn more about this art in
order to lead their groups into more rewarding levels of
performance include a host of teachers, drama and
music directors, youth workers, high-school principals,
ministers, and many others.

Just as there is "no one thing that a verse choir is," so
there is no one kind of person who should direct. Each
and every one directs differently and so he should, for
as he guides the choir through the poem he is expressing that part of himself that is a unique and singular
contribution that only he can give. This fact has been
proven many times in our verse-choir directing classes
when different students chose the same poem, each giving it the flavor of his own interpretation. Another extremely satisfying fact that was evident in these classes
was the marked improvement and growth made by these
students each time they tried a new poem.

The Director

Nearly every book on the subject of choral speaking
lists *love of poetry* as the first requisite for the director,
and ours should be no exception. I beg leave, however,
for our purpose to expand the meaning of "poetry" to
include all literature that is rhythmical and dramatic and
elicits a vital response from its readers and hearers, for
there is much prose of this nature that is good grist for
the verse-choir mill. If we may call this *living literature*
and equate it with poetry we can surely say it is the
fountainhead from which all the good expectations of
this work derive, and one must love it to achieve its values.

Love for people must come next because it is for our choir members, the audience, and all others involved with us for whom we are working—and there will be times when any other motive but love will wear too thin.

A keen *perception* of hidden values in chosen material and an *ingenuity* for the "right" right way to cause the choir to bring them out are two "executive officers" without whose services the love of poetry will remain an unrequited frustration. A large *storehouse of material* at your mental fingertips will be very useful, especially on rainy days.

There are so many other characteristics and abilities that are helpful in getting the directing job done that after listing them the director may appear to be a "paragon of miscellany."

But for the record: the director should be *fluently expressive,* both in voice and body, should command *respect* without demanding it, and should emanate *composure* under stress. He must have the ability to *organize* people, programs, and schedules, and the *determination* with *tact* to carry out plans compatibly in the complex environment of the institution that is hosting the choir. A *sense of humor* will lubricate the whole procedure. The director must also be able to *communicate* with people of all intellectual and social levels.

No person I know carries this entire portfolio, but if each item is kept in mind the right one may surface just when needed.

Three Directing Principles

Now we come to actually "getting your hands up" and taking charge of the choir. Some books give detailed descriptions and diagrams of actions, corresponding to time patterns, that bring good results to many and they may be helpful to you in refining your procedures.

I would rather take the approach of presenting and emphasizing the *underlying principles* that have proven to be effective in our choirs and in others that I have observed. These principles may better encourage your own creativity and "leave room" for the discovery and development of your individual set of actions and "signals" that will best communicate with your particular group.

The first principle is that it is not only the hands but the *entire body* responding to the rhythm and total dynamics of the poem that signals to the choir the nature, degree, and timing of their response.

This can range from subtle "gesture degree" movements to large and vigorous actions that match the scope of the poem. It can also include expressive body movements, such as abstract and realistic pantomimes, improvisations and deeply felt responses that suggest the nature and spirit of the concept being evoked from the choir.

These you will "find yourself doing" and therefore you will be natural and unselfconscious and will not attract undue attention but will communicate effectively with the choir in a nonverbal "felt" manner. In fact, when sensitively and appropriately done, these will express the inner essence of the poem visually as the choir is doing it orally and so will add a helpful dimension of communication with the audience.

Once these expressive movements have proven to be effective they must be consistently used and made a part of your directing procedure for that poem. The choir will expect them and will be confused if they are omitted or changed.

The second principle is that *consistency is compatible with variety.* Consistency relates to what you do with each poem, as described above. Variety develops when each new poem you do brings out a different set of movements, signals, and responses. The sum of all these, reflecting different poems, becomes the sum total of your directing procedure—a varied, interesting, and valid part of the choir's performance. They will also save you from "directing everything the same way"—with elbows flapping.

The third principle is that the choir's responses to the poem can become so well set that the *director does not have to actually be present during the performance* but can remain backstage or in the audience. I confess to being unable to bring a choir to this state of self-reliance but Orlin Corey, Mary Gwen Owen, William J. Adams, Clayton Liggett, Eugene Bahn, Albert Johnson, Agnes Curran Hamm, to name only a few, have succeeded very well in doing it. It is a major achievement in speech education for it gives each individual a sense of self-reliance within a complex group.

As the supreme example of this "remote control" miracle we can remember that Arturo Toscanini's N.B.C. Philharmonic Orchestra returned one year after his death to play a concert dedicated to his memory. Music critics reported that they played as if their genius conductor were on the empty podium!

Directing in Rehearsal

Whether you intend to direct from the stage or to have the choir perform independently, these suggestions should help you prepare them for performance.

It is not a way of doing certain things but the "certain way the director does everything" that holds the choir up to its best. This can be reduced to these definite techniques:

(1) *Cause the choir to understand and feel* the meaning and emotion of the poem by *working it out with them.* The director will be expected to have his own response to the poem in mind when he first presents it and must express this fully and clearly. But from then on he listens to individual opinions expressed in open discussion, *senses what most of the choir members respond to most vitally and naturally* in early rehearsals as they both search for the *greatest common denominator.* The director must be the final arbiter and will be respected if he *listens* to suggestions and *explains* why some cannot be used and why others will enhance the interpretation.

With this approach the choir feels involved in planning the interpretation and with the rapport thus established will follow his direction with "whole person" cooperation. (This is the basis for commanding rather than demanding respect, as mentioned earlier.)

(2) *Firmly take charge of the rehearsals* to accomplish this interpretation. The director is now functioning as the catalyst that helps the choir realize its desired interpretation. His explanations must be clear and explicit. His actions and signals must be definite and consistent and so well-related, "geared," to the responses they evoke from the choir that there is no uncertainty.

This definiteness results in a comfortable atmosphere that makes possible the enrichment of the interpretation by building from one rehearsal to the next. (Its antithesis is the confusion that results from experimenting with *new interpretations* late in the rehearsal schedule.) It is possible, and healthy, to accept suggestions from choir members regarding a better way to *express the decided-upon interpretation,* but each new idea must pass this test.

(3) *Correct mistakes when they happen.* Seemingly minor mistakes will affect everything that follows and they have a way of becoming habitual and difficult to root out if not dealt with *now.* It also keeps the choir "on their toes" and each individual more alert when he realizes that "my mistake" may be the reason for stopping an otherwise smoothly flowing run-through. In doing this the director is also representing the audience, which is often prone to spot the flaws.

(4) *Insist on the constant attention* of each choir member throughout the entire poem, *whether he is speaking or not.* This assures total concentration on the poem, a necessary thing, and prevents missed cues and trying to get back into the spirit and rhythm of the poem. One person trying to find "Mom" or some other friend in the audience can destroy what the entire choir has worked so long and hard to achieve.

Directing in Performance

If you decide to direct from the stage these are some suggestions that may be helpful to you. They represent experiences culled from directing various kinds and sizes of choirs and are intended as starting points from which you will find the procedures that work best for you.

(1) Before going onto the stage "get loose" with the choir by body and voice exercises. (The Coreys take a full hour for this before each rehearsal as well as before performances.) This is extremely important, for people arrive with all their emotions and tensions, which must be relieved before they can concentrate on the performance. Some may be directed at you so it is good to demonstrate general good humor; and perhaps the right words to the right people may have therapeutic value

for both the choir member and yourself. The human equation is a powerful force and a clear, positive atmosphere is essential for creativity.

If there is not time for any of this, there are some sample warm-up exercises suggested in Chapters 8 and 14 that can be done in front of the audience in a "get-acquainted" style that puts everyone at ease. From these you can create your own to fit your choir.

(2) Find the fastest and most orderly manner of getting onto the stage. The one used by the San Dieguito Drama Choros should work well for most choirs. It can be speeded up by having the two halves of the choir approach from opposite sides of the stage.

(3) Be sure you have everyone's eye before you begin the first number. Intended unity is not enough; it must be *demonstrated* by a poised, ready-to-take-off posture with focus on the director.

(4) The down-beat that starts the choir is really a two-part beat, though a surprising number of beginning directors try to start on the "down" stroke. The choir needs to be prepared for a unified beginning so the following procedure is suggested:

> Hold both hands comfortably in front of you at about chest level as a signal for attention. When you have everyone's eye raise your hands to about eye level for the preparation part of the beat. If everyone will take a breath at this upward motion the entire choir can be both physically and mentally ready for a sharp and "clean" beginning when you bring your hands down to complete the first beat. There is no hesitation at the top for it is a unified beat, as all others are.

(5) Use the whole arm or arms freely to establish the rhythm but keep the elbows close to your sides. (They aren't very expressive when flapping.) If you concen-

trate on the hands and fingers, which will express the subtleties, the whole-arm movements will be natural and flowing.

(6) Remember to let the whole body express the poem freely, as developed in the first directing principle.

(7) Be careful that the choir does not trade speed for interpretation and that your own enthusiasm does not cause the tempo to "run away." When this happens I find it helpful to point with one finger to the opposite hand, which is slowing the beat to the proper tempo. Similarly, by pointing to your lips you can ask for sharper articulation.

(8) After finishing one poem, make a definite transition to the next. We accomplished this by making abbreviated motions in the rhythm and tempo of the new number to establish its spirit before starting the downbeat. In case the poem should lag, you can signal for them to lift the spirit with a sharp upward movement of the hand not beating the rhythm, with the palm up. Conversely, the palms of both hands may be turned down as they beat the rhythm to ask for a more subtle or subdued treatment of a passage. The normal position for the hands is a natural open one with the palms toward the choir.

(9) Generally, smaller movements call for a quieter sound and larger ones ask for greater power and projection, but these will result naturally from your own response to the number.

(10) You can keep your choir at ease and in a positive "up" mood by an informal yet dignified manner. Compliments and corrective directions between numbers will work wonders and help the transition to the next poem. In case of a mistake, or even a ruinous breakdown that

cannot be "pulled out" by aforementioned signals, a relaxed and "no blame" huddle will mend the technical fault, restore the spirit of the group and demonstrate to the audience that you have an intrepid though "human" organization working. In fact, "having fun" between the director and the choir is acceptable on most occasions. A cheerful choir begets a receptive audience.

(11) We have found that even in the most informal situations the choir appreciates being recognized by bows from the director. Sometimes I "took off my (nonexistent) toupee" to our choir as an "in" joke, (but not everyone will be so nonequipped for this.) Similarly, soloists, narrators, the choir manager, and any others who have had special responsibilities feel an extra satisfaction at being recognized separately. Some directors feel that this causes an unwanted break in the "one for all" group aspect of the choir. You choose.

(12) The choir can demonstrate its appreciation for the all-important audience by bowing sharply on signal to recognize their applause. On some occasions when the audience has joined us in a simple number, such as "The Lion Hunt," we have applauded *them*. Once, at a predominantly black high school the choir joined the audience for the "The Lion Hunt," becoming one large choir—and received one of our few standing ovations.

The Directing of Sister Rose Terrence

This master teacher, who has developed a verse choir of 70 girls at Rosary High School in Detroit, Michigan, demonstrates how to do all this in a crisp and inspired way. These notes were taken the day we heard her choir:

Her direction is superb; it inspires, frees, and disciplines all at once. Its source is her keen intellect and sensitivity to the whole poem—all its facets. Visual aspects show great variety from large movements of the entire person to small hand and even finger signals; sometimes she counted each beat of the rhythm, at others she pointed only a few emphatic peaks in sort of an "overdrive" manner; her facial expression *mirrored the poem, not anxiety* for how it was sounding, helping the choir to concentrate on this first thing; motions were always definite and clear, following no set pattern but reflecting the thought and feeling of the instant; the total effect seems to be an adroit representation of the poem in expressive pantomime that manages never to be too much nor to draw attention from the choir.

We can still remember the immediate, almost simultaneous, response given by the girls in response to each change in pace, power, phrasing, and all other subtleties called for by her direction. Their attention was so acute, they seemed poised in mid-air expecting her next motion.

These classes meet every day and the girls stand for the entire period, resulting in "tall-alive" posture. They memorize all their numbers, including some well-selected patter exercises. Materials cover a wide range of religious, secular and humorous numbers, all worth remembering.

Performing with Books in Hand versus Committing Material to Memory

Choirs that use books in performance have the distinct advantages of confidence and being able to cover far more material than if they committed their poems to memory. After a few performances they find they can take their eyes off the books most of the time, and after a few numbers the audience is not conscious of their use as they become a "part of" the performer. Both drama choroses give brilliant performances while using books, even when the director is not on stage with them.

In our choirs we have tried both systems and have chosen to have the material memorized. We believe that more complete involvement can be attained when everyone in the choir has mental mastery of the numbers and can give full attention to the director, who is then able to make subtle changes in the interpretation as they are needed.

There are two disadvantages in this system. The first being that when someone fails to master the poem his uncertainty causes fuzziness in attacks and articulation. He indeed has not only failed to be a positive force but has become a dangerous negative one. The other is that we lose time in rehearsal in that we cannot work on the finishing refinements in interpretation until the poem is committed to memory.

However, there is nothing quite like the sound of a choir, large or small, doing a poem with precision and sensitivity from memory and expressing their joy in this accomplishment. It also increases their mental acuity and clinches another poem for that "storehouse of treasured memories."

Directing Group Scenes in Plays

There is of course no formal direction possible from the stage during the action of a play but this can be overcome by having a *central person* begin the passage and, if it is complex, to have *sub-leaders* control the part their particular group contributes to the whole. All this is done by agreed-upon sight cues that are a part of the body movements of the characters the leaders are portraying.

The choir of *townspeople, soldiers, or whatever characters the so-called "extras"* are playing should be rehearsed as a combined group to feel the unity of their part in the scene then divided into sections or banks, each operating independently even to making separate entrances from different places at different times, possibly beginning their lines from off-stage. In this case each sub-group becomes a separate verse choir operating as an integral part of the whole, much as any other actor in the scene.

In the case of a *Greek play,* the chorus would be so well rehearsed and coordinated with the play as to function as another character, each member speaking his lines as if he were the only one responsible. Leaders are still used and their timing and interpretation is taken as the model, with small group and individual variations that have been built in by the director during the rehearsal period.

Shakespeare gave his crowds little to say though he indicated when they were to be heard. This calls for the director to give each section a different set of short sentences that they repeat according to the action of the play. These also should be rehearsed and integrated into the scene. This planning and rehearsal takes the place of ad-libbing, which is undependable and therefore dangerous.

In cases where only a low-key mumbling or rumbling is called for as *background sound,* one suggested technique is to give the entire choir one long sentence to commit to memory. Then each section should begin the sentence at different times, similar to singing a "round." This will give variety to the total sound and provide a gradual build. Another advantage is that if any part is spoken loudly enough to be heard it will relate to the play. This will supplant the age-old practice of having the crowd members say the word *rhubarb* in varying degrees of intensity. Yes, there was the time when one loud RHUBARB topped the rest of the crowd and even the dialogue of the scene.

Recruiting a Verse Choir

One effective way of recruiting a verse choir is to *start a group with a small number* of interested people and let it grow as the word spreads that "something is cooking" in the drama room. Clayton Liggett brought a small group to our class in verse-choir directing to read "A Man Dies" and the resulting interest gave him a group of 20 the following semester. This has gradually and solidly grown to a healthy 70 at this writing and their brilliant performances have won for them an invitation to enter an international speech festival in Hawaii.

A simpler and ready-made procedure is to introduce a verse choir into the *program of any given class* as an adjunct to their regular studies. Most appropriate subjects are history, literature, social science—though one former student taught his physiology class the bones of the body in high-spirited verse-choir style! (He is now a Superintendent of Schools.) Many other subjects can be served by the verse choir magic.

Still another alternative is to offer it as a *separate class* that spends all of its time in this activity. One thrilling group, still remembered after many years, was a class of 66 people at Hoover High School in San Diego made up of some people who loved poetry and many who "wanted to get out of English." Their memorized program included a vigorous treatment of Lindsay's "The Congo," and the most poignant rendering of Johnson's "The Crucifixion" that we have managed since, even with college choirs.

However your people come to you there are two philosophies at work as to how to arrive at the ultimate personnel of the choir. The first is to *choose the most capable* with the best voices and form a well-balanced choir capable of the finest interpretation of the highest-grade material and establishing the art of choral speech on or above the level of other fine groups in the expressive arts. This the Johnsons have done with *Everyman* and Milton's *Paradise Lost,* and the Coreys with *Job* and *Romans,* all winning international acclaim for their achievements. How fortunate it is for the movement that there are groups such as these! It has been generally estimated that 36 is the maximum number with which such artistic heights can be reached, and certainly great dedication and years of working together are necessary for the mastery of such works. Some of the *Job* and *Romans* casts have been with the Coreys for nine years and are still continuing.

The other philosophy is to *accept all who come* and to try to blend them into a group that will be able to do numbers of varying difficulty well enough to give "the greatest good to the greatest number"; which is also a worthy educational principle. You may have your people for only one semester, perhaps two, or for only one special project but two things will likely happen to them. They will have found a new dimension in the capacity of their speaking voices; and they may seek to find, or

start, another such group in another place at another
time.

The key word in directing is *communication*—for the
contagious something that infects everyone is brewed in
the heart of the poem, distilled into an interpretation as
the director and choir respond to it, and swells into a
wave of living literature that washes through the choir to
the audience.

8

Voice and Articulation Applied to the Verse Choir

Before we go into the chapters that deal with materials and procedures for interpretation, we must take up a mundane, sometimes tedious, but *absolutely necessary* subject—*the mechanics of voice production and the mastery of the articulators.* These are the "finger exercises" for the art of speaking and are basic to the success of individual speakers and especially so for the verse choir.

Definitions

For our purposes let us define *voice* as the sounds that are produced by the human vocal mechanism, and *articulation* as the manner in which these sounds are modified, or articulated, to become meaningful speech symbols.

162

The Obvious Need

It is obvious that an effective voice is needed to make the message *loud enough to be comfortably heard* and that articulation must be *clear enough to make the words easily understood.* Even these necessities are sometimes neglected.

Let's begin with an individual speaker presenting a poem to an audience. It is easy to stop too soon in the total procedure of preparing the work without giving due attention to how it is to be carried to the audience.

I well remember a tall, handsome student with a deeply felt and keenly perceived conception of Poe's "Annabelle Lee." But the half-pronounced and nonprojected sounds of this beautiful love poem reverberated somewhere between his Adam's apple and alveolar ridge! He received the full power of Poe's message but it failed to reach the waiting audience.

When we multiply this careless performance by twenty or a hundred people in a verse choir, the poem will remain on stage in a mishmash of confusing sound. No wonder people ask, "How can you understand so many people talking all at once?" But you can.

Fred Waring feels so strongly about clarity that he spells out each sound of every word to insure uniformly clear diction and pronunciation in the songs his inimitable "Pennsylvanians" sing. He does the same for their remarkable choral readings, especially of Johnson's "God's Trombones."

The Hidden Need

A less obvious but even more important need is to speak the message so that the *subtleties of its full intellec-*

tual and emotional meaning will be highlighted for the hearers. A more complete use of the voice and diction mechanism is needed here, for these subtleties are usually carried by the *second half* of the words.

It is easy for a speaker to accent the first syllable of a word and feel he is giving it adequate emphasis. The other syllables of course should not be accented with force equal to the first but should receive *proportionate* treatment, according to their importance in the total meaning.

For instance, the word *livelihood* when given with a positive feeling would be "LIVE-li-hood," with the last two syllables receiving unaccented emphasis—but enough to make them heard and to have them count. The continuing vowel sound in "hood" gives a further opportunity for a full-bodied ending, finalized with a distinct but unobtrusive "d" sound. Similarly, the phrase, "A memorable happening," is rich in good vowel sounds and continuing consonants that can demonstrate to the audience how the speaker relishes his poignant memory.

These are analogous to a full tennis stroke with a complete follow-through that gives the ball its critical spin that delivers it to the exact spot for which it is intended. A "MEM-r-ble happ-nin'" is more like a "slap stroke" that can send the ball anywhere—or nowhere.

This follow-through in speech, or *proportionate sounding* of all the elements in the words, has been called "quantity" or "continuance" in speech texts. Radio and television people call it "voice presence," and singers refer to it as "singing on the hum." By any name it provides the words a chance to deliver their complete message. Its antithesis is "staccato speech," which sounds more like a typewriter!

Be careful, though, for when one has achieved this ability he is in danger of "falling in love" with the sound of his voice and therefore depriving it of its primary function of *unobtrusively* carrying the message. "The best art is the hidden art."[1]

A further bonus is that this manner of speaking will make a *nervous speaker sound at ease* until he feels so. It also induces self-confidence and a note of unassuming authority. It may have had something to do with the New Testament report that Jesus "spoke as one having authority," and the ability of the Old Testament prophets to confront kings with things they did not wish to hear.

The Speech Mechanism

It is important to have a brief introduction to the physical mechanism that makes possible the wonderful sounds of human speech so you can better understand the reasons for the exercises that follow and the improvement they will give you.

There are four major parts to the speech mechanism. Each part has an influence on the performance of the others so our goal is to achieve a *well-coordinated operation of the mechanism as a whole.* This short chapter will allow only a much-simplified treatment of how each part can be made to produce effective speech sounds while depending on the other three parts.

---

[1] Cornelius C. Cunningham, *Making Words Come Alive* (Dubuque, Iowa: William C. Brown Co., 1951).

The Motor

The principle muscle of the motor is the dome-shaped *diaphragm,* that forces the air out of the *lungs,* (which have no muscles), through the *bronchial tubes* to the *trachea,* or "wind pipe," that houses the *larynx* where the sound is made. The *diaphragm* is aided strongly by the *abdominal muscles* and, to a lesser degree, by the *costal muscles* that control the rib cage, or chest.

These three sets of muscles also help us to breathe in two distinctly different ways. First, they *operate automatically,* even when we are asleep, to allow us to breathe to *sustain life.* This automatic rhythm, however, does not meet the demands of speech. Second, these three sets of muscles *must be controlled* to provide the *steady outflow* of air needed for speech and singing. This action is called "central breathing."

Central Breathing

Central breathing may be most easily learned by first exhaling all the air possible from the lungs. (A certain amount of residual air will always remain.) This *exhaling* action is demonstrated by Diagram 8, which shows the three sets of muscles operating as follows:

The *abdominal muscles contract* by being "squeezed in." This will *push the diaphragm up,* forcing the air out of the lungs. The *costal muscles* will contract the rib cage at the same time, completing the exhalation phase.

This action should be done vigorously to increase the tone of the muscles and to gain control over them. A further value is that when "all" the stale air is expelled a

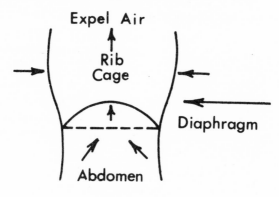

DIAGRAM 8

lungfull of fresh air replaces it. The "bonus value" to speakers of expelling "all" the air is that by doing so the abdominal muscles have *pushed the diaphragm up*, putting it in the proper position for the *down stroke* of the inhalation phase, thus helping a person to "find" his diaphragm—perhaps for the first time.

To *inhale* the process is reversed, as shown in Diagram 9.

> The *costal muscles* extend the *rib
> cage outward* as the *diaphragm pushes down*.
> This in turn pushes the *abdomen
> forward*, completing the inhalation
> phase.

For the purpose of exercising these muscles and mastering their control both phases of the central breathing process should be done vigorously and with increasing speed until you can "pant," feeling and seeing the action of the diaphragm reflected in the abdomen.

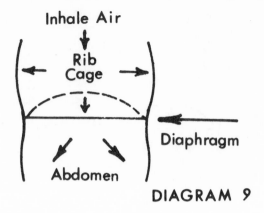

DIAGRAM 9

For the purpose of speaking or singing the act of exhaling is prolonged, resulting in a steadily controlled column of air passing through the vocal folds to activate
them and thus produce, or "phonate," the vocal sounds.
The fact that only a relatively small amount of air is
needed for this phonation shows the importance of this
prolonged control.

Several things need to be remembered in regard to
central breathing:

1. Do not allow the shoulders to move *up and down*
   because this encourages shallow, "costal," breathing.
   (The *shoulder blades* may be drawn together *laterally* to
   facilitate the rib cage expansion of the inhaling
   phase.)

2. Central breathing is different from "costal breathing," which uses only the costal muscles controlling
   the chest and results in shallow breathing and insec-
   ure speech.

3. Central breathing is different from "abdominal breathing," which uses only the muscles of the abdomen

and therefore loses the supportive power of the diaphragm and costal muscles.

4. Central breathing results from the *concerted action* of the diaphragm, the abdominal muscles and the costal muscles and results in a "solid" and controlled voice for speaking or singing.

5. Those of you who may fear that central breathing might enlarge the middle of the body may rest assured in the fact that the strength and tone thus given to these sets of muscles will provide firm and natural figure control.

The Vibrators

The vibrators are the *vocal folds* and they are housed in the *larynx,* sometimes called the "voice box" or "Adam's apple." They are activated by the moving column of air passing through the trachea. At this point *air pressure changes to sound waves!* (In fact it takes relatively little air passing through the vocal folds to produce sound waves.)

It is critically important to control these three sets of muscles in such a way that they will send *just enough air past the vocal folds to activate them in an orderly fashion!* This will result in a relaxed and solid (nonbreathy) voice, which will be capable of many variations easily achieved by the speaker and pleasant to hear for the listeners, maintaining absolute and comfortable control while speaking.

If this control is not maintained, the result will be a disorderly action of the vocal folds caused by too much air passing through. This in turn will spawn many other speech faults; such as breathiness, nasality, stridency, hoarseness—who needs more?

The vocal folds are capable of vigorous and extended use when the power comes from central breathing, for then they are relaxed and "poised." Many actors and opera singers test their voices severely with long and demanding daily rehearsals and performances. Their tours often last for periods of months and years, and although they themselves become tired, their well-conditioned voices suffer no ill effects.

It is when the person uses *costal breathing* that the danger arises. *Costal breathing results in a stricture of the neck and throat muscles,* which in turn tightens the vocal folds. This introduces a thin, nonresonant, raspiness into the voice that reduces its flexibility and causes it to tire quickly. When a person finds this happening he should immediately return to central breathing and a relaxed voice, for *continued misuse of the vocal folds can cause serious damage.* In some cases this damage has been permanent and tragic.

The Resonators

The three primary resonating chambers are the *pharynx* (throat), *oral cavity* (mouth), and *nasal cavities* (the cavities in and behind the nose). These three chambers serve to *amplify* the relatively small sound that emanates from the vocal folds and to give the voice its *individual quality* by determining the kind and degree of resonation that will make up its final character.

But we are not at the mercy of the sounds made by these resonating chambers in their *static* condition, for the effect of each one *can be changed* with careful thought and practice. The *throat* can be kept open and relaxed to produce a smooth, relaxed sound. Most of our students could accomplish this by saying the phrase, *wide-open throat,* with a large, free voice. It helped us to imagine the sound going through a stovepipe while doing this.

The *mouth is capable of many changes* in its shape that will in turn change the resonance and character of the sounds passing through it. The lower jaw and lips are mainly responsible for these changes in the shape of the mouth—and the resultant "shape" of the sounds.

The shape of the *nasal cavities cannot be changed*—but we can *control the volume of sound* that reverberates through them. Too much will produce a *hyper-nasal voice,* not enough will give a *dry, hard, nonresonant voice,* both of which are unpleasant and reduce the versatility of the speaker's vocal control.

Just enough sound passing through the nasal cavities will add to and *enhance the effect* of the other two resonating chambers, resulting in a *voice with well-balanced and rich resonance.* This voice will be capable of many variations and great changes, which an imaginative speaker or creative actor can use to increase his *expressive capacity and ability,* as the latter catches up with the former.

There are other secondary resonating chambers in the upper part of the body and the head that serve to supplement the total resonation of the vocal sounds.

The Articulators

These are sometimes called the *modifiers* because they change, or modify, the sounds as they pass through the mouth, having the *last possible effect* on the voice by the speech mechanism. This effect is tremendous when we consider that it is largely responsible for making clear the sounds and words not only in the languages and dialects of our country but in the hundreds of languages and thousands of dialects spoken throughout the world. There are five of these articulators:

(1) The Lower Jaw.

This has been called the "open door" because if it does not drop down far enough for each sound, the other articulators do not have sufficient room to work. It should be about halfway down for the sounds "AY" and "EE," and all the way down for "AH," "OH," and "OO," to give the lips room to complete the shaping of the sounds. We will use these five simple *vowel sounds* as the basis for demonstration and exercise. Please notice that they are different from the *names* of the *vowels*, being: "A," "E," "I," "O," and "U."

(2) The Lips.

There is no good reason for the "lazy lip" habit that has captured too many people. The lips are surrounded by circular muscles, which are supplemented by the other muscles of the face, waiting to be used to make the many subtle shapes that add accuracy to the sounds. They represent our last chance to modify the sounds and if they are allowed to just "hang there" they can ruin much of the effort we have expended so far. Their vigorous use will also *improve your appearance* as well as your expressiveness.

The lips are open widest on the sound "AH," for the jaw has been dropped to its lowest point. Why not try it? Now leave the jaw down and bring the lips around for the "OH" sound. (If the jaw does not stay down, there will not be enough room for the lips and the throat will have a tendency to tighten.) With the jaw still farthest down, bring the lips in to a small circle, almost as if you were going to whistle, to give the "OO" sound its best shape and to "aim" it for better projection.

For the "AY" sound the lower jaw should come to a half-way-down position and the lips can be relaxed to allow a free flow for the sound. It may surprise you to realize that the jaw and lips can maintain these same positions for the best articulation of the "EE" vowel sound, for the back of the tongue will hump up to make the difference between the two vowels. It is a mistake to stretch the corners of the mouth back to make the "EE" sound for this tightens the throat and tends to add a too-nasal quality to what will be a relaxed and clear sound if produced as suggested above.

(3) The Tongue.

The tongue is a large muscular mass attached to the floor of the mouth. It has a tip, blade (middle), and heel (back), which are all involved in the articulation of speech sounds.

You will find charts in books on voice and diction that will indicate the highest point the tongue will assume when articulating each of the front, middle, and back vowels. In working with a large verse choir we have found this to be a too-meticulous approach that can become frustrating. Instead we have found that if the group hears the word with the critical vowel pronounced accurately by the director and then "thinks" it, with careful attention given to the other articulators, that the tongue will find its proper position.

It is essential that the tongue be exercised vigorously so that it will be nimble and precise in articulating with the teeth, alveolar ridge, roof of the mouth, and soft palate for crisp sounding of the consonants, vowels, and diphthongs. Cornetists have excellent tongue action in speech because of the "triple-tonguing" demands made by their instruments.

(4) The Teeth.

Most books count the teeth as an articulator and they are, in a supportive sense. They function more as a stationary "banking board" for the tongue to articulate against for the "T" sound, as does the alveolar ridge for the "D." Several other sounds use these banking boards, among which are both the voiced and unvoiced "TH" and the "S," as in "this thistle."

Again, for work with the verse choir it is important for the members to be aware of the part the teeth and alveolar ridge play in articulation so they can be sure of a definite contact and a cleancut breakaway as called for by the words in question.

(5) The Soft Palate.

It is a surprise to most people that this articulator can be controlled as indeed it must be, for it determines the volume of *sound* that enters the nasal passages. The degree of nasal resonance can be lessened or increased by the *deliberate action* of the soft palate. This fact should be encouraging to people with too much or too little nasal resonance—but they must take the deliberate action!

A person can become aware of his ability to control the soft palate by dropping his jaw down, keeping his lips closed and consciously trying to yawn. Doing this latter action in rapid succession will strengthen the musculature and increase the control. Then pronouncing words with varying degrees of nasality consciously "built in" will prove that one can be free from a former speech fault, unless there is a pathological reason for it, in which case a speech clinic can help him.

"Placement?"

Before leaving the articulators we should say a word about "front placement." This is a practice from out of the past that was used as an antidote for voices that were rumbled and mumbled in the back of the mouth and even in the throat, not giving the articulators a chance.

But placing every sound at the front of the mouth brought on other problems. It resulted in a *tight, less-resonant voice and awkward pronunciation* that limited the total potential of the voice and caused the speaker to sound unnatural, often to the point of affectation.

Actually speech sounds are not "placed" in any one area but are *shaped* in different parts of the mouth where the *articulators change rapidly and drastically* to accommodate their demands. Remember that they are also *enriched* by the primary and secondary resonating chambers, given a *solid* sound by the vocal folds, and firmly *projected* by the diaphragm and abdominal muscles. The entire mechanism must be considered, for each part makes its important contribution to the total sound.

When a professional golfer was asked if every time he stroked the ball he thought of all the many parts of a golf swing that he had learned, he said, "No, just one, and then the others fall into place."

Different "keys" work for different people but most of my students have found that thinking of the *down stroke of the diaphragm* is the best way to start the smooth and efficient operation of the speech mechanism and to insure a good final sound. This must of course be preceded by concentrating on the total meaning of the word or phrase being expressed. This the golfer also does in planning his shot before he swings.

Group Exercises to Improve Voice and Articulation

Many good exercises that are pertinent to the particular needs of *individuals* may be learned from teachers and coaches of voice and articulation, from books on the subject, and from speech pathologists.

In dealing with *large groups* we have the responsibility to choose exercises that will do the *greatest good for the greatest number in the shortest period of time*—and it will help if they are fun to do. Full-choir participation is necessary for success—especially for those few who "just don't feel like it this morning," because they need it most. Students with physcal or pathological problems should of course not participate in any exercise that is not indicated for their particular condition.

The speech act involves the entire body so the following series is designed first to *relax the body,* then to *condition the speech mechanism* for strenuous work, and finally to *prepare for the first poem* we will be rehearsing. These eleven exercises have been selected from many that we have used over the years and they seem to get the job done in the most effective way. You may find or create others that will work better with your group.

1. *The Sky Reach:* With the feet slightly apart extend both arms upward as far as they can comfortably go. Then reach up higher with the right arm until you feel the muscles stretch down the side of the body. Do the same with the left arm.

2. *The "Ad-Lib" Stretch:* Place the feet a little farther

apart, bend the knees slightly, bounce a little, and then enjoy your own delicious stretch, being sure to involve the back, legs, and arms.

3. *Turn the Arms Inside-Out:* Hold the arms out as if you were carrying a large beach ball. Then bring the hands in toward the chest and twist the wrists and arms as you extend them outward, finishing with the palms out. Then turn them in and repeat until the arms and shoulders feel good. Now shake the arms and wrists.

4. *Leg-Twist and Toe-Point:* Raise the right foot off the floor until the knee is well bent. Then twist the foot and leg around, finishing with the toes pointed forward. Repeat with the left leg. Then give each a good "shake-a-leg" treatment.

5. *The Head Roll:* It is important to begin this exercise slowly, taking at least a full minute for the first time around. First, extend the head comfortably upward, then let it fall backward as far as it will go. Let it remain there until you feel the muscles of the throat stretch and relax. This *unhurried relaxation* is the purpose of this exercise.

Next let the head fall over to the right side and move it slightly to "find its notch." As it rests there wait until you feel the *muscles on the opposite side of the neck relax.* When the head falls forward it should remain there longer because the muscles at the back of the neck are stronger and need more time to relax. The head should be "way down" for this. Then let the head move over to find its notch on the left side, and wait until the muscles on the right side relax.

Repeating this "four-step" rotation twice should relax the neck and throat muscles enough for free operation.

Now you are ready to do what most books recommend:
roll the head in a wide, free circle several times.

6. *The Jaw Roll:* Simply lower the jaw as far down as it
   will go, take the chin in the fingers and roll the jaw
   around in its widest arc. Let the jaw do this independently as soon as it is able, to strengthen the muscles
   that control it.

7. *Relaxed-Tall Posture:* Push the *crown* of the head up
   as far as you can, as if you were holding up the ceil-
   ing. This will bring the chin in and align the head,
   shoulders, hips, and knees in a balanced and relaxed
   manner—and will extend the rib cage outward.

8. *Central Breathing:* With the ribs remaining out push
   the air out of the lungs by the action of the *abdominal
   muscles.* "Push the abdomen in with the hand," if
   necessary, until you learn to do it. Then consciously
   force the abdomen forward with the action of the
   diaphragm. You can "push the hand out with the abdomen" to identify this most important "happening."
   Repeat this slowly at first, increasing the speed until
   you can master the action with a rapid "panting" motion. *Note:* This may not happen the first day, or
   week, for it takes concentration and practice. Although when I first told Asradt Wolde, from
   Ethiopia, about this, he said, "Oh, you mean instead
   of breathing like this [heaving his chest], I should
   breathe like this?" [pumping his diaphragm and
   abdomen]!

9. *Lip Shaper:* The circular muscles around the lips can
   best be strengthened by dropping the jaw down and
   distinctly sounding the "OO-AH-OH-OO" sequence
   of vowels, *leaving the jaw down.* Then close off the
   "OO" sound by bringing the lips into a tight circle,

and releasing it with a sharp "WUH." Do not allow this sequence to become "WOW" because accurate lip shapes can be gained only when each vowel is articulated distinctly, especially the "OH." Repeat this until *after* these muscles become tired to increase their strength and tone.

10. *Tongue Tingler:* First find the tongue by touching it to the roof and floor of the mouth alternately, then from one side to the other. Extending it far out and wagging it will increase the strength of its larger muscles. The tingle results from trilling it against the teeth and is especially good to prepare the tip to articulate such sounds as "L" and "T." This is a new experience for some people but it can be learned by holding the tongue in a relaxed and "neutral" position; then activate it with short, sudden bursts until sustained trilling can be accomplished.

11. *Control the Soft Palate:* The easiest way to "discover" the soft palate is to run the tongue back over the firm hard palate. When the tongue passes the half-way point the contact becomes indefinite, due to the fact that both the tongue and soft palate are soft.

Now close the lips, drop the jaw far down, and try to yawn. You will feel, and hear, the action of the soft palate. Repeat this rapidly, leaving the jaw down and the lips closed, to strengthen the muscles and increase the control.

Now test your control over nasality by saying the phrase: "Down in the valley," first with too much nasality, then with none, and finally with just the right balance of oral and nasal resonance—being certain the vowels are clear.

If too much nasality still persists try the non-nasal

phrase: "Jack Spratt could eat no fat, his wife could eat no lean"—but look out for the "EE" sound in "lean" because it may be affected by the nasal sound of the consonant "n." This is called "assimilated nasality."

If these eleven exercises seem too many or too much on certain days, or if your time is limited before a performance, numbers 3 and 4 may be omitted—depending on the "Ad-Lib Stretch" to relax the arms and legs. The only way to receive the full benefit of their cumulative effect is to run through the full series diligently before each rehearsal and performance. Once the choir has learned them they can be done in a short five minutes, and they do become a source of fun and satisfaction.

Rhythms

The following four vocalizing exercises have arranged the five simple vowel sounds as rhythms to increase their fun value and to unite the choir. Doing them faster and faster will improve articulation accuracy. Stop just before the point of phonic chaos.

1. Extend the first "La-ay" for several seconds and then continue with "Lay lay lay lay— —" with varying degrees of power, being careful that the sound does not become strained as it is made louder. Bring it down to the softest solid sound possible. Treat the other vowels in this same manner. Breathe as often as is necessary for there is no merit in seeing how long you can speak on one breath.

2. In doing this second one you should emphasize the crispness of the consonant sounds:

"*Lay* le *Lee* le *Lah* le *Loh* le *Loo*, *Loo* le *Loo* *Loo* le *Loo* le *LOO* *LOO!*"

Repeat the same rhythm with "Tay," "Bay," "Way," and

others of your choice, checking the sounding of these five vowels and the crispness of the consonants.

3. This third one varies the rhythm somewhat. It uses a rhythm your people may have learned in camp. It will be used in the introduction number so will do double service.

It also represents the first time we have used different voice groups of the choir. They are indicated in the margin by L, M, D, or All, and within a line they will be in parentheses. To save repetition the first indication will work until there is a change to a different group or solo.

L   *Lay Lee Lah Loh,* loo *Loo,* loo *Loo*
M   *Tay Tee Tah Toh,* too *Too,* too *Too*
D   *Bay Bee Bah Boh, Bay Bee Bah Boh,* (All) *BOO!*
All   *Boo* boo *BOO, boo* boo *BOO, boo* boo *Boo* boo *BOO BOO!*

4. The fourth rhythm is simply the alphabet, with variations. After giving them a sample let the group "ad-lib" it, first, using their own individual inflection patterns and making it "say" whatever they like. Then give them a sentence, such as "What a gloomy morning we are having—but tomorrow may be sunny again!" See what they do with it as a choir. This sentence should take the entire alphabet; the first half from "A" to "O" and the second from "P" through "Z," for speed enhances flexibility of both pitch and phrasing.

This is a good time to introduce phrases from the poems you intend to rehearse; allowing the choir to respond to them with this free use of the alphabet will excite their imaginations and save them from narrow and stilted patterns.

We will be using this paraphrasing technique a great deal, and in different ways, in the next chapter on "Group Oral Interpretation" so it is good for the choir to become familiar with it in this informal way.

Practice Sentences for the Vowels and Consonants

In identifying a sound for practice it is better to simply articulate it rather than to name it, for its name will often involve other sounds.

You may wish to choose a few of these for repeated use—and memorization—or to choose two or three a day and thus cover the sounds in the English language by completing both lists. They are designed to place the critical sound next to various other sounds for forced practice in clearer articulation. This is especially useful in avoiding assimilated nasality—allowing the nasal consonant to affect the vowel sounds that precede or follow it.

Our people made a game of counting all the critical sounds in each sentence and comparing notes. They are easy to miss. It is also a creative experience to have your class make up their own practice sentences, thus assuring vocabulary that fits the group's age level.

You, yourself, can have the most fun by presenting each sentence with *varying emotions;* such as anger, surprise, fear, consolation, suspicion, and others. These should bring forth some strange and wonderful inflection and phrasing patterns, as you have fun with them, which they will return to you. This approach will make of these exercises a welcomed *fun experience* and at the same time gain improvement in all the skills of voice and articulation. It will also give them experience in group oral interpretation, which is the concern of the next chapter.

PRACTICE SENTENCES FOR THE VOWEL SOUNDS:

KEY
WORDS:

Front Vowels

H*E*:   The eerie eel was even greener than Clarice
          perceived.
W*I*LL: Here it is, Dick. Near the Virginia
          Veterinarian's office.
P*A*Y: They hastened to make a lazy haven for the
          enraged reigning male.
TH*E*M: The ebbing echo beckoned the daring men to
          the very edge. The end.
B*A*CK: Frank shall carry the family parrot back and
          forth and back.
L*A*ST: Laugh is pronounced halfway between calm
          and cat, so is half.

Middle Vowels

B*I*RD: The Colonel ascertained when the first
          excursion would return.
B*U*(R)N (Use the above sentence, omitting the "R"
          sounds as in Southern and Eastern dialects.)
C*U*T   The troublesome flood does much damage as
          it comes down the valley.
(Stressed)
*A*BOVE   I am amazed that you allow the gorilla to select
          the vegetables.
(Unstressed)

Back Vowels

WHO: The moody ruler swooned at the rumor of the spoofing buffoon.

WOULD: The wolf stood in the woods and shook the brook full of wool.

* GO: Oh, go blow your oboe before you stub your toe, Joe.

CALL: I thought Shaw was the author, to my sorrow.

ON: Morris caught cold hauling logs across the soggy bog.

FATHER: Father's barber was calm under the balmy San Juan palms.

* RIDE: I tried to climb the fire escape twice to hide the pie.

*HOUSE: No doubt they found the sauerkraut downtown.

* *Diphthongs*

* BOY: The Doyle boys, Lloyd and Floyd, adroitly avoided the oysters.

* CUTE: Hugh viewed the beautiful new suit at Hubert's New York shop.

* AIR: Who cares where the lions have their lair, as long as they stay there.

* NEAR: Come here, dear, so I can dry your tears.

* TOUR: The poor travelers toured the rough contour of the moors.

PRACTICE SENTENCES FOR THE CONSONANT SOUNDS:

MUM: The diaphragm is the dome-shaped muscle that surmounts the abdomen.

NONE: Definite sentences are commonly accompanied by downward inflections.

SING: Frank Manning is going to bring me a singing monkey, Bing.

PAY: Do you suppose that Paul appreciates painting and sculpture?

BE: Anybody who believes that fable is probably as gullible as a baby baboon.

TO: What did you do today, Tait, rotate?

DO: Tait didn't. He was hidden deep in the garden under the mullioned window.

KEY: The cocky cook baked a chocolate cake for the picnic in the park.

GO: Gregory the Great forgot his hunger and staggered through the fog.

ROAR: ** If you can say brew and wary you can surely pronounce February accurately.

LILLY: Calla lillies and little Lulu's family live in a low valley.

FAN: San Diego's far flung fishing fleet found fifty-five porpoises.

VAN: The diver, with nervy verve, vivisected the vivacious octopus.

THIN: Do you think the thimble will help you thrust the thread through the cloth?

THEN: The heather withers in this weather whether or no.

SIT: "Mississippi" looks a little like "Missouri" but has a dissimilar sound.

** Semi-vowels or glides

ZOO-:   There are zebras, monkeys, and weasels in the zoo.

SHE: Emotion should surely be shown by facial expression.

VISION: He usually filled his leisure hours with casual pleasures.

CHEW: The child's chair became chunks of charcoal, but his "choo-choo train" survived.

JUDGE: George's heart jumped a beat when the judge asked the jury for its verdict.

HE: Who says a mahogany highboy isn't heavy, Hugh?

WHET: The whirring ship whistled through his whiskers as he wheeled around.

WET: **Hugh usually awakened at once when Wendell threw water through the window. Wouldn't you?

YES: ** It would amuse you to know the value of that yellow New York yacht.

* * * * * * * * * * * * *

At the end of his first inaugural address, Lincoln said, "I am loath to close." I feel the same at this point for the principal emphasis of this chapter may be lost if we are not reminded that voice and articulation are the *servants of the meaning* they are expressing and not ends in themselves.

If the voice becomes too mellifluous and "pretty," and diction over-exact, "nasty-nice," and pedantic, they miss their primary function of expressing the speaker's sincere involvement with the author's idea and emotion.

They can only perform this function when they *result from* the author's total meaning.

Success in doing this is more easily attained when the speaker is surrounded by others engaged in a friendly, cooperative effort—as in the verse choir. Each individual will also gain the lasting values of disciplined speech, sensitivity to great and small meanings, and the need to cooperate with others.

Part Three

Materials and Procedures
for All Age Groups

9

Group Oral Interpretation, Programming, Rehearsals, and Performance

Many of the problems encountered in causing a group, whether large or small, to interpret a poem with coherence and a unified spirit may be solved by wise selection of materials.

Selecting Materials

The four principal characteristics that render material easily adaptable for group interpretation are *universality, rhythm, euphonic quality,* and *appropriateness for the group.*

Universality.
This is the "central something" to which everyone the world over can respond. We will refer to it as the

"Greatest Common Denominator." It is necessary for the involvement of the total choir and for the response of the audience, for we are communicating from "people to people."

But before we concede that universality limits us to "life, death, sunshine, and rain" we must remember that most people are interested in many things, and also that it is possible to awaken interest where none had been before—nor even suspected.

More critical to universality than subject matter is the *manner in which the material is treated by the author*. His frame of reference can be so narrow that few beside himself can understand and share his view, giving it limited potential. This could be true even if his subject were the sky! On the other hand, a personal subject can be given universal appeal, and the choir, being "one great voice," can represent the unifying element that makes it a common experience for all.

A good example of this "plural" treatment of an individual's personal feelings is found in Elizabeth Barrett Browning's love sonnet written to her husband, Robert Browning. When she says, "How do I love thee? Let me count the ways— —" our first inclination is to read no further, for these must be intimacies belonging only to these two people. But as we do read on we find that she is expressing personal love in ways that we can appreciate and indeed would like to have initiated ourselves. "I wish I had said that" really applies here.

Other examples of this "central something" are: Walt Whitman's *love for life* presented in his "Miracles"; the *painful poignancy* of Edna St. Vincent Millay's "The Harp Weaver"; the *agony* with which Kipling endows "Danny Deever"; the *fear of death* that pervades Goethe's *The*

King of the Elves; pomposity exposed by Shelley's "Ozymandias"; and even Robert Burns' *sympathy for a field mouse* is not too small a thing to be included.

Rhythm.

Rhythm is useful to the choir because it is a strong, unifying element. Unlike music, which has many "built in" controls, this *felt beat* is the strongest factor we have with which to build the other elements of our interpretation. Rhythm also is the key to the inner life of the poem and helps us focus our interpretation on this central thing. (Rhythm has been more fully discussed in Chapter 6 under "Phrasing," one of the seven variables.)

Euphonic Quality.

Beauty of sound can be a dangerous thing in interpreting a poem for we can become so captured by it that it can overshadow the meaning. It is the "Lorelei" of group oral interpretation.

This tendency should not prevent us from making full use of the *resounding vowel* sounds and the cellolike *continuing consonants* in highlighting the meaning and bringing it more pleasurably to the audience. Nor are these the only sounds to be considered, for the sharp tinkling that Poe gives "To the tintinnabulation that so musically wells— —" adds to the gaiety of the sleigh ride. There is even a rugged kind of beauty in his harsh introduction: "Hear the loud alarum bells—Brazen bells! What a tale of terror, now, their turbulency tells!" Beauty is where you recognize it.

Perhaps we will be close to the truth if we maintain that an important part of euphony is *fitting the sound to its subject* so well that it helps to bring it to the consciousness of the audience. This refers not only to onomatopeia but also to adroit use of the language. Tennyson rewrote some lines thirty times to achieve this accuracy.

Appropriateness for the Group.
The following guidelines may be applied to groups of all ages. An excellent learning opportunity is presented here in having the members of your group help choose the poems. This process will not only make them aware of values but will also assure their interest.

1. *Difficult enough to challenge the choir.* San Dieguito High's Drama Choros found that Toche's "Geographical Fuge" took considerable work but was within their capability span—and gave them great satisfaction. Pride in achievement results from doing numbers considered "too difficult." By the same token, "Two Little Kittens" gave a mentally retarded class of five and six year olds the same psychological boost when they reached to the top of their ability to give it a joyous rendition filled with elaborate inflections that demonstrated their love for the kittens. The challenge serves both of these groups, and all others in between, equally well by making them stretch above their present ability toward their total capability.

2. *Novel and spectacular for flair.* Try Robert Louis Stevenson's "Windy Nights" for younger people, or any of Vachel Lindsay's works for "growing-ups" and adults.

3. *Simple and serious for depth.* John Donne's "For Whom the Bell Tolls" is superb for this. We have used it as a "signature" number. Religious writings can be done in schools as art numbers.

4. *Light and "fun-for-its-own-sake" for relief.* A. A. Milne's "The King's Breakfast" and "A Musical Trust" will do well for nearly any age. Dr. Seuss' works have limitless possibilities. His early poem, "And to Think that I Saw It On Mulberry Street" still stands as a masterpiece of imagination.
5. *Representative of many cultures.* "A Hanukkah Top," by N. D. Karpinver; "The Creation," by an Objiway Indian; Johnson's "God's Trombones"; "Songs of the Slums" by Kagawa; and Lorca's works are five of the many directions that may be taken.

Marjorie Gullan's Seven Best Choices.

Miss Gullan gives us seven poems that she considered most representative of the five following categories of subject matter suitable for the verse choir:

1. *Melody:* Nashe's "Spring."
2. *Rhythm:* Belloc's "Tarantella," and Stephens' "The Fifteen Acres."
3. *Prevailing emotion:* Shakespeare's "Under the Greenwood Tree."
4. *Climax and anticlimax:* Masefield's "Cargoes," and Kingsley's "The River."
5. *Thought moving majestically:* Shirley's "Death, the Leveler."

Finding the Greatest Common Denominator

The greatest common denominator of a piece of literature is that part of its intellectual and emotional message to which the greatest number of people can respond. It is also called the "central core" or "central essence."

I submit that the plural aspect of the verse choir provides a ready-made opportunity for finding this central essence, through the free and immediate response of its members. It is at once a workshop to discover the greatest common denominator and an arena to test its validity.

There is also a greater likelihood of the group's finding this central core than an individual interpreter might, for although he has the opportunity to develop a uniquely different treatment of the poem he may be drawn to an *attractive facet* of the meaning or become *singularly subjective* in its interpretation. The numbers in the group serve as a "check-and-balance" safety measure to guard against these two limitations.

It is fortunate that this central core is usually closely related to the *rhythm* of the poem, which gives it easy access into the consciousness of the choir members. Rhythm becomes a bridge from the poem to the choir, assisting greatly in striking the common chord.

Also, if the poem possesses the quality of *universality,* discussed at the beginning of this chapter, the choir members will have little trouble agreeing on the greatest commonality that ties them together—and to the audience.

Two factors that *operate against* a poem having a broad enough meaning to evoke a response from many in the choir and audience are:

1. The author's having written it from a *"singular"* or *narrow point of view.*
2. The poem promoting a *narrow partisan position or call for action* that does not win broad advocacy or support in the choir and audience.

This second factor is an especially good reason for the

choir at every age to be organized on *democratic principles and procedures* where each and every member can feel free to express his particular perception of the meaning. The best time for this is when the poem is first presented and in the early stages of its preparation. It is this procedure that promotes, and should insure, the complete involvement of every choir member—the factor that is so vital to the spirit of creative unity that makes each choir unique. The same person "came out" differently in succeeding semesters due to the particular personnel of each choir giving its own fresh response to its inner life.

Using the Resources of the Growing Person

There will be some age diversity in the personnel of even these loose groupings due to individual differences, environment, and learning opportunities.

1. *Children's Emotional Spontaneity:*

Pre-school and primary children have no difficulty in getting into the central spirit of the poem, immediately and completely. They can quickly respond to the strange and wonderful characters in any of Dr. Seuss' magnificent stories, and they give complete empathy to whatever is presented to them. Luckily they know the difference between "pretending" and reality, which protects them from some of the grim tales in earlier children's literature. While children's literature is improving in this regard, the bombardment of violence and terror through general television offerings is causing serious psychological damage. So let's give them more healthy experiences through the verse choir.

2. *Reflective Thought in Children:*

Similarly these young children have no problem in discovering what poems and jingles of many subjects are about for they are interested in everything—they are discovering their world. This perception soon becomes reflective thinking, which should be listened to for it will give us a valid insight into the "child mind." So here are two examples:

When three-year-old David Sanders was caught in an especially heavy Illinois thunderstorm he ran, dripping, to his mother to ask confidentially, "Mom, did we really need all this rain?" When our own son, Richard, was in the first grade the dawn was mentioned at the dinner table. His contribution was, "I was out in the dawn once. That's when God doesn't hang out the sun all at once. He just scoots it up over the edge a little bit." (When you write a book you can tell what *your* children have said.)

These random efforts of young children to understand the wonders of nature can be directed to analyzing their poetry on an intellectual as well as an emotional level—even to the point of objectively finding its greatest common denominator that all in the class can agree upon.

3. *The Growing-Up Years:*

As children become "growing-ups" through the intermediate, or "middle," grades and secondary schools they can contribute more deeply and astutely to the *intellectual analysis and interpretation* of the increasingly complex poetry that matches their advancement. While this is happening, their *emotions tend to become submerged* so our problem is to show them it is acceptable to be "childlike" or "naturally responsive" enough to feel and express the emotion that is also a apart of the total experience.

4. *The College Years–"The Age of Reason":*

This is the period in which the person should have reached a *high degree of acuity* in both the intellectual and emotional (or cognitive and affective) realms. His total educational experience has been directed toward the acquisition of knowledge and an understanding of himself that should bring both of these areas into balance.

This balance, in turn, makes possible deeper analysis not only of the obvious concepts in the poem but the subtleties as well. It will take more discussion as there will be more divergent views but when their commonly agreed upon interpretation has been formulated, it should be closer to the author's intention and inner essence of the poem than any earlier group could achieve. As the college student's potential is greatest at this point, so is the college verse-choir director's opportunity.

The Director's Opportunity and Responsibility

After this central meaning has been understood and accepted and the spirit of creative unity established it is then the director's responsibility to apply the principles, tools, and procedures of directing to the job of delivering the poem to the audience in the clearest and most exciting way—using the resources of the choir as a responsive instrument.

At this point the director changes his function from a *discussion leader* to an *"artistic dictator"* who uses his creative ability to conduct, or "play," the choir. This accounts for variations in the basic interpretation of the same poem by the same choir when conducted by different directors.

Arranging A Poem for the Verse Choir

There are many ways in which the director communicates his ideas to the choir: by explanation, paraphrasing, evocative statements, or by presenting the passage orally as he "hears" it. Finally it must be put down on paper as an "arrangement sheet," and the following format is suggested as being the simplest and most workable under rehearsal conditions.

In the first example the full choir does the entire poem so the emphasis will be on the *paraphrasing and evocative statements* running down the right margin. They will function best if they epitomize the interpretation of the particular phrase and if they are kept short. Sometimes they are single words that call to mind the feeling or essence of thought that should pervade the reading of the phrase or passage.

This poem by John Donne, a contemporary of Shakespeare's, first made us realize that large groups can express subtleties, if there is complete unity of thought and feeling. The author has given his work two admirable qualities: it is a *monolithic poem about one idea*, the interdependence of mankind; and, in restating this central theme he has *clothed it in subtleties* that "open up" its interpretation, saving it from being intoned in solemn monotony. The director can point up these subtleties with such statements as appear in the right-hand margin. The basic message calls for the poem to be done in unison.

FOR WHOM THE BELL TOLLS

No man is an island,
   entire of itself.

            (A simple fact firmly stated,
            with no "dramatics.")

Every man
   is a piece of the Conti-
     nent,
   a part of the main.

            (As if the author leaned over
            to us and said: "In other
            words.")

If a clod be washed away
   by the sea
   Europe is the less

As well
   as if a promontory were;

            (The analogies in these next
            three lines become increas-
            ingly personal, narrowing
            down to, "thine own."
            They also make a good
            build.)

As well
   as if a manor of thy
     friend's
   or of thine own were.

Any man's death di-
   minishes me,
   because I am involved in
   mankind;

            (Firm simplicity again for this
            "core" statement.)

And therefore—
   Never send to know for
     whom
       the bell tolls:

            (Once accepted, this inevita-
            bly follows.)

It tolls for thee.

            (Simply and quietly.)

The second example is the fourth stanza from Edgar Allen Poe's "The Bells." It also uses the full choir at times, but makes use of four *different voice groups to represent different elements in the poem* and to capitalize on the versatility of the choir in expressing the nuances of the poem. The full text of "The Bells" is given with suggestions for the director in Chapter 14.

In breaking up the "one great voice" of the choir it is imperative that care be taken at the following points. These principles operate with all choirs, regardless of the number of sections, solos, narrators, musical accompaniment, sound effects, or cooperating groups of dancers or actors.

(1) Each section, and all solo voices, must be synchronized accurately so that transitions will be smooth—giving the illusion that it is still "one great voice" speaking.

(2) All other elements in the production are governed by this same necessity.

(3) Solo voices or voice groups may well be used for a short phrase, or even one word, as a special emphatic "spike" that will sharpen the total meaning of the passage.

(4) When a voice unit is designated in the left margin or within the line, it will work until a change is made.

(5) When voice groups in a four-voice-group choir are combined or discontinued, their numbers reflect these changes, as: 1-12-123-All, 234-34-4; or other combinations.

(6) All voice units used within a line will be designated in parentheses.

(7) Do not become so fascinated by all these possibilities that the interpretation becomes "splintered" and detracts from the poem's spirit or message.

THE BELLS
Edgar Allan Poe (Fourth Stanza)

Legend: 1—Light Women, 2—Medium Women,
3—Medium Men, 4—Dark Men

4   Hear the tolling of the
      bells—Iron bells!   *(Velvet melancholy)*
    What a world of sol-
      emn thought their
      monody compels!
    In the silence of the
      night,
1   How we shiver with a-
      fright   *(High and frightened)*
2   At the melancholy (3)
    MENACE (4) of
      their tone!   *("Attic to cellar")*
    For every sound that
      floats
    From the sound within
      their throats—is a
      groan.
12 And the people—ah,   *(Eerie, but with sympathy)*
    the people—
    They that dwell up in
      the steeple, all
      alone,
4   And who tolling, tol-
    ling, tolling
    In that muffled   *(The smooth groundswell that be-*
      monotone   *gins here tops out at "glory"*
34 Feel a glory in so rol-   *and falls off at "heart a*
    ling   *stone.")*
    On the human heart a
      stone—
12 They are neither man
    nor woman—

34 They are neither brute
      nor human—
4 They are ghouls—
   And their king it is   *(From the bottom of the well)*
      who tolls;—
   As he rolls, rolls, rolls,
      rolls
   A paean from the
      bells!
34 And his merry bosom   *(Faster, with poltergeist aban-*
      swells   *don.)*
   With the paean from
      the bells!
   And he dances and he
      yells;
All Keeping time, time,
      time, in a sort of
      runic rhyme,
   to the paean of the
      bells, of the bells
   Keeping time, time,
      time, in a sort of
      runic rhyme
   To the throbbing of
      the bells—
   Of the bells, bells,   *(Begin slower tempo at "throb-*
      bells—   *bing". These "bells" and*
   To the tolling of the   *words are soft and musical.)*
      bells—
34 Of the bells, (12) bells,
      (34) bells,   *(Maintain a constant pitch and*
   (12) bells,   *stately rhythm. Accent every-*
34 bells, (12) bells, (34)   *other beat to the end.)*
      bells—
All To the moaning and
      the groaning
   Of the bells.

These *arrangement sheets* represent the verse choir's nearest proximation to a musical score so should be constructed and adhered to very carefully.

Rehearsing a Verse Choir

Rehearsals are work sessions that can be made enjoyable and efficient, each adding to the other. You may wish to consider the following suggestions, in relation to your own techniques and procedures.

At whatever age level your choir may be it is good to begin with appropriate relaxing and muscle-toning exercises to free the entire body from tensions and to render the speech mechanism ready for beyond-the-ordinary work. Eleven such exercises are presented in Chapter 8.

If unity and morale are needed "that morning" it is good to do a familiar and well-liked number first. If the choir is "ready," a new number will provide fresh interest.

Regular attendance, concentrated attention on the task of the moment, and *committing poems to memory* are obvious necessities. *Willingness of spirit* is a great boon. Without it the whole procedure becomes an ordeal—with it everything comes to life. A willing spirit should result from making the rehearsals and performances well-planned and meaningful experiences.

Each rehearsal should move the choir forward toward a polished execution of each number, keeping the *well-known* fresh and bringing the *new* nearer to "performance pitch." In this process we found it helpful to set definite graduated goals for each rehearsal. These include "roughing out" or "breaking open" a new poem and refining the interpretation of familiar ones. This "working by steps" gives the choir a sense of *daily accom-*

plishment. Expecting the finished product at each rehearsal breeds frustration, but experiencing solid progress each day promotes confidence.

Give definite directions and accept only full achievement of your goal for the passage in question. Compliments will work wonders when deserved, and so will definite analysis of the mistakes and of your expectations. Stop the choir *at the point of the mistake,* correct it, and then run over the passage until it is "theirs."

Have fun when fun happens, work hard when working—but don't mix the two, not even with a "fun" poem. Just as comedy demands more careful timing and acting skill than a straight drama, so does a light-spirited number require more work to achieve the vocal precision and shades of meaning involved. The ultimate enjoyment will result from achieving final mastery of the poem, or the part you are working on.

As soon as possible run the entire program in order to make clear transitions from the mood of one poem to the next, and to get the feel of the program as a whole. Timing each number and the entire program is necessary for radio and television broadcasting and for tight time requirements of school assemblies, and other occasions.

Rewards provide worthy motivation. At the college level the announcement that we would leave five minutes early if we finished our work for the day was appreciated and brought results. In schools where this is not possible the reward might be doing a favorite number "after we have worked hard on the new one." Playing a word game is also fun—and it builds vocabulary painlessly.

Ideally all rehearsals should be accomplished in a

good spirit of cooperative, businesslike effort. But there will be days when no one feels like working, not even yourself. At these times you must find the key that will get the whole thing moving again.

It may be a *radical change of approach* such as a brief discussion of something in which they are all interested; an athletic event, a play, or social function—or even a serious experience they all have shared. Having focused their interest you can move on to the one best suggestion in the above list, or from your own resources, that will get the rehearsal moving.

It may be necessary to *give up your entire rehearsal period* to a discussion of some problem that is holding them captive. Such a "true session" will likely clear the atmosphere and strengthen their rapport with you as one who is interested in them as people and not merely as "voices."This could be the key thing that will bring them back to their next rehearsal with new insights and ready for work.

Careful Programming

This is similar to window-dressing in showing each number to its best advantage by its placement in the program as a whole. The following seven things should be considered in arranging the poems:

1. *Age level of the choir:* This extremely flexible criterion for choosing materials is treated in detail in Chapters 10 through 14.

    An interesting principle operates here. It is to *"Look ahead for challenge–look back for depth and new findings."*

    Often a choir will exceed its own, and its director's,

expectancy by "reaching" to do a creditable job of a number that is beyond its full comprehension, and be better for the experience. A different kind of value will come when a choir does a "younger" number than is expected of its age level, finding new meanings and appreciations passed over before.

There can be no condescension, undue exaggeration, nor "cuteness" when an older choir does a poem written for younger people. In a real sense it takes an older person to fully appreciate a child's poem or song. But the older choir must really "look back in hunger" to find the deeper experience.

The juvenile "A Musical Trust" provided our college choir with great fun as we rolled back the years; and we reinforced its "All for one and one for all" meaning by our unabashed acceptance and spirited rendering of the poem. Similarly "Little Boy Blue" caused us to understand parent-grief and little-boy insight better from the vantage point of our budding maturity.

The depth is there in children's literature. It was no accident that Igor Stravinsky found enough in "The Owl and the Pussy Cat" for a major musical composition. Educators may well ask themselves "Who was that little lamb that followed Mary to school that day.?"

There is no one absolute best age to do a number. There are many best times to accomplish various purposes for various age groups.

2. *Variety for balance:* It is good to start with short, attractive numbers and move into heavier material as you build to your featured number, ending with your

"signature" poem, which will leave a lasting impression of both the program and the choir. Longer programs need to be relieved by short, fun poems. If carefully selected and positioned, their contrast will add to the poignancy of the more serious numbers.

3. *Fitness for the audience:* Choosing from your total repertoire it is good to add to the "sure-fire" numbers others that will stretch their appreciation potential. Both you and they may be surprised by this "carrot-dangling."

We found a strange phenomenon here. Young children were filled with wonder at the rhythm, sounds, and complexity of our heavier numbers even though they understood little of their content. Of course, the fun poems are their special "dish," especially if they can participate in them, as in "The Lion Hunt."

4. *Keep with the trend and mood of the times:* Maintain a careful balance to assure clear perspective. Our *"High-Time, America"* program looked at the past, present, and future of our country. It may be found in Chapter 13 under the title "A Past to Remember—A Future to Mold."

5. *Special themes:* An entire program can be developed around a single theme and presented to many different audiences. We recorded one using poems about and by Abraham Lincoln. It also included the contrapuntal spoken arrangement of *The Battle Hymn of the Republic* and *Dixie,* given in Chapter 16. A "single-author program" will be interesting if his poems have sufficient versatility.

6. *Fitness for the occasion:* Until you have developed a

large repertoire it will be impossible to do a complete program of poetry especially suited for different occasions. You can, however, develop one poem that will serve this purpose and place it at a featured spot in your program, at the top of the "build" mentioned in the paragraph on "Variety for Balance," thus paying homage to the special nature of each occasion.

7. *Rearrangement of material* can sometimes be surprisingly helpful. Shortly before our choir was to appear on the campus of Arizona State College two of their strongest student leaders met tragic deaths within the period of one week. In consultation with Mr. Jon Guthrie, a former student who is now chairman of the speech department, we decided not to cancel but to proceed with the program in the following way:

We fortunately had some serious numbers which we grouped in the first half of the program and dedicated them to the two young men, ending with John Donne's "For Whom the Bell Tolls." At this point we reminded the student audience of the manner in which the Dixieland bands in New Orleans conducted their funeral processions. On the way to the cemetery they played *When the Saints Come Marching In,* and other spirituals in slow measured time in keeping with their grief at losing their friend. But when they had left him and were returning to the city they played the same numbers in jazz rhythm for they were re-entering the world of the living and they faced it with a joyful spirit, as they believed their friend would desire them to do.

We then finished our program with light-hearted numbers, and subsequent reports showed that many of the students were freed from the pall of shock and grief that had gripped them since the tragedies.

This general principle of rearranging program material will operate in many instances.

The Performance

Everything we have dealt with in these nine chapters has pointed to this vital culminating experience filled with rich human values for everyone involved: the choir members who give of the author and themselves; the individuals in the audience who receive the living poem and give back a response; the director whose satisfactions match his responsibility and effort; the production workers who have provided the physical necessities; and the author who knows that his work has completed its cycle.

The strange acuteness of a verse-choir performance reaches unusual proportions at times. This is due not only to the novelty of hearing many people speak with variety and meaning but to the *unadorned directness* that adds such a personal dimension to this form of communication.

Many choir members have attested to this strange quality of experience in such terms as: "You could *feel* the audience"; "I thought it would be fun, but nothing like *this;*" "I feel wonderful inside"; "Did you see those kids' eyes"; "I didn't know there was so much in that poem"; and "I felt I was 'going all out' for myself and still blending with all the others—it was sort of a miracle."

Other aspects of the performance are given in greater

detail in Chapters 4, 5, and 7. However, these few reminders may be helpful to you and your choir:

A crisp, orderly movement onto the stage will give your audience a feeling of expectancy and set a good mood for the performance.

Expect to be thrilled in giving each number. This will assure your deep satisfaction and the best response from the audience.

Take time to establish the mood of each poem with the choir. It will help to beat the rhythm and tempo before actually starting the poem.

Concentrate on each poem—and watch the director!

No matter how tired you all are, approach each performance as if it were the "first time." This spirit of enthusiasm is your best stock in trade and the audience will find it contagious, and you will all be refreshed.

10
Young Children

As we learn more about individual differences, cultural backgrounds, disparity of earlier learning opportunities, language facility, and motivational factors we see that children of any one chronological age cannot be optimally served in a single grade level.

Indeed some schools find they can best serve their children by becoming ungraded, by combining several grades in one group and by varying their organizations in other ways as they find workable factors for determining groups with the greatest educational facility. A child may even be placed in classes of different age levels that match his potential in various subjects.

It is also good practice, in using the verse choir, to give an "older" poem to a younger group, or vice versa, to stretch their abilities in the first case or to encourage them to find greater depth in the latter.

For these reasons the grade and age connotations at the heading of this and each of the next five chapters are meant to serve only as general guidelines.

Most of the principles and procedures we have covered so far will relate to those of you who work with young children, reduced in complexity by the age of your people and the simplicity of the poems. Here are some additional ideas that pertain directly to this particular age span.

From the very beginning of awareness of the sound of poetry, and on through the primary grades, children are attracted by its "jingle" quality. Very young children will respond to this element long before they can speak.

The jingle quality is a combination of *distinct meter, rhyme, and inflection patterns.* Although we have minimized these, as such, for other age groups they are important at this beginning stage and therefore you should make the most of their intrinsic value—especially as they excite the imagination and lead into visualizing and catching the spirit of the subject of the poem.

This enticement will help children, as they begin to speak, in their natural desire to *give generous vocal expression* as they become further involved in the story and characters of the poem, including the animals, trees, wind, and abstract concepts that only a child can conjure up.

You can encourage this by an *animated presentation* of the poem and the "living out" of each character in your own way, extracting all the fun you can by generous facial expressions and strange and wonderful vocal changes. They will love it, and you, for doing it; and it will establish a rapport that could ease if not dissolve some stubborn problems.

When the teacher "has fun" with the poem the flood-gates are open for the spirit of the children to follow; and, once under way, they can be directed to even greater heights than they thought possible. This wave of fun can carry them well past the short attention span usually expected of this age.

Beginning with pre-schoolers and progressing through the third grade these suggestions may be helpful:

1. The most likely subjects to begin with are animals they know and love, then move from these into new and broader subjects.
2. They love nonsense words and sounds. Short words are best at the beginning, but the interest engendered by group speaking will speed up their vocabulary growth.
3. The boy-girl organization will likely work best but this can be varied by smaller groups and child-a-line arrangements.
4. Child-a-line arrangements will also strengthen individual recognition. This will help the transition from self-concern to group-awareness as the children grow through this age span.
5. Verbal perfection is not as important at the beginning as enjoyment of the poem. So accept what the children do and use their momentum for later improvement in language skills.

When the children express a desire to, as they will say, "act out" the poem, they have an unusual opportunity to do so through the verse choir for it allows each and every child to simultaneously live each character, animal, and element as it appears in the poem. This leaves no one out, reinforces the expression of each individual, and gives the whole group the growth value of the experience. The need of this age group for physical activity is also met, to the degree each child has room to move in the group arrangement.

Here we have another growth opportunity through a vocabulary change. Instead of the child's term "acting out," why not introduce the more meaningful one "living out"? "Acting out" carries an insipid suggestion of artificiality and unwanted exaggeration, while "living out" keeps the experience closer to real-life values.

Threshold to Creative Dramatics:

The door is now open and the momentum is mounting to further enrich the children's experience by working out a creative dramatics treatment of the poem.

With guidance the children could participate in choosing the cast of characters from those who proved themselves to be "most like" the various characters in the verse choir experience. Several more "run-throughs" of the poem may be necessary—but this is all to the good.

Another growth opportunity is presented in the term "most like," which emphasizes the imaginative portrayal of the character, while the word "best" tends to evaluate the person. There usually is a "best" person who can garner all the richer parts, whereas a submerged individual may be "most like" a certain character—and get his chance!

Simple scenery, properties, and other production elements will provide more creative opportunities and lead your people into other areas of learning. Simple pieces of costume that merely suggest the character are often better than fully developed outfits since they allow room

for the imagination of the child to "fill it out." One boy
was disappointed when his teacher brought him a crown
she had worked hard to make—because he liked the one
he imagined better.

The following five poems indicate the great variety of
subject matter, style, and form found in poetry written
for this age group. The suggestions you will find in the
two margins are intended only to guide you in finding
the most imaginative treatment of these and the many
other numbers that are available. The "most right" interpretation will be the one you and your group create
together.

Miss Elizabeth Dresser is a dedicated teacher with a
giant-size imagination and a love for nature and children to match. These three charming poems are published here for the first time. The first should be within
the reach of kindergarteners, the second and third will
find homes in the hearts of older primary children as
their language skills increase.

BABY HORNED TOAD
Elizabeth Dresser

All The grass blades
     glowed
  And the sand was
     bright,
  The red-gold sand
  In the sun's warm
     light;
  I went to look for
     something—
  A lizard, bug, or
     sprite.

"What a day for bug hunt-
ing!"

Boys   The wind called,
      "Where?"   A lo-ong question.
                                  "We're getting closer!"
Girls   And a bird sang,
      "Here!
      "On shining sand
      "Where the sunlight's
        clear
      "You'll find the bug
        or something—
      "He's staying very
        near!"

All   I looked and looked   "Wonder what it will be?"
     On the stream's dry
       bed,
     And found him there
     Where the sand
       gleamed red—
     A smiling little crea-   "There it is!"
       ture
     With horns around
       his head!

SINGING BUSHES
Elizabeth Dresser

Girls   I heard a noise in
      the bushes,   *(The boys could investigate the*
     A thin, bright noise.   *exact sound crickets make and*
      (Listen)   *reproduce it softly throughout*
     Could it be the fairy   *the first two stanzas, making it*
      children   *stronger as the girls listen at*
     Playing with their   *intervals)*
      toys? *(Listen)*
     Could it be a hum-
      ming bird

Humming   out   a
 tune? *(Listen)*
Could it be a little
 skunk
Calling to the moon?
 *(A giggle would be
 in order here)*

Boys   All the night was   *("We were right there in the*
 full of hushes   *middle of it!")*
Except in the noisy
 bushes.
When I went up close
 to see
They started singing
 right at me.
Do you know what
 was singing,
Singing in the night.
With a queer little
 tune,
Sharp and bright?

All   It was some little
 crickets
Playing music in the
 thickets.

In this next poem the use of boy-girl groups is suggested because of their suitability to catch the inherent
quality of each stanza assigned to them.

WIND TALK
Elizabeth Dresser

Girls Outside the shining
window
I heard a little sound,
And saw the leaves
begin to whirl
Round and round
and round.

(With wide-eyed wonder)

Boys "Ah, ha!" thought I,
"There's a wind out
there!
He's come to play
with flowers and
leaves
From his cool, dim
lair."

("Of course, I know what it
is!"*)*

Girls "Wheeeeeeee!" called
the little wind.
My! he was having
fun;
He was a little pixie
wind
Who liked to laugh
and run.

*(Gaily—with some added gig-
gles.)*

Boys I wanted him to come
inside
And bounce from
chair to chair
And climb upon the
table
And shake his wild,
green hair.

*(Wistfully—as if wishing for a
playmate.)*

Girls So I opened wide the window
And cried, "Come in, small elf!"
"Hushshshsh," I heard; it was that wind
Shushing up himself.

(Loudly. "Of course he'll come.")

("Well, now, that's funny.")

Boys When I closed the window up,
"Wheeeeee!" he called again;
And he tumbled in the tree-tops
And squealed as he ran.

("What has gotten into him?")

("Look at him go!")

Girls Then I thought to talk to him
In his native tongue;
So I yelled "Wheeeee!" out the window
'Till I almost burst a lung.

("I know what I'll do.")

Boys Ah, me, I guess I yelled too well:
He must have thought me rough,
Because all I got for answer
Was "Puff-puff-puff-puff - puff."

("Wups, too loud, I guess.")

All   It was the frightened
            fairy wind
      Panting   hard   for
            breath;
      Poor, small, sobbing
            wind, I must
      Have   scared   him   ("I'm *sorry*, little wind, I really
            half-to-death!   am!")

   This poem lends itself to several other treatments,
such as assigning smaller groups or soloists to play the
wind and carry the dialogue. Another, and simpler, arrangement would be to let a large part of the choir serve
as the narrator with a special group playing the wind.
This group would also join in the narration when possible to make transitions smoother. This latter arrangement has the added advantage of causing each person
helping to tell the story to stretch his voice to meet the
demands placed on the choir as a whole, for story telling
is a special art.
   The author of "Socratic" presents a scene that is too-
often enacted in our homes—when a young child tries to
tell an important incident to a parent who is engrossed
in some minor adult occupation, like getting dinner, or
painting the living room—or "just reading." Let's let the
boys play the father, who is trying to read the evening
paper, while "listening with one ear."

SOCRATIC[1]
Hilda Doolittle

The Little Girl:	The Father:
Girls:They cut it in squares.	
Sometimes it comes in little jars—	Boys: O—?
Under the trees—	Where?
By his *sheep* pen.	Whose?
The man who brings the eggs:	
he put it in a basket with the moss	What?
Why, the little jar.	What for?
Why, to carry it over—	Over where?
The field to Io's house.	Then?
Her mother took it out of the moss, opened it—	What?
The little jar.	And then?
We each *had* some	What?
Why the thing in the little jar	
they got from the straw huts.	What huts?
Why, the little huts under the apple trees,	
Where they live—	Who live?
Why, the *bees!!*	— —OH—H—H!

[1] From John Ciardi, *How Does A Poem Mean?* (Boston: Houghton, Mifflin Co., 1959).

Every young choir should try Eugene Field's whimsical flight into his rich imagination with "Wynken, Blynken and Nod." Even our college choir enjoyed doing it, making a serious effort to return to the childlike credulity that the poem demands. It is a good example of the rewards awaiting a group that is willing to "go back down the age ladder" to find greater depth and poignancy in a seemingly simple poem.

Any combination of voice groups or soloists can take the six parts of: Narrator, Moon, Stars, and the Three Sailors—and the Director must stay awake at the last stanza. However, the going-to-sleep and sudden-awakening will be most effective if the entire choir plays the Narrator.

WYNKEN, BLYNKEN, AND NOD
Eugene Field

Narrator	Wynken, Blynken, and Nod one night
	    Sailed off in a wooden shoe—
	Sailed on a river of crystal light,
	    Into a sea of dew.

Moon	"Where are you going, and what do you wish?"
Narrator	The old moon asked the three.
Wynken	"We have come to fish for the herring fish

Blynken   That live in this beautiful sea;
Nod   Nets of silver and gold have we!"
Narrator   Said Wynken,
                                 Blynken,
                                 And Nod.

The old moon laughed and sang a song,
    As they rocked in the wooden shoe,
And the wind that sped them all night long
    Ruffled the waves of dew.
The little stars were the herring fish
    That lived in that beautiful sea—
Stars   "Now cast your nets wherever you wish—
    Never afeard are we";
Narrator   So cried the stars to the fisherman three:
                                 Wynken,
                                 Blynken,
                                 And Nod.

All night long their nets they threw
    To the stars in the twinkling foam—
Then down from the skies came the wooden
    shoe,
    Bringing the fisherman home;
'Twas all so pretty a sail it seemed
    As if it could not be,
And some folks thought 'twas a dream they'd
    dreamed
    Of sailing that beautiful sea—
But I shall name you the fishermen three:
                                 Wynken,
                                 Blynken,
                                 And Nod.
Wynken and Blynken are two little eyes,
    And Nod is a little head,
And the wooden shoe that sailed the skies
    Is a wee one's trundle-bed.

(Slightly slower as drowsiness sets in.)
So shut your eyes while mother sings
　Of wonderful sights that be,
(Slower still; they are all nodding.)
And you—shall see—the beautiful things
　As you rock—in the mis-ty sea,
(They will all be asleep with chins on chests after Blynken.)
Where　the　old—shoe　rocked—the fishermen—three
　　　　Wyıken—
　　　　Blynken—

Director:　Ps-s-st — Ps-s-ST! — PS-S-ST!!
(All heads snap up on cue.)
All　　　AND NOD!!

Here are some selected poems, with their authors, that have been recommended by teachers of pre-school and primary children who liked doing them:

1. "Arithmetic," by Carl Sandburg.
2. "Ballad of the Happy Christmas Wind," by Mary Madeleva.
3. "The Bashful Armadillo," by Mary Parrish.
4. "The Bubble Elf," by Marjorie Barrows.
5. "Choosing Shoes," by Frieda Wolfe.
6. "Deep Sea Song," by Marjorie Barrows.
7. "The Elf and the Doormouse," by Oliver Herford.
8. "Horton Hatches the Egg," said to be Dr. Seuss' favorite.
9. "The Little Whistler," by Frances Frost.
10. "The Mocking Bird," by Maurice Lesemann.
11. "Marco Comes Late," by Dr. Seuss.

12. "My Problem," by Jacqueline Rowland.
13. "The New Puppy," by Aileen Fisher.
14. "Rain on the Pane," by Eleanor Svaty.
15. "The Secret," Anonymous.

11

Intermediate Children

Intermediate children are in their active years, when the emerging identity is centered in physical prowess. It is also a time when the mind is whetting its appetite. Some individuals in this span are mastering subjects and concepts that earlier generations struggled with in high school—and some new ones belonging only to the present. So how do we interest them in the verse choir?

Three approaches are suggested: The first is to capitalize on their group loyalty and introduce the verse choir as "the next thing we will do," assuming that they will all be interested. Those who aren't at first may sit in a comatose condition that will become increasingly untenable as the enthusiasm of the others mounts.

The second is to form an extra-curricular choir as an after-school activity—or at a class period when all volunteers can be present. This depends on some initial stimulation that could be provided by a record or tape of a successful group, or hearing one do a live program.

A third way to introduce the choral speaking approach is to say "I know a poem that says this very thing" to a class that has demonstrated a vital interest in a given subject or direction of thought. It can also work with a class that *needs* to show a vital interest. There are poems on every subject going in many directions—and if you do not have time to read—read—read, why not form a reading committee of the precocious youngsters who need something more to do?

In any case the next step is to choose the right poetry. For the physical aspect, "Casey at the Bat" comes first to mind and Sandburg's "Arithmetic" should be fun for some mental gymnastics. "Fifty Nifty United States," by Ray Charles, is another that will keep them on their toes. It may be remembered that the 12-year-olds are sensitive to idealistic and spiritual values, making poems in these categories rewarding material. It is best to introduce them after the choir is under way and confident of its ability.

Now for *directing techniques*. This age level usually equates "loud and fast" with good expression or interpretation. This is best handled on your part by strong and definite actions that will keep the tempo and decibels in control.

Definite directing actions are necessary in giving the rhythmic beat and indicating subtleties in interpretation. These actions can be large or small to suggest loudness or softness of the sound—but they must be definite, especially for this age group.

You may wish to improvise a set of definite hand signals to further refine and sharpen your communication with the choir. These will be especially helpful in performance. For instance, both hands extended up at about shoulder height with palms toward the choir means "Stop—and wait for the next signal"; a finger held over your lips and your other hand beating the time with palm down would ask for less power and a more subtle treatment of the passage. Turning the palm up and using larger movements with the other hand beating the time would ask for a more spirited and larger sound.

The bright, lively passages may best be signaled by sharp movements of the hands and quick actions and formations of the fingers. Youngsters need to be reminded that they "may speak as fast as they can be understood." You will find many more right signals to communicate effectively with your group. (Grasping your hair with both hands and pulling hard would be the last signal—and you may wish to try it sometime.)

The wonderful energy, dynamics, and keen perceptions of this age deserve to be expressed and constructively channeled—and these children need the freeing and disciplining values of the verse choir.

In addition to the above suggestions regarding materials for this age span it is good to reach ahead into "older" materials to stretch their potential—for once started these youngsters "don't know what they can't do."

This first poem by John Masefield should answer the spirit of adventure and desire for action, especially of the fifth and sixth graders—but who can say when these begin?

As a young man John Masefield loved the sea and followed it as a sailor, storing up many memories of the joys and hardships of sailing before the mast. When he was Poet Laureate of England these memories pulled him back to the sea so strongly it nearly became an illness, which he calls:

SEA FEVER
John Masefield

All   I must go down to *(Irresistible attraction)*
      the seas again
      to the lonely sea
      and the sky,
    And all I ask is a tall *(Joyous anticipation)*
      ship
      and a star to steer
      her by;
    And the wheel's kick
      and the wind's
      song
      and the white sails
      shaking,
Boys And a gray mist
    on the sea's face
Girls and a gray dawn
      breaking.
All   I must go down to *(On deck in a gale! Revelling in*
      the seas again, *vibrant, all-out participation.)*
      for the call of the
      running tide
    Is a wild call and
      clear call
      that may not be
      denied;
Boys And all I ask is a
      windy day
      with the white
      clouds flying,
    And the flung spray
      and the blown
      spume,
Girls and the sea gulls
      crying.

All   I must go down to the seas again, to the vagrant gypsy life,

(Nostalgic retrospect. Savoring all the memories.)

     To the gull's way (Girls) and the whale's way where the wind's like a whetted knife;

(The gulls suggest the easy-going tropics—the whales the icy North.)

Boys   And all I ask is a merry yarn from a laughing fellow-rover,

All   And quiet sleep and a sweet dream when the long trick's over.

(Draw out the vowel sounds and continuing consonants to add substance to the dream.)

Here is another Masefield poem that can usher your people into a deeper understanding of the three periods of history referred to through the movement and cargoes of the ships of those periods. An investigation into the oar, wind, steam propulsion used by each craft will set the rhythm and tempo, which vary markedly with each vessel. To gain a sense of unity the entire choir should do all three stanzas:

All   Quinquireme of Nineveh from distant Ophir Rowing home to haven in sunny Palestine,

(A slow, inexorable, non-stoppable, unchanging rhythm and pace.) (The "sweet white wine" can break the spell, with "doubletime")

With a cargo of ivory,
And apes and
    peacocks,
Sandalwood, cedar
    wood, and sweet
    white wine.

Stately Spanish gal-   *(With "Pouter-Pigeon Pride.")*
    leon coming
    from the Is-
    thmus,
Dipping through the
    Tropics by the
    palm-green
    shores,
With a cargo of
    diamonds,
Emeralds, amethysts,
Topazes, and cinna-
    mon, and gold
    moidores.

Dirty British coaster   *(This is the time to use "staccato*
    with a salt-caked   *speech." The words "Tyne*
    smoke stack,   *coal, Road rails, Pig lead"*
Butting through the   *can be done in "half-time," re-*
    Channel in the   *turning to staccato for the last*
    mad March days,   *line.)*
With a cargo of Tyne
    coal,
Road-rails, pig-lead,
Firewood, iron-ware,
    and cheap tin
    trays.

Here are two nature poems by Elizabeth Dresser the girls should like, and the boys may surprise themselves. The first one could be used together with Carl Sandburg's famous "Fog." "Invasion," like "Fog," should be done as one continuing, moving sentence that carries the silently pervading action of the fog.

All   Up our canyon, cool and still,
The fog-sprites dance in shoes of lace,
Through the bushes and up the hill
Covering all, till only a trace
Of outline, shadowy-pale,
Is left of tree and house and stone,
Till a silver sea spills over the trail
And the world belongs to the fog alone.

(Please see the chapter on Voice and Diction for "quantity," "continuing sounds" and "presence.")

(Individuals should "take a breath" as needed to insure continuity of the sentence and full breath support.)

"Sky Child" likely belongs to the girls because of its delicate subtlety. Its marked change of mood makes it a good exercise in perception. (Well—if the boys want to, they might do, or join in, the second stanza, which carries more action.)

SKY CHILD
Elizabeth Dresser

Girls   Moon puts its head *("Winsome" is the key word.)*
on a pillow of cloud,

Slim little sky child
    curved to the
    night,
Resting a moment in
    delicate pleasure,
Winsome and elfin,
    poised for new
    flight.

Sharp as a flame,   *("Zip—zip!")*
    through black
    caverns gleam-
    ing,
Moving like laughter,
    Moon sped away,
Piercing the hills of
    the ebony night
    lands,
Silver child racing,
    bright-shod for
    play!

The next nearly forgotten poem by the beloved James Whitcomb Riley deserves another hearing, for the humor of its last line if nothing else. But there is plenty more to recommend it to an audience and to make it attractive to intermediate children. The dialect should be played for its full and complete value. We are not teaching our children to speak with a nineteenth-century mid-west dialect—just to appreciate it and to get the feel of the times, and the author's spirit. The boy-girl arrangement is suggested for the sake of variety, though it could well be done in unison by a flexible choir. In any case the first and last stanzas should be in unison.

THE TREE TOAD
James Whitcomb Riley

All   " 'S Cur'ous like," said the tree-toad,
        "I've twittered fer rain all day;
        And I got up soon,
        And hollered tel noon—
        But the sun, hit blazed away,
        Tel I jest clumb down in a crawfish-hole,
        Weary at hart, and sick at soul!

Girls "Dozed away fer an hour,
        And I tackled the thing agin;
        And I sung, and sung,
        Tel I knowed my lung
        Was jest about give in;
        And then, thinks I, ef hit don't rain now,
        They's nothin' in singin', anyhow!

Boys "Onc't in a while some farmer
        Would come a-drivin' past;
        And he'd hear my cry,
        And stop and sigh—
        Tel I jest laid back, at last,
        And I hollered rain tel I thought my th'oat
        Would bust wide open at ever' note!

All   But I fetched her!—O I fetched her!—
        'Cause a little while ago,
        As I kindo' set,
        With one eye shet,
        And a-singin' soft and low,
        A voice drapped down on my fevered brain,
        A-saying,—"Ef you'll jest hush I'll rain!"

The rollicking spirit with which Robert Louis Stevenson invests "Windy Nights" should be highlighted by absolute and unabashed adherence to the predominant rhythm. It is a "rhythm poem" if there ever was one. In fact, if the transitions from the girls and boys groups causes this flow to hesitate an instant the whole poem should be done in unison. The interpretation suggestions in the right margin also must be kept within the galloping rhythm.

WINDY NIGHTS
Robert Louis Stevenson

Girls   Whenever the moon
    and stars are set,
  Whenever the wind
    is high,

Boys   All night long in the
    dark and wet,
  A man goes riding
    by.

All   Late in the night
    when the fires
    are out
  Why does he gallop
    and gallop about?

Girls   Whenever the trees
    are crying aloud,
  And the ships are
  tossed at sea,

Boys   By, on the highway,
            low and loud,
            By at the gallop
        goes he.
All   By at the gallop he
            goes, and then
        By he comes back at
        the gallop again.

Eugene Field's own personal loss is said to have prompted him to write "Little Boy Blue." This may be why its sharp poignancy is recognized as a valid experience by each generation. While it "belongs" to young children there is so much more in it than can be seen at the first look that an older choir should also sound its depths. When our college choir did it we assigned different lines to three voice groups in an attempt to express the subtleties of imagery and emotion. Perhaps a young choir should do it in unison, representing the child who "kissed them, and put them there."

LITTLE BOY BLUE
Eugene Field

All   The little toy dog is
            covered   with
            dust,
        But   sturdy   and
            staunch   he
            stands;
        And the little toy sol-
            dier is red with
            rust,
        And his musket
            moulds in his
            hands.

Time was when the
little toy dog was
new
And the soldier was
passing fair;
And that was the time
when our Little
Boy Blue
Kissed them, and
put them there.
"Now, don't you go
till I come," he
said.
"And don't you
make any noise!"
So, toddling off to his
trundle-bed,
He dreamed of the
pretty toys;
And, as he was
dreaming, an
angel song
Awakened out Lit-
tle Boy Blue—
Oh! the years are
many, the years
are long,
But the little toy
friends are true!

Ay, faithful to Little
Boy Blue they
stand
Each in the same
old place—
Awaiting the touch of
a little hand,

The smile of a little
face;
And they wonder, as
waiting the long
years through
In the dust of that
little chair,
What has become of
our Little Boy
Blue,
Since he kissed
them—and put
them there.

Three Ideas to Promote Interest

1. Mrs. Elizabeth Rice Johnson, a former student, used this cluster of poems about the weather as choral readings in her fifth-grade class:

1.	"The Weatherman"	by Richard Armour
2.	"The Wind"	by Christina Georgina Rossetti
3.	"Lightning"	by Grace Barker Wilson
4.	"A Rain Song"	by Clinton Scollard
5.	"Rain"	by Robert Louis Stevenson
6.	"Clouds"	by Christina Georgina Rossetti
7.	"Cold Fact"	by Dick Emmons
8.	"Sing a Song of Seasons," from "Autumn Fires"	by Robert Louis Stevenson
9.	"Wind is a Cat"	by Ethel R. Fuller
10.	"The Year's at the Spring"	by Robert Browning

2. Another student, Mr. Bruce Bikson, developed a Choral Speaking Festival which was held as an early

evening event in a large community center to accommodate all the parents and friends and get the children
home early.

Six schools participated with their choirs ranging as
follows: one second grade, one fifth grade, three sixth
grade and one from the junior high age. This wide span
gave mutual encouragement which was Mr. Bikson's
goal. There was no competitive aspect to the program
but most of the selections challenged the choirs to
"reach ahead of themselves" for they wanted to do their
best.

3. Each spring the San Diego State Verse Choir invited
choirs ranging from the first grade through senior high
school to our University Theatre for a Verse Choir
Spring Festival. Over the years every grade was represented and choirs came from all areas of the city and
county. Again competition was ignored, the participants
being more interested in hearing the wide range of materials and techniques used by the various groups. Pride
of achievement was enough incentive for each choir to
stretch to its best performance. At the close of the program each choir stood for a round of applause while
their directors were being presented. Also each choir
member was given a "Participation Award" signed by his
director and the director of the college choir, which presented its program last. The fact that so many "big people" were also engaged in this activity was especially encouraging to the younger ones.

The following poems may suggest others for you to
try. They have all been successfully produced by
fourth-through sixth-grade verse choirs:

1. "Columbus" by Joaquin Miller
2. "The House I Live In" by Lewis Allan

3. "Little Brown Baby" by Paul Lawrence Dunbar
4. "Magic Books" by Pearl Sandburg Henschel
5. "Nancy Hanks" by Rosemary Benet
6. "The Owl and the Pussy Cat" by Edward Lear
7. "Pirate Don Durk of Dundee" by Mildred Plew Merryman
8. "The Potato Dance" by Vachel Lindsay
9. "Roll Down to Rio" by Rudyard Kipling
10. "The Squaw Dance" by Lew Sarett
11. "The Story of Ferdinand" by Munro Leaf
12. "Sweet Little Jesus Boy" by R. Morris
13. "Tiptoe Night" by John Drinkwater

12
Junior High Students

Some educators believe that this is a "difficult" age to interest in the verse choir. True, people in junior high are seeking an individual identity, a search which tends to lead them away from organized group activity. The insistence of many of them to get an immediate emotional or physical thrill out of anything they invest in does seem to work against the necessities of reflective thought and personal discipline that are so much a part of this "cultural" activity.

However, people in this age span do tend to be one-hundred percent either for or against a given proposal. There is strong evidence, represented by the many successful choirs that I have heard or have been reported by their directors, that a great many junior high students have chosen "for" the verse choir.

Students of this age are also attracted by *unusual, clever material and by outstanding achievement* in any field of endeavor. Both of these are well within the possibility of the verse choir, and success can result in a sense of pride in achievement and satisfaction in being connected with a clever program. (Why shouldn't we use showmanship?)

The "key" to working at this level, according to their directors, is to demonstrate your *regard for them as individuals* and your *faith in their potential* to understand and enjoy literature and their willingness to meet the responsibilities of choir membership. This direct and seemingly idealistic approach has worked in a culturally deprived school between an all-black sixth-grade class and its white teacher, Mr. Arthur Dan Willson. Most of his people began as nonreaders but learned to enjoy literature by "living it" through the verse choir. A back-door approach, perhaps, but it worked!

Mr. Willson is now teaching in a junior high school and is so successful in involving his students in literature that some of them gain permission to return to his class as often as four times in a day to participate in the living experience he provides through choral speaking. He further states that control and discipline problems melt away on the wave of enthusiasm that develops. His secret is to "let myself go and have fun with the poem, and all the rest follows."

The most critical need of some young people at this age is to *have an adult recognize and believe in them.* The director of a verse choir is in a unique position to establish this rapport which, as with Mr. Willson's people, may break the logjam holding back other interests, emotions—and abilities.

The verse choir is a natural and likely arena in which to have this major miracle happen and the director, or teacher, has a better chance of helping to bring it about if his *interest in his people* and his *enthusiasm for living liter-*

ature both "show." An imaginative and attractive program, with many performances, will further promote this entire human-growth process.

These "pre-adults" may surprise themselves in what they can do. Two numbers that have proven successful are the difficult but rewarding "Jabberwocky" by Lewis Carroll and Norman Corwin's warm-hearted dog story, "The Odyssey of Runyon Jones," which is reinforced by many spectacular space-age sound effects the choir can do vocally—with relish. They both follow, with arrangements and suggestions targeted for this age span.

"Jabberwocky" is a fooler. It is not easy but is extremely rewarding, in many ways. First, your students will find some of the "foreign" words in the dictionary—a search that will not hurt them a bit. Second, once you decide on the best pronunciation of those they won't find you can have great fun in giving them all a little more than their just dues by way of *energetic articulation,* remembering accuracy. Third, this is a truly dramatic story, melodramatic in fact, and is a good vehicle for budding histrionic abilities that need expression.

Our college creative dramatics people found their imaginations could spiral higher with this poem because the "strange" words did not confine them as tightly as others that were well-defined. Even when Alice first encountered it behind the looking glass she said, "Somehow it seems to fill my head with ideas—only I don't know exactly what they are!" This is a strange phenomenon that I hope works with your group, both to enrich their verse-choir treatment and possibly to inspire a creative-dramatics living-out experience.

The poem provides such a long stretch of the imagination ·and vocal mechanism that the more people you

can involve, the better. The entire choir could tell the
story if they can "let themselves go," but anything less
than their best is too little. However you decide to do it,
the following suggestions may be helpful:

JABBERWOCKY
Lewis Carroll

All:	'Twas brillig, and the slithy toves Did gyre and gimble in the wabe; All mimsy were the borogoves, And the mome raths outgrabe.	*(Set an ominous mood, perhaps in the "gouhl-haunted wood-lands of Wier.")*
Kind Father:	"Beware the Jabberwock, my son! The jaws that bite, the claws that catch! Beware the Jubjub bird, and shun The frumious Bandersnatch!"	*("He's one of life's greatest dangers—along with these others!")*

All:	He took his vorpal sword in hand: Long time the manxome foe he sought— So rested he by the Tumtum tree, And stood awhile in thought.	*("If Saint George can kill a dragon— — —!"*
Burbling	And, as in uffish thought he stood,	*("Yikes! It's bigger than I thought!")*
Jabberwock:	The Jabberwock, with eyes of flame, Came whiffling through the tulgey wood, And burbled as it came!	
Valiant Son:	One, two! One, two! and through and through	*("But not too big for little old ME!")*

Son: The vorpal
                    blade
                    went
                    snicker-snack!
All: He   left   it
                    dead,
                    and with
                    its head
                    He   went
              galumphing
              back.

Kind,   "And   has   *("Hail Caesar!")*
                    thou
                    slain the
                    Jabberwock?
Jubilant   Come   to
                    my
                    arms,
                    my
                    beamish
                    boy!
Father: O   frabjous
                    day! Cal-
                    looh!
                    Callay!"
                    He   chor-
              tled in   his
              joy.

All: 'Twas brillig,   *("Everything is now peaceful and*
                    and the   *serene at the old homestead.")*
                    slithy
                    toves
                    Did   gyre
              and gimble in
              the wabe:

> All   mimsy
> were   the
> borogoves,
>   And   the
> mome   raths
> outgrabe.

"The Odyssey of Runyon Jones" is a major poem that has been making eyes "puddle up" ever since Norman Corwin first put it on the air as a radio program. It is just now being made into a musical comedy for children, and all the rest of us. He also anticipated the space age when he sent his intrepid young hero, Runyon, through various stations in outer space looking for his loyal Pootzy until he finally arrived in Curgatory. We hope you will enjoy the quest, with all the sounds and feelings, as much as we did. The individual characters may stand in front of the choir in a group, or, if there is room and if the nature of the program permits, they can indulge in more elaborate dramatic action.

This arrangement of the drama is intended for a four-section choir but it can be adapted for any organization you choose. While any age choir will greatly enjoy doing this heartwarming number we believe the junior highs deserve "the first crack at it."

THE ODYSSEY OF RUNYON JONES
Norman Corwin

CAST OF CHARACTERS:	SOUND EFFECTS:	LEGEND:
NARRATOR	GOLDEN ESCALATOR (12)	1—Light Women
CLERK	CLOCKS, BELLS, GONGS,	2—Medium Women
GUIDE	CHIMES (1234)	3—Medium Men
RUNYON	INTERSTELLAR TRAVEL	4—Dark Men
FATHER TIME	(1234)	
CHAIRMAN OF THE BOARD	RESPONSES (1234)	
BOARD OF DIRECTORS (34)		
POOTZY (12)		

RUNYON:	(timidly) Is this the department of lost dogs?
CLERK:	YE-E-e-e-e-ESSS!
RUNYON:	I'm looking for my dog.
CLERK:	(perfunctorily) Your name?
RUNYON:	Runyon Jones.
CLERK:	Runyon?
RUNYON:	Yes, sir. It's a terrible name. The other boys call me Onion.
CLERK:	What's the name of your dog?
RUNYON:	Pootzy.
CLERK:	(disdainfully) Pootzy?
RUNYON:	Yes, sir. He's very smart, sir.
CLERK:	When did you lose him?
RUNYON:	Yesterday morning.
CLERK:	How?
RUNYON:	Chasing automobiles. He wanted to bite the tires, I think.
CLERK:	Front or rear?
RUNYON:	All of them.
CLERK:	What happened?
RUNYON:	The car ran over him.
CLERK:	And then?
RUNYON:	He was killed, sir.
34:	Oh-h-h-h-h-h-
12:	Poor Pootzy

(This first sign of sympathy should take the form of low murmur, to contrast with stronger expression later.)

CLERK:	Then you're on the wrong floor. This is the Department of Lost Dogs. What you want is the Department of Deceased Dogs.
RUNYON:	Where is that, sir?
CLERK:	Two flights up. Here, take this slip and hand it to the man at the desk.
RUNYON:	Thank you, sir. *(He runs in place.)*
RUNYON:	Is this the Department of Diseased Dogs?
GUIDE:	Deceased, not diseased! Let me see that slip. Pootzy Jones . . . one and a half years old . . . inveterate auto chaser . . . mm. (Toy Runyon) Young man, in the case of Pootzy, he is down in the files as an inveterate auto chaser and tire nipper, Class 4. Also, it is known that he has resisted leashes, that he bit a dog-catcher, and that he stayed out all night on three separate occasions. I'm sorry to say he's not in Dog Heaven.
ALL:	Not in Dog Heaven!?
RUNYON:	(freshly disappointed) No? Gosh! Well, where is he then?
GUIDE:	In the place where all ill-behaved curs are punished. Curgatory.
34:	Oh-h-h-h-h-h-,
12:	Curgatory!
RUNYON:	Where's that? I'll go there.
GUIDE:	Oh, no. Impossible.
RUNYON:	But he won't chase any more automobiles—I swear it! Look—honest. I'll spit on my hand and touch my forehead three times. *(Spitting.)* Pft—foo.
GUIDE:	What's that mean?
RUNYON:	That's the secret oath of the Elmwood St. A.C., which means pledge of honor!
ALL:	Pledge of honor!
GUIDE:	Nevertheless it will be impossible.
RUNYON:	But Pootzy will be lonely without me. I have to find him.
GUIDE:	Oh, very well, Mr. Jones, this is what you do. There is only one person that I know who can possibly set you on the right track, and that's Father Time. His place is quite far, and—Oh I'll have to take you.
RUNYON:	Thank you, sir. Gosh, Pootzy's sure gonna be glad to see me!

GUIDE: Don't be too sure you'll find him, because you're liable to be disappointed. Now, young man, if you come with me we'll take the Golden Escalator.

RUNYON: All right, I'm coming.

SOUND OF GOLDEN ESCALATOR:
                (This is done simultaneously by 1 and 2.)

1:              Zip zip zip zi-i-i-i-i-i-IP, zip zip zip zi-i-i-i-i-IP *(Repeat 3 times)*

2:              Z-z-z-z - z - z-z-z- z - z-z-z-z-z- ZIP, Z-z-z-z-z- z - z-z-z-z--z- ZIP *(Repeat 3 times)*

12:             *(Stopping)* ZIP-ZIP-ZIP-zip - zip-zip—zip!

GUIDE: Here we are!

RUNYON: Gee whillikers!

TIME SOUNDS: *Pattern of (1) Cuckoo Clock, (2) Trill Ring, (3) Tick tock, (4) Big Ben Bongs, ending with (All) Tower Chimes.*

(Cumulative effect results from adding each pattern, letting the bedlam continue a few beats, and ending with dignified Tower Chimes.)

FATHER TIME: Now what was it you wanted, little man?

RUNYON: Well, sir, could you tell me how to get to curgatory, because my dog Pootzy?

TIME: Was he a delinquent dog?

RUNYON: No, SIR. He was a MONGREL!

NARRATOR: When you hear the musical note it will be the hundred seventy-second millionth anniversary of the birth of the first dinosaur.

34:            BONG-NG-NG—(Add 2) Ng-ng-ng—(Add 1) Nn, ng-ng—*(Take it up in pitch as high as your voices can reach.)*

TIME: Remind me to send an anniversary message of felicitations of M.N.

GUIDE: Yes, sir.

TIME: *(To Runyon)* Where did you say the dog was?

RUNYON: In Curgatory. I just want to know how to get there.

TIME: (He *is* a fuddy-duddy) Well, now Sonny, I don't even know where Curgatory is. It used to be on Sirius, the Dog Star, but the neighbors on Furud, Murzim and Adhara complained about the piteous howling and whin-

	ing that came from there; so they had to move.
RUNYON:	*(fearing the worst)* Er—why was there howling and whining?
TIME:	Because all the dogs in Curgatory are tortured, of course.
RUNYON:	Does—does it hurt them bad?
TIME:	*(laughs)* Well, naturally! What a question! Why, I've heard there are fleas in Curgatory as big as a lion! That's only one of the attractions. Hee—hee!
RUNYON:	Uh—well—is there some way I could find out how to get there?
TIME:	Well, the only one I know who could possibly help you is M.N.
RUNYON:	M.N.?
TIME:	Don't you know anything, lad? Mother Nature!
RUNYON:	Oh.
GUIDE:	Hold tight, here we go!

SPACE TRAVEL SOUND:

> *(12) Eerie siren modulating in pitch and power.*
> *(34) Low hum, sustained. (Both held under Narrator.)*

NARRATOR:	So Runyon Jones visited Mother Nature who gave him a charm so he could understand the Harpy's language. And the Harpy sent him to the Giant who FINALLY told him how to get to Curgatory, where the Board of Directors have FINALLY reached a decision on what to do about Pootzy.
34:	BONG-NG-NG!! *(If a BONG was ever important-sounding, make this one so.)*
CHAIRMAN:	Gentlemen of the Board, this is Mister Runyon Jones of Earth whose request to be reunited with his dog Pootzy, Number seventeen billion, six million twelve, we have just discussed.
34:	
	How do you do, Mr. Jones. *("Looking down their noses.")*
CHAIRMAN:	Jones, we have gone into this matter most carefully— — —
RUNYON:	That's good.

CHAIRMAN: We fully appreciate the pains to which you have gone, and the trouble . . .

RUNYON: Oh, it was nothin'.

CHAIRMAN: —you have taken. We are also aware of the unusual devotion you have shown the said Pootzy, and all these factors have entered into our decision.

RUNYON: Yes, sir. Then can I see Pootzy and have him back?

CHAIRMAN: The unanimous decision of the board of directors is that you may NOT!

34:           You may NOT!

RUNYON: What? You mean I can't see Pootzy for just a minute?

CHAIRMAN: Sorry, Jones.

RUNYON: Not even for a teeny-weeny second? Just to peek at him through the bars and whistle once? Like this? *(He tries to whistle, but cries instead.)*

CHAIRMAN: We are all very sorry, Jones, But it may be of some consolation to you to know that there are no bars in Curgatory.

RUNYON: That's good. Do you torture Pootzy bad? He's got a lame foot, you know.

CHAIRMAN: Just a moment, Jones. I am proud to say we do not torture any dogs in Curgatory. Where did you get that terrible idea?

RUNYON: Father Time told me.

34:           That old-fuddy-duddy!

12:           They say he chews his whiskers! *(Why not add a giggle?)*

CHAIRMAN: Father Time? Why, don't take stock in anything he says, Jones. I shouldn't like this to get back to Father Time, but between you and us—strictly entre nous—that job of his seems to have made him a little tick-tocky.

34:           That torture talk is nonsense!

CHAIRMAN: Yes, indeed. . . . Well, we've got a big docket to clear. I'm afraid that closes the case. Sorry.

RUNYON: Can I say just one more thing, gentlemens?

CHAIRMAN: Well, you'll have to make it fast.

RUNYON: *(pleading)* Pootzy is a good dog. He didn't mean to bite those tires. He just wanted to race the cars to show me how fast he could

	run. And he could of run faster if he wasn't lame in the leg.
34:	Lame in the leg!? *(Their pomposity now changes to sympathy.)*
RUNYON:	And about his staying out all night, that was because he saw me talking to Eddie Mazer's bulldog, and he got jealous. You can't blame a dog for that, can you?
34:	Of course not! *(They are silenced by a look from the chairman.)*
RUNYON:	Honest, Pootzy is the best dog in the world, or else would I have come all this way for him?
CHAIRMAN:	What about the day the auto ran over him and killed him? Didn't he break away from your leash?
RUNYON:	No, sir, the leash broke.
CHAIRMAN:	*(severely)* Are you sure of that, Jones? *(Silence.)* Jones?
RUNYON:	*(defeated)* No, sir.
CHAIRMAN:	Then the said Pootzy did break away?
RUNYON:	*(now crying)* Yes, sir.
CHAIRMAN:	Well, there you are. Again, please understand that we are sorry, but there is nothing we can do. Next item, gentlemen.
GUIDE:	This way out, Runyon. *(Sadly)*
RUNYON:	Good-bye. And tell Pootzy I—I . . . (He can't finish.)
CHAIRMAN:	Yes. I'll tell him.
RUNYON:	*(going off)* Good-bye *(Shouting.)* GOOD-BYE, POOTZY! CAN YOU HEAR ME!?
CHAIRMAN:	*(gravely)* No, he cannot. I will tell him good-bye for you.
RUNYON:	Thank you, sir.
CHAIRMAN:	Wait a minute, Jones. Where did you get that mark over your right eye?
RUNYON:	Oh, that's nothing. I got that in the accident.
CHAIRMAN:	What accident?
RUNYON:	When I tried to keep Pootzy from being run over.
CHAIRMAN:	Well, didn't you reach Pootzy in time?
RUNYON:	No, sir. Almost—but, you see, the car ran over me first.
THE BOARD:	*(shocked)* It did?!

RUNYON: Yes, sir. That's how I got killed.
34:            Got Killed!!?
CHAIRMAN: Well, now . . . Ahem—just a moment, Mr. Jones.
34:            (An indistinguishable ad-lib conference. At length.)
CHAIRMAN: Jones, the status of the case is changed by the fact that you gave your life to save your dog. That comes under the Priorities Ruling affecting the Seventh Clause of the Constitution of Curgatory.
RUNYON: (not getting it) I see. Well, goody-bye gentlemens.
CHAIRMAN: No, no—you don't understand! You may have the said Pootzy back!
34:            Pootzy back! (From here on their sympathy is enhanced by spontaneous support.)
RUNYON: (incredulously) I can see Pootzy?
CHAIRMAN: Yes, sir. We'll release him from Curgatory in your custody.
34:            In your custody!
RUNYON: You mean—now?
CHAIRMAN: (pleased as Punch—no, more so) Yes! The guide will take you! A-hem!
GUIDE: Come on, Mr. Jones.
RUNYON: Yes, right away. Gee!
GUIDE: He's down at the end of the corridor. (Runyon and the Guide walk in place.) Well, here we are. He's right inside that door.
34:            Inside that door!
RUNYON: (hardly able to control his voice) Is he? Right inside there?
GUIDE: Yes. Just open the door and walk right in.
34:            And walk right in!
RUNYON: Er—wait a minute.
GUIDE: What's the matter?
RUNYON: Do I look all right?
GUIDE: (chuckling) Oh, yes, Mr. Jones.
(Runyon opens door and steps toward 12)
RUNYON: Pootzy!!!
12:            (Gleeful barks and yelps—Pootzy's unbridled glee is too great for one voice, it needs all the girls' voices.)

At first glance, "The Horse's Version of the Ride of

Paul Revere" belongs to the boys, and they could have a fine time giving this new perspective to the famous ride of the intrepid Paul Revere. But then—the horse *was* named "Bess," and the girls just might want to get in on the fun. It is more within the range of the seventh- and eighth-graders, and could be used as an encore number, or for humor relief, in any choir.

THE HORSE'S VERSION OF THE RIDE OF PAUL REVERE
Anonymous

Listen, my jockeys, and you shall hear
How I carried my master, Paul Revere.
From the bank of the Charles at the midnight hour,
When the lights flashed out in the belfry tower.
The British had landed! Paul gave me a pat
And said, "Well, Bess, old gal, that's that."

And off we sped through the country wide—
And maybe I didn't give Paul a ride!
But honest, I had to laugh at the folk
We waked, who said, "What's this, a joke?"

(Subtlety should be locked in the closet when you do this poem.

It is an all-out prideful telling of a "once-in-a-lifetime" event and our intrepid "Bess" should be endowed with a gusty voice that equals her equine stature and historic deed.)

And one old party, a
    Cambridge squire,
In nightgown and helmet,
    yelled, "Where's the
    fire?"

And, of course, as I
    couldn't talk, you
    know,
I just whinnied, "You tell
    'em, Paul; let's go!"
Then away we flew
    through village and
    town.
I don't know the route but
    it's all set down
In Longfellow's poem, I
    simply said
"We'll make the grade if I
    don't drop dead."

Well, I didn't, and when
    that ride was done,
And Paul said, "Bess,
    there's Lexington."
And I saw a stall and a
    pile of hay,
Well, I just lay down and I
    passed away,
And when I woke up next
    day and heard
What the minutemen had
    done—my word!
I wobbled up and gave
    three horse cheers
For that ride of mine—and
    Paul Revere's!

Forty Poems about American History

These following forty poems were selected and anno-tated by Mr. John F. Smith, now Chairman of the Speech Department at Mesa Community College, San Diego County, to cover four major periods in the history of America. He chose them especially for eighth-grade students but they may well be used by younger or older people. The bibliography from which these poems were taken follows the last period.

Poems for the Early American Unit:

1. "Christopher Columbus" by Rosemary and Stephen Vincent Benét: a light poem, pointed at how Columbus expected to find China.
2. "Landing of the Pilgrim Fathers" by Felicia Dorothea Hermans: a poem expressing what the Pilgrims sought in the new world.
3. "Concord Hymn" by Ralph Waldo Emerson: a poem dedicated to those who died for freedom at Concord.
4. "The Green Mountain Boys" by William Cullen Bryant: the spirit of Ethan Allen and his Green Mountain Boys.
5. "The Yankee's Return from Camp" by Edward Bangs: the poem that became the song *Yankee Doodle*.
6. "The Fourth of July" by John Pierpont: rejoicing at the adoption of the Declaration of Independence.
7. "The Battle of Trenton," author unknown: how the battle of Trenton gave heart to Washington and the patriots.
8. "Defeat and Victory" by Wallace Rice: Captain

James Lawrence's famous saying "don't give up the ship."

9. "Old Ironsides" by Oliver Wendell Holmes: a protest to the plan for destroying the ship *Constitution*.

10. "O Beautiful, My Country" by Frederick L. Hosmer: a man sees in his country the beauty of its freedom.

Poems for Westward Growth Unit:

1. "Daniel Boone" by Arthur Guiteman: the life of Daniel Boone containing many facts and expressing the spirit of the westward movement.

2. "Lewis and Clark" by Rosemary and Stephen Vincent Benét: the adventures of the Lewis and Clark expedition.

3. "Pioneers, O Pioneers" by Walt Whitman: a poem that captures the spirit and courage of the early settlers.

4. "The Gold Seekers" by Hamlin Garland: a poem telling of the rush to California for gold, and the hardships and despair that had to be faced.

5. "Bill Peters," author unknown: a cowboy ballad depicting the adventure of driving a stage in the West.

6. "The Defense of the Alamo" by Joaquin Miller: a poem that combines the spirit of the Alamo with the names of the famous men who fought there.

7. "The Passing Herd" by Kenneth C. Kaufman: a young boy experiences the great cattle drives of the West.

8. "Song of the Forerunner" by Karle Widso Baker: the type of people that settled Texas and their dream for their state.

9. "Betsy from Pike," author unknown: a ballad that describes the trip from Pike County, Missouri, to California.

10. "Thunderdrums," author unknown: the Chippewa Indians' resistance to the white man's advance upon their lands.

Poems for a Civil War Unit:

1. "John Brown's Body" by Charles Sprague Hall: this poem symbolizes the North's feeling toward slavery.

2. "We Conquer or Die" by James Pierpont: a call to arms for all Southerners to defend their freedom.

3. "The Brigade Must Not Know, Sir," author unknown: this poem tells of the fear that the news of Stonewall Jackson's death might get to the troops. It is a dedication to his courage and inspiration.

4. "The Gettsyburg Address" by Abraham Lincoln: this is really a free-verse poem and makes a powerful verse-choir number.

5. "Sherman's In Savannah" by Oliver Wendell Holmes: a poem expressing joy at the success of the Northern Armies.

6. "Clara Barton" by Rosemary and Stephen Vincent Benét: the accomplishments of Clara Barton and her spirit of humanity.

7. "The Surrender at Appomattox" by Herman Melville: the meaning of victory and peace are expressed in this poem.

8. "O Captain! My Captain" by Walt Whitman: an expression of grief at the loss of President Lincoln.

9. "The Conquered Banner" by Abram Joseph Ryan: the sorrow and weariness of the South at the end of the war.

10. "The Blue and the Gray" by Francis Mils Finch: this poem reflects the idea that respect should be given all those who fought in the Civil War.

Poems for America as a World Power Unit:

1. "How Cyrus Laid the Cable" by John Godfrey Saxe: the story of the struggle to lay the Atlantic cable.
2. "My People Came to this Country" by Burt Struthers: the feelings of a man for the peace and safety America gave him.
3. "The Name of Old Glory" by James Whitcomb Riley: a poem telling how our flag came to be known as "Old Glory."
4. "The Thinker" by Berton Braley: the importance of man even in an industrial era.
5. "Abraham Lincoln Walks at Midnight" by Vachel Lindsay: a poem directed toward the idea that America, as symbolized by Lincoln, should be concerned with the happenings in Europe.
6. "Armistice Day" by Roselle Mercier Montgomery: a sober thought about the price we had to pay for the Armistice.
7. "The New Crusade" by Katharine Lee Bates: this poem presents the idea that World War I would be the war to end all wars.
8. "What Does It Mean to be an American?" by Roselle M. Montgomery: the great heritage that is the birthright of all Americans.
9. "The United States in 2033" by Rosemary and Stephen Benét: a look ahead that gives us a view of history and our place in it.
10. "Prayer of a Soldier in France" by Joyce Kilmer: this poem expresses the thoughts of a soldier as he compares his suffering and sacrifices to those that Christ suffered for him.

Bibliography for Poems on Four Periods of American History:

1. Ansorge, Elizabeth F., and Lucas, H.M., (Eds.) *Prose*

and Poetry of America. L. W. Singer Co.: New York, 1942.

2. Bailey and Leavell. *The World of America.* American Book Company: New York, 1952.

3. ———. *Worlds of People.* American Book Company: New York, 1951.

4. Chamberlain and Winn. *Tales and Trails.* Iroquois Publishing Co.: Syracuse, New York, 1949.

5. Holliday, Robert (Ed.). *Joyce Kilmer.* George H. Doran Co.: New York, 1918.

6. McClure and Yarborough. *The United States of America.* State Department of Education: Sacramento, California, 1947.

7. Moore, Carpenter, and Paquin. *Building A Free Nation.* Charles Scribner's Sons: New York, 1953.

8. Reynolds and Deming (Eds.). *Reading for Enjoyment.* Noble and Noble, Inc.: New York, 1936.

9. Stevenson, Burton (Ed.). *American History in Verse.* Houghton, Mifflin Co.: New York, 1932.

10. Tower, Russell and West (Eds.). *Prose and Poetry Journeys.* L. W. Singer Co.: New York, 1945.

Here are another dozen suggested poems with a broader variety to match the widening interests and growing ability of the junior-high-school age:

1. "Brotherhood" by Edwin Markham
2. "A Hannakuh Top" by N. V. Karpinver
3. "Cracked Record Blues" by Kenneth Fearing
4. "High Flight" by John Gillespie Magee, Jr.
5. "The Kalliope Yell" by Vachel Lindsay (Mr. Lindsay's spelling)
6. "The Maid Servant at the Inn" by Dorothy Parker
7. "Ozymandius" by Percy Bysshe Shelley

8. "The Plaint of the Camel" by Charles Edward Carryl
9. "Something Told the Wild Geese" by Rachel Field
10. "Shadrach" by Robert McGimsey
11. "Sudden Storm" by James Russell Lowell
12. "Unicorn in the Garden" by James Thurber
13. "Uphill" by Christina Rossetti

Before we put a lid on the capacity of Junior High students we should remember that Arthur Dan Willson's ninth-grade people were successful in doing T. S. Eliot's *Wasteland* and Book Nine from Milton's *Paradise Lost!*

13
Senior High School Choirs

New Adults.

For many individuals adulthood begins somewhere in this age span. Certain aspects of adult behavior, such as *self-control, cooperating with others,* and *trying to do your best* are so much a part of the verse choir procedure and expectancy that it again provides a fertile environment for such growth. The third aspect, "trying to do your best," is the key to working with people in this group, for it not only makes the other two necessary but it capitalizes on the natural desire to excel that motivates senior-high-school students.

Desire to Excel.

This competitive spirit is usually associated with athletic teams and other organizations that represent the school. Even some drama and speech activities still use interscholastic competition as a motive, more's the pity, so that some one person or group emerges as the "best." Fortunately, there is a new emphasis that rates the top degree of competence as "superior," achievable by many, and uses "excellent" and "good" as milestones on the way up.

Choir Competes with Itself.

The desire to excel, when used by the verse choir, is focused on "doing better than we did last time." Each individual is actually in competition with himself so that his improved performance—comprising better memorization, understanding of the material, vocal skills, and all the rest that it takes—will contribute to a more-polished and effective performance by the choir. Thus, he is working for "our choir" and a share in the resulting pride in achievement.

Such motivation is also better than working to please the director, which is a valid supplement and welcome bonus. This personal element, however, could take a turn for the worse and become a "choir versus director" affair, which puts the onus on that lonely person to "pull a performance" out of an indifferent group.

Their Best Equals Adult Level—with Rewards

So we hold Senior High School students up to their best and show how that puts them on a plane with adult achievement and performance, and we give them experiences that will bring admiration for their work by both their peers and adults. Many adults have been heard to say, "I wish they had had something like that when I was in school."

A further reward will come when a high school choir performs for younger children, whose exorbitant appreciation will leave its indelible mark. Even our returning college choir members still say, "Remember those kids in Calexico?", being unable to hide the something more than pride in their voices.

"You will never be the same again—"

A Fresh, Challenging, and Powerful Patriotic Program

The following numbers are well within the interest and capability span of Senior High School people for they contain *humor, subtle innuendo, colorful action, human values,* and a deeply rooted challenge, all presented in a straight-forward way.

The use of the narrator is especially helpful in this total program for his informal manner not only provides natural transitions but also aids in condensing over three-hundred years of human experience on this continent into a concise "telling" of America's story. For the sake of smooth transitions and dramatic vitality he should not announce the titles of the numbers in parentheses.

This program proved to be a deeply moving experience for our college choir as well as for our audiences, both young and mature, for the poems have great variety and wide appeal. The familiar selections, found in our early documents, take on new meaning when they are seen to be the most vital parts of the living story as it unfolds.

A PAST TO REMEMBER—A FUTURE TO MOLD
or HIGH-TIME, AMERICA
    Legend:
    N — Narrator
    L — Light

M — Medium
D — Dark
S — Solo
G — All girls
B — All boys
All — Everyone
(   ) — Suggestions to the Director

Narrator: Our program honors The American Dream. It is a simple, unadorned appreciation of our past and an urgent call for us all to unite to complete this "greatest human experiment ever attempted." It is particularly meaningful as we approach our Two-Hundredth Anniversary and should be a guide to us in the far future—for none of us have yet reaped the full harvest of its blessing.

We begin with a poem written by D. K. Stevens for children because children's literature usually carries a deeper meaning "between the lines." So we offer it to you at its face—and full—value.

(The marked rhythm of this number is an inherent value and you can enjoy it best by adhering strictly to its beat, adding to it all the other variables to highlight the subtleties of its seemingly simple story.)

(*The Musical Trust* by D. K. Stevens)

L   There was once a man who could execute
"Old Raccoon" on a yellow flute,
    And several other tunes to boot,
But he couldn't make a penny with his tootle-ti-toot.
    Tottle-ootle-ootle—tootle-ti-toot!
    Tootle-ootle-ootle-tootle-ti-toot!
Though he played all day on his yellow flute,
He couldn't make a penny with his tootle-ti-toot.

M   One day he met a singular
        Quaint old man with a big tuba,
        Who said: "I've traveled wide and far
     But I haven't made a penny with my oom-pah-
     pah."
        Oom-pah! Oom-pah! Oom-pah-pah!
        Oom-pah! Oom-pah! Oom-pah-pah!
     Though he played all day on his big tuba,
     He couldn't make a penny with his oom-pah-pah.

D   They met two men who were hammering
        On a big bass drum and a cymbal thing,
        Who said: "We've banged since early spring,
     But we haven't made a penny with our boom-zing-
     zing."
        Boom-zing! Boom-zing! Boom-zing-zing!
        Boom-b-b-boom-boom—zing-zing!
     Though they banged on the drum and the cymbal
     thing
     They couldn't make a penny with their boom-
     zing-zing.

L   So the man with the flute
        Played tootle-ti-toot,
M   And the other man played oom-pah-pah
D   While the men with the drum and the cymbal thing
        Went: Boom-b-b-boom-boom—zing-zing!
All And they traveled wide and far.
        Together they made the welkin ring-ng-ng
L   With a Tootle-ootle! (M)Oom-pah! (D)Boom-zing-
     zing!
     Tootle-ootle! (M)Oom-pah! (D)Boom-zing-zing!
L   Tootle-ootle! (M)Oom-pah! (D) Boom-zing-zing!
All And Oh! the pennies the people fling! When they
     hear the
L   Tootle-ootle   (LM)   Oompah   (All)
     Boom-b-b-boom-boom—zing-*ZING!!*

N   You see, it doesn't *zing* until everyone gets in on it.
     And it's the same with the American Dream—It
     means everyone, and it needs everyone to bring it
     off. —It began with a courageous declaration:
     (Deliberately and firmly, making each word count. It is a
     beautiful passage.)

All We hold these truths to be self-evident, that ALL
     men are created equal! That they are endowed by
     their Creator with certain unalienable rights! That
     among these are Life, Liberty and the Pursuit of
     Happiness!!

N   And it became a soul-honest Document which
     began:
     (This begins the same way, then mounts inexorably, as in
     "progressive jazz," to its "all-out" crashing climax.)

All We, the people of the United States, in order to
     form a more *perfect* union,
     Establish justice, Insure domestic tranquility,
     Provide for the common defense, Promote the
     general welfare
     And secure the blessing of Liberty for ourselves
     and our posterity,
     Do ordain and establish This Constitution—
     For the United States, of America!!

N   Who were these "people"? They were those who
     dared to venture from their stifling homelands, be-
     lieving there had to be a fairer land and a freer
     way to live. They found the wholecloth from which
     to fashion their dream on our bleak Atlantic shore
     where Robert Frost describes their "Gift Outright":

(*The Gift Outright* by Robert Frost)
(*This could be done by a strong solo voice within the choir*)

S   The land was ours before we were the land's.
(Or   She was our land more than a hundred years be-
All) fore we were her people.
        Such as we were we gave ourselves outright
        To the land, vaguely realizing westward,
        But still unstoried, artless, unenhanced,
        Such as she was, such as she would become.

N   And the Black Man was here from the earliest be-
        ginning, contributing his labor, his blood in all of
        the country's struggles, his talents, his inventions
        and his discoveries. With it all he breathed out the
        depth of his hope and his desperate desire to be
        free through his songs and poetry—one of his later
        poets, Langston Hughes, hears him say:

(*The Negro Speaks of Rivers* by Langston Hughes)
S   I've known rivers:
(Or   I've known rivers ancient as the world and older
All) than the flow of
        human blood in human veins.
All   My soul has grown deep *(Whether this is done as a solo or*
        like the rivers.   *not the entire choir should do*
        I bathed in the Euphrates *last line of the first and last*
        when dawns were young *stanzas, for added support.)*
        I built my hut near the Congo and it
        lulled me to sleep.
        I looked upon the Nile and raised the pyramids
        above it.

I heard the singing of the Mississippi when Abe
Lincoln went down
    to New Orleans, and I've seen its muddy bosom
turn all golden
      in the sunset.

I've known rivers:
Ancient, dusky rivers.

All My soul has grown deep like the rivers.

N   But wait! Before either of these there was the Indian; that near-forgotten one on whose unsuspect-
ing forested door we knocked and gained entrance,
only to push him westward and more westward
until, empty of hope and weighted with despair, he
sat his horse at the end of the trail—only dimly
remembering happier days such as Lew Sarett recalls in his "The Squaw Dance."

(*The Squaw Dance* by Lew Sarett: second stanza only)

B   Medicine men on the *(The rhythm must be absolute*
        medicine drum,   *throughout, the Boys' and*
      Beating   out   the *Girls' sections, making the*
        rhythm with a   *transitions smoothly to keep the*
        steady thrum.   *dance beat going.)*

G   Medicine gourd with
        its rattle, rattle,
        rattle,

All Flinging wild with the
        call of battle.

B   Beaded   drummers
        squatting in the
        ring

All   Leap to its challenge
        with a crouch
        and a spring;

B   Weathered old bucks
        that grunt and
        wheeze

G   As they jangle bells
        on their wrists
        and their
        knees—
     Shining new and
     olden bells,

B   Silver, copper, golden
        bells,

G   Cow-bells, (B) toy
        bells, (G) ringing
        sleigh-bells,

B   Beaded dance bells,
        (G) "give-away"
        bells,

All   Jingling, Jangling,
        Jingling bells,   *(The changes in subject matter*
     Set-the-toes-a-tingling   *and mood give many other*
     bells,   *opportunities for variety.)*
     To the beat, beat,
     beat, beat, beat upon
     the tom-tom,
     Beat, beat, beat, beat,
     beat upon the drum;
     And a shuffle to the
     left, a shuffle to the left, a shuffle, shuffle to the
     left, to the left—

G   Hoy-eeeeeeee-yah!
        (B) Hoy-
        eeeeeee-yah!

All   Hi! Hi! Hi! Hi! Hoy-
        eeeeeeeeeeeeeeeeeee-YAH!

N   This elemental exhuberance was too soon stifled when the Indian was set apart to live enclosed on patches of the land he once roamed free with the buffalo, the deer, and the soaring eagle—and still others came to claim their share in the seemingly inexhaustible bounties of the developing America. Emma Lazarus welcomes them with this greeting inscribed on the base of the Statue of Liberty.

            (*The New Colossus* by Emma Lazarus)

S   Not like the brazen   *(Clear contrast.)*
       giant of Greek
       fame,
    With conquering
    limbs astride from
    shore to shore,
    Here at our sea-
    washed sunset gates
    shall stand
    A mighty woman with
    a torch, whose flame
    is the imprisoned
    lightning,
    And her name,
    Mother of Exiles.

G   Keep, ancient lands,   *(Great compassion.)*
       your storied
       pomp
    Cries she with silent
    lips,
    Give me your tired,
    your poor, your hud-
    dled masses, yearning
    to
    Breathe free,

The wretched refuse
of your teeming
shore.
Send these, the home-
less, tempest-tosst to
me.
I lift my lamp beside
the Golden Door.

N   Some expected to find the gold in nuggets on the
streets, but it was soon clear that opportunity was
the gold she offered. Each man set out to find his
own, with little beside his own conscience to guide
him. It was a "free country," wasn't it? It was the
honor system on a nationwide scale, with some living up to the high demands of the American
Dream, while others made their own rules, spawn-
ing myriads of problems that plague us today.
—This burgeoning, little-controlled self-seeking effort caused a city to grow in the middle of the
country, its gusty spirit coming to us as a great
shout in Carl Sandburg's electrifying poem
"Chicago."

All   Hog Butcher for the   *("All-out gustiness" is the key to*
          World   *interpreting this poem.)*
Tool Maker, Stacker
of Wheat,
Player with Railroads
and the Nation's
Freight Handler;
Stormy, husky, brawl-
ing,
City of the Big
Shoulders:

(All solos will be more
effective if they come
on strong from within
the choir.)

Solo They tell me you are   *(These three solos show the*
wicked and I be-   *human cost.)*
lieve them,
for I have seen your
painted women under
the gas lamps luring
the farm boys.

Solo And they tell me you
are crooked and
I answer:
Yes, it is true I have
seen the gunman kill
and go free to kill
again.

Solo And they tell me you
are brutal and
my reply is:
On the faces of
women and children
I have seen the marks
of wanton hunger.

Solo And having answered   *(This fourth solo continues the*
so I turn once   *bragging.)*
more to those
who
sneer at this my city,
and I give them back
the
sneer and say to
them:

G   Come and show me   *(Observe nuances to keep it from*
another city with   *"running away.")*
lifted head

singing so proud to
    be   alive   and
    coarse   and
    strong and cun-
    ning.

B   Flinging   magnetic
    curses amid the
    toil of piling
job on job, here is a
tall bold slugger set
vivid against the little
soft cities;

All   Fierce as a dog with
    tongue lapping
    for action,
cunning as a savage
pitted against the wil-
derness,
Bareheaded, Shovel-
ing, Wrecking, Plan-
ning, Building, break-
ing, rebuilding,

G   Under the smoke,   *(Begin the final build here.)*
    dust all over his
    mouth, laughing
with white teeth,

B   Under the terrible
    burden of des-
    tiny laughing as
    a
young man laughs,

All   Laughing even as an
    ignorant fighter
    laughs who has
never lost a battle,
Bragging and laugh-   *(Make each word mount up to*
ing that under his   PROUD, *which is the peak of*

wrist is the pulse, and
under his ribs the
heart of the people,
    Laughing!
Laughing the stormy,
husky,   brawling
laughter of Youth,
half-naked, sweating,
PROUD to be Hog
Butcher, Tool Maker,
Stacker of Wheat,
Player with Railroads
and Freight Handler
to the Nation.

*the poem. The rest stalks
firmly downhill!)*

N   This same spirit was rampant throughout the land,
flinging men to the farthest reaches of her fron-
tiers, filling the empty places in between, crowding
her cities and threatening to smother the very life
of the nation with too many people building too
many houses and factories, and later driving too
many cars too fast on too many streets and free-
ways. Richard Armour describes this seething
tangle as it threatens to strangle his beloved
California.

    (I Loved You, California by Richard Armour)
*(The soloists must synchronize well to keep the rhythm of this
delightful poem flowing smoothly, just as care must be taken in
all the transitions. There is good expectancy value in giving the
boys the sharp "tag ending" each time, though this pattern is
reversed a few times for surprise value.)*

All California, here they come:
S   Doctor, (S) lawyer, (S) merchant, (S) bum.

G   They come by car and train and plane,
B   Straight from Kansas, Georgia, Maine,
S   Massachusetts, (S) Minnesota,
S   Iowa and (S) North Dakota.
S   Rich folk, (S) poor folk, (S) young folk, (S) codgers,
All Moving westward (B) like the Dodgers.

G   Here they come, and here they are,
      Living, dying in a car,
      Ever moving, dawn to dark,
B   Looking for a place to park.

B   Drive-in movies, drive-in cleaners,
G   Drive-in spas for burgers, wieners,
B   Drive-in banks and colosseums,
G   Drive-in (one-way) (B) mausoleums.

G   Under and over
        In Chevy or Cad,
      Some, caught in a clover-
        Leaf, (B) slowly go mad;

B   While some, with scant leeway,
        Slow-reaction-time men,
      Miss a sign on the freeway,
G   Aren't heard of again.

All Here, superlatives abound;
      "Best" and "most" are all around:
      Finest roads and oldest trees,
      Biggest universities,
      Hottest day and highest lake,
      Lowest point and hardest quake,
      Most of most, no ifs or buts,
      First in peaches, pears—(B) and nuts.

G   Divorce?
B   Of course.

G   Build a house upon a hill,
      Or a cliff, so that you will
      Get a view of row on row
B   Of other houses down below.
All   Out with trees, and don't lament;
      Fill the valleys with cement.
      Thus is nature redesigned
All   Of other houses down below.
      Fill the valleys with cement.
      Thus is nature redesigned
B   By the modern one-tract mind.

All   Bulldozers aren't dozing
        By night or by day;
      They're opening, closing
        And gnawing away,
      Making molehills of mountains
        (The golf course now rules),
      Turning lakes into fountains
        And swimming pools.

All   Hail the warming sun above,
      Golden Bear and poppy love;
      Hail the jackpots, crackpots, crooners,
      Fog and smog and displaced Sooners.
      Life begins at sixty-five,
      When the pension checks arrive;
      Then, with smiling, carefree faces,
      Off to Bingo or the races.

G   So leap with joy, be blithe and gay,
B   Or weep, my friends with sorrow.
All   What California is today,
       The rest will be tomorrow.

What California then will be
Is something I'd as soon not see.

N   Again the poet speaks for the whole nation. Indeed
if the "too-many-people" problem is not solved we
may be too late to deal with the myriad others.
—But we will try, for we Americans do not believe
a thing cannot be done. But how? Well, for a star-
ter we could return to our early commitment.

All   *(Rediscovering its meaning)* We hold these truths to
be self-evident, that ALL men are created EQUAL!
N   For this commitment is high enough, deep enough
and wide enough to encompass all the perplexities
that confuse and torment us now.—

(Your Dream Is Nearer than You Know, Original)

All   *(Interrupting)*—Look UP, America,
Your dream is nearer than you know!
Two hundred years of searing strife
Have rendered you a mighty Giant
Whose generous hand has thrice made whole
A war-torn world.

D   But with purpose fixed on distant lands,
L   And toward the sky,
D   You could not feel your own deep needs.

All   So heed them now, your inner ills,
And use the sinews of ALL your brood,
Their rich array of race and creed and special
gifts;
Unite them, with one will, to gain
The fullness of your early dream!

(America the Beautiful by Katherine Lee Bates)

(As at the beginning of the Preamble to the Constitution this should be spoken deliberately and firmly, making each word and idea count. Now, remembering "voice presence," let this passage build inexorably in power to the key word, "brotherhood"—to which you all add an "of course" implication.)

All   Oh, beautiful for patriot's dream that sees beyond the years,
Thine alabaster cities gleam, undimmed by human tears, (*)
America—America, God shed His grace on thee,
And crown thy good with BROTHERHOOD, from sea to shining sea!
(*) *(This certainly does not mean that there have been no human tears, but that they have not dimmed the ultimate hope for our cities.)*

G   *(Sing the first phrase)* Oh beautiful— *(Then hum the remainder of the stanza under the poem to provide a counterpoint musical background.)* *(Do this twice, if necessary, and join in singing the last line when the boys have finished the poem.)*

(For Whom the Bell Tolls by John Donne)[1]

B   No man is an island,   *(A simple fact, firmly stated with*
     entire of itself.   *no "dramatics.")*

[1] (This poem was "found" in a paragraph of one of John Donne's devotional writings entitled, "The Tolling Bell." His thought was so rich in rhythm and poetic expression that it needed no further refinement to reach this exquisite form that has been an inspiration to people for over three centuries. It now serves as a fitting lodestar to "mold the future" of America.)

Every man
   is a piece of the
Continent,
   a part of the main.

(As if the author leaned over to us and said: "In other words.")

If a clod be washed
away by the sea
   Europe is the less

As well
   as if a promontory
were;

As well
   as if a manor of thy
friend's
   or of *thine own*
were.

(The analogies in these next three lines become increasingly personal, narrowing down to "Thine own." They also make a good build.)

Any man's death di-
minishes me,
   because I am in-
volved in mankind;

(Firm simplicity again for this "core statement.")

And therefore—
   Never send to
know for whom the
bell tolls:

(Once accepted, this inevitably follows.)

It tolls for thee.

All   (Singing) And crown thy good with brotherhood, from sea to shining sea.

Bands Are "Saying What They Cannot Play"

A new development in choral speaking is coming about in senior high schools, and from an unexpected quarter—their symphonic and marching bands.

Its beginnings are found in Karel Husa's monumental work *Prague,* wherein this patriotic Czechoslovakian composer tried to encompass the mountainous heartbreak and anger engendered by the Russian take-over of his beloved country in 1968.

His composition begins with the clear, sustained, un-protected notes of a single piccolo soon joined by com-binations of instruments that give the ominous warning of tragedy. What follows is difficult to assimilate, or to understand—only to feel.

He brilliantly and painfully uses the total range of his orchestra to sweep his listeners into the vortex of over-powering emotion directly caused by inescapable clamor, unexpected crashing climaxes, tantalizing quiet inter-ludes with soft flutes shattered by a cacophony of mounting sounds from unusual combinations of instru-ments whose dissonant chords represent the sustained agony and futile cries for deliverance of the helpless people.

But even this is not completely satisfying, for though it holds the listener in a vise-grip of sound that com-municates to his whole being and leaves him exhausted, it has not really and clearly stated his case. Music critics have said that in this heroic work Husa has carried his mastery of technique to the limits of the capacity of mus-ical instruments.

In his next band composition, *Apotheosis of This Earth,* he sought and found another supportive means of communication. He called on *speaking voices* to express feelings that had been unattainable by the band medium alone. He used them at times in a subordinate way, with nonverbal utterances held under instrumentation, and at other times to speak out strongly in direct statements over a cluster of instruments.

This does not place musical instruments and speaking voices in competition. It does welcome the speakers to add their easier flexibility and direct word-communication to the great family of expressive sounds that are the unique contribution of instrumental music.

Other young composers have been inspired by this new approach, including Brent Heisinger who uses it in his composition, *Statement*. Many other similar things may be found in catalogues of Aleatoric Music for symphonic bands, orchestras, choral compositions, including speaking, and books for the classroom on the aleatoric style. One such source, the *Aleotoric Catalogue of Symphonic Band* may be found in the Bibliography.

When you need a poem to especially "light up" a program here is one that has proven its ability to do so many times when used by the Drama Choros of San Dieguito High School, whose director, Clayton Liggett, has given it this happy arrangement. He uses Light Medium and Dark sections with six solos. If possible, you should heed the author's wish to give S2, Jane, a "Selma Diamond" voice.

The author is certainly no ordinary person. We first saw "Sadie Lou" building scenery in the early days of the San Diego State Theatre where her acting, directing, and writing quickly pushed her to the top. After significant contributions to the Old Globe Theatre in San Diego, she began a promising motion picture career —that she cut short in favor of a family that reflects her special brand of all-encompassing love, yet she still finds time to direct a community theatre of high standard.

She dashed this gay number off one day when, preparing lunch, she found that even this seemingly simple subject proved to be hiding something beneath the surface.

NON-CONTROVERSIAL—PEANUT BUTTER by Sadie Lou Tieri
(Published here for the first time by special permission from the author and arranger.)

All   What can we talk about that won't be controversial?
LM   War?
MD   Sex!
LM   Death?
MD   Taxes!
All   Social Theories!
L   Philosophical queries?
All   How can the government efficiently demonstrate
      Its fullest capacity to wisely administrate?

      Will we ever have an electric car?
      Or will the polluters drown us in oil and tar?
      How much can a student agitate
      And still manage to graduate?
LM   Pros and Cons;
MD   Cons and Pros!
All   We grab at theories that don't equate.—
      Let's find one thing to which we all relate!

LM   Apple pie?
D   Apple pie and mother!
All   I know! Peanut butter!
      Everyone likes good old peanut butter
      Peanut butter,
      Peanut butter,
        Moist but nicely thick to chew!
      Peanut butter,

     Peanut butter,
         Nutty-crunch and creamy, too!
L   It's not debatable.
M   It's not inflatable.
D   It's absolutely non-demandatory!
All You can say without equivocation that
     It's bland, Man!

     In fact it's quite foreseeable
     That mankind will learn to negotiate
     With this greatest common denominate:
     Peanut butter!
     To be used by the United-Nations-Delegations-
         Summit-Meetings - top - Diplomatic Relegations.
     Before battle begins at the peace-talk table,
     Before one angry word is allowed to be uttered,
     Everyone should be made to eat—
     A great big sandwich—peanut buttered!

Sl   Peanut butter on thick slices of freshly baked,
     homemade bread.
All Umm-umm!
Sl   With real butter!
All And mayonaise and bananas!
S2 Mayonaise and bananas?
All With cream cheese!
S3 Kosher dills and onions, please!
S2 Yuk!

All Peanut butter and strawberry jam!
S4 With chocolate chips and bacon bits!
All Or honey and ham, thank you, ma'am!
S2 Anyone vote for just plain?
All Or carrots and raisins, on certain occasions!
     Peanut butter,
     Peanut butter,
         Moist but nicely thick to chew!

   Peanut butter,
   Peanut butter,
     Nutty-crunch and creamy, too!

   Peanut butter, however it's served,
   Is definitely food with a certain verve.
   But of course if you wish to guild the lily—
     RASPBERRIES!

S5	Grapelade!
S6	Boysenberries!
LM	Marmalade!
MD	Green peas!
All	Cream cheese!
	Strawberry jam!
	Honey and ham!

S2	Please!—Plain?
All	Jane!
S2	Just plain?
All	Oh Kay, Jane!
	Peanut butter,
	Peanut butter,
	Plain or fancy—
	PEANUT BUTTER!!
D	m-m-m-m (DM) M-M-M-M (All) M-M-M-M! GOOD!!!

List of Suggested Poems:
  These dozen and a half poems introduce the great versatility of the senior high school people:
  1. "Aim for a Star," Marshall.
  2. "Blowin' In The Wind," Dylan.
  3. "The Congo" and others by Lindsay.
  4. "Desiderata," Max Ehrmann

5. "Father William," Carroll.
6. "Geographical Fuge," Toche.
7. "How Jack Found that Beans May Go Back on a Chap," Carryl.
8. "The Center of your Soul," Kavanaugh.
9. "Jazz Fantasia" and others by Sandburg.
10. "The Listeners," De la Mare.
11. "Old Friends," "Sound of Silence," Simon and Garfunkel.
12. "The Road Not Taken" and others by Frost.
13. "The Shaggy Dog Stories," Miles Kimball Co. (Good relief materials.)
14. "Sound of the Sea," Longfellow.
15. "Take my Hand," Steffy
16. "Turn, Turn, Turn," Seeger.
17. "A Wanderer's Song" and others by Masefield.
18. "You've Got to be Taught to Hate," from *South Pacific,* Hammerstein.

(There are many, many others.)

14

College People and Other Adults

All the material in the foregoing thirteen chapters, along with these few observations, should help you understand and work with these young adults—for they have passed through all the stages with which we have dealt. These observations may help you in working with them:

(1) College students may have developed a set of inhibitions brought about by their preoccupation with classes and educational hurdles, or a reticence to break away from the norm of their particular group—or simply the "encasement" that often sneaks up on a person at this age if he hasn't found some means of self-expression.

(2) Once these inhibitions have been overcome, college adults have the greatest potential of any previous age, for they have spent their entire lives amassing knowledge, forming opinions, broadening apprecia-

tions, developing skills, acquiring a belief in themselves and a willingness to try new things. This maturity makes them "ripe" for the verse-choir experience, even if they have not been exposed to it before.

(3) For these reasons people of this age can grasp finer subtleties and express more shades of emotion than younger people—and, best of all, they can discipline themselves to control these and reproduce them at will. Their voices are mature enough to respond to vigorous training and their bodies are highly coordinated so that they can master detailed group movement and even refined choreography.

In the presence of these latent resources a verse-choir director should be able to develop a mature and artful rendition of any material he and the choir find attractive and worthy of their effort.

(4) The great majority of college students will appreciate the values of this work for themselves, and many will pass it on to others. Having attempted to work with every age group dealt with in this book, I have found experiences with the college adult to be the most richly rewarding and deeply satisfying.

(5) Other values of the maturity found in this group are their ability to do "younger poems" with relish and abandon, and also their willingness to take time and care to do imaginative rhythms and other creations with precision.

Such a sequence is presented here. This three-part introductory number serves to establish immediate audience rapport, and to relax and "tune up" the choir. Its span of success ranges from elementary school assembles to a non-worship evening church program. It of course would not be used when it did not fit the mood of the occasion.

The value of the entire choir talking at random and then going through the "All right, all right" sequence demonstrates how choral speaking brings order out of chaos—if it is planned.

SOUNDS TO REMEMBER—Original

Legend:

D — Director	S — Solo
1 — Light	N — Narrator
2 — Medium	All — Everyone
3 — Dark	( ) — Suggestions for
M — All Men	the Director.
W — All Women	

Opening: Introductory remarks by the Director, to cue: "(Your own)

Verse Choir, Circa————!"

All *(Interrupt the D to talk at random, until your group joins him.)*

D   All right, all right, (D1) all right, all right, all right, (D12)
     right, right, All right, All right, (D All) all right, all right,
     all right, right right!

D   Well, how's your sequence?

All Just real real good, good good.

     ("Demonstrating" their sequences.)
1   Lay lee Lah loh, loo loo, loo loo
2   Tay tee tah toh, too too, too too
3   Bay bee bah boh, bay bee bah boh *(All)* Boo!
     Boo boo BOO boo boo BOO boo boo BOO boo
     boo BOO

D Oh, you are bright today. *(cue)* But do you—
   ("It's fun to interrupt the Director.")

All Boo boo BOO boo boo BOO boo boo BOO boo
   boo BOO

D Yes, you said that. But do you know any words?

All Why yes, of course! Articulation, Modification, Tin-
   tinabulation!

D Mercy me, and such big words, too.—This is the
   unpredictable, incorrigible *(Your own)* Verse Choir
   warming up for a program.
   And what is a verse choir?
   ("Well now, we'll just tell you.")

All A verse choir is nothing I guess
   But a whole lot of people who want to more or less
   Talk together—like this:

1 We have light voices (2) Medium (3) Dark voices,
   too.

All We talk all together (1) Or sometimes just a few

All And we'll say a something now if we thought that
   you—
   Would like to hear some sounds to re
   MEMMMMM ber.

FAREWELL TO THE STEAM LOCOMOTIVE-
               —Original
*(This sound represents the mechanical "panting" of a standing
locomotive so continue in constant rhythm, tempo and power
under NARRATOR until ESCAPING STEAM.)*

M CANH canh canh canh CANH canh canh canh
   CANH canh canh canh CANH canh canh canh

W   HISSsss   HISSsss

N   Now there's one sound I never want to forget; the sound of a locomotive. And I mean a STEAM Locomotive! An old-fashioned, iron-mongered, bell-ringin', whistle-tootin' wonder with a play-for-keeps COWWWWW-catcher on the front and a tender on behind! — — I can see it now, standin' in the station on a bright, windy winter day with the gray and white smoke a-billowin' from its stack and the steam a-spurtin' and a-hissin' all around!

S   All-l a bo-o-o-OA-OAOOARD—bo-o-OARD!
(This is the Conductor's chance to crow and he loves it.)

All   (ESCAPING STEAM) PSH-SH-SH-SH-SH-SH-SH-SH-sh-sh-sh-sh
S   (HIGH WHISTLE, with an after escaping steam)

W   TRAIN WHISTLE, 2 short, "OO-OO"
(with various pitch levels to get the right discord.)

     ENGINE BELL, (W)"CLING-G," "CLANG-G"
(Alternate at same pitch until the WHEEL SKID)

M   CHOUG * * * CHOUG * * * CHOUG * * CHOUG * *
(Increase speed slowly)

M   (WHEEL SKID, *jumbled*) CHOUG CHOUG CHOUH CHOUH choug choug choug

All   CHOUG * * CHOUG * * CHOUG * CHOUG * CHOUG *
(Increase speed slightly. –Note that the "rest" beats are diminishing.)
M   CHOUG choug choug choug CHOUG choug choug choug CHOUG choug choug choug

W   CLICKETY CLACK click click
     (Repeat this "clickety-clack" sequence once, running a lit-
     tle faster.)
M   CHOUG choug choug choug CHOUG choug
     choug choug CHOUG choug choug choug
W   CLICKETY CLACK click click

M   CHOUG choug choug choug CHOUG choug
     choug choug CHOUG choug choug choug
W   (WHISTLE FOR CROSSING: 2 long—2 short)
     oooooo—oooooo—oo—oo
M   CHOUG choug choug choug CHOUG choug
     choug choug CHOUG choug choug choug
     (Take enough "running time" to approach the crossing.)
M   CHOU chou chou chou CHOU chou chou chou
     CHOU chou chou chou CHOU chou chou chou
     (We're running too fast for the final "g's") ding
     ding ding ding DING DING DING DING ding
     ding ding ding!
     (Repeat sequence from "WHISTLE FOR CROSS-
         ING," running at full speed.)
W   CHOU chou chou chou CHOU chou chou chou
     CHOU chou chou chou CHOU chou chou chou
M   RU-U-U-UMMMMMMMMMMM
     BLLLLLLLLLLLLLLLLL RUMBLE bumble
     BUMBLE
     (These running sounds continue until—DRIFT INTO
     "CASEY JONES".)*

CASEY JONES
(An American folk ballad arranged for the verse choir to follow
"Farewell to the Steam Locomotive".)
Legend:
W — Women
M — Men

C — Casey
F — Fireman

W   *(Continue train sounds, under.)*
M   *Come* all you *rou*nders
        for I *want* you to
          hear
     The *story of* a *brave* eng*ineer*.
     Casey Jones was the *rounder's name*
     On a *big* eight-*whee*ler of a *mighty fame*.

W   *Caller* called *Casey* 'bout *half*-past *four*,
     He *kissed* his *wife* at the *station door*,
     Climbed to the *cab* with his *o*rders in his *hand*
     And said, (C) *"This* is my *trip* to the *Holy Land!"*
W   *(2 short whistle blasts. Then moan-n, under.)*

M   *Out* of South *Mem*phis *yard* on the *fly,*
     Heard the *fire*man say, (F) "You *got* a 'white *eye'!"*
M   Well, the *switch*man *knew* by the *en*gine's
     *moa*n-n-n-n-*n*-n-n-n
     That the *man* at the *throt*tle was (C) *"CASEY
JONES!"*

W   The *rain* was comin' *down* 'bout *five* or six *weeks,*
     The *rail*road *track* was like the *bed* of a *creek;*
     It *slowed* her *down* to a *thir*ty-mile *gait*
     And the *South*-bound *mail* was *eight-hours-late.*

M   *Fire*man said, (F) "*Casey*, you're *run*nin' too *fast,*
     You *ran* the block *board* the last *sta*tion we *passed!"*
M   *Casey* said, (C) *"May*be, but *we'*ll make it *through,*
     For she *steams* a lot *bet*ter than *I* ever *knew!*
     Come on, *Fire*man, *don't* you *fret,*
     Keep *knock*in' at the *fire*door, *don't* give up *yet*.

I'm gonna *run* her 'til she *leaves* the *rail,*
Or *make* it on *time* with the *South*-bound *mail!"*

W   *(4 long whistle wails under the next stanza.*
    Then increase Moan-n-n-n to the wreck.)
M   *Around the curve* and *down* the *dump*
    Two locomo*tives* was *bound* to *bump!*
    (F) *"Look* out, *Ca*sey, it's *just* a*head,*
    We *might* jump and *make* it or we'll *all* be *dead!"*

M   *Around* the *curve* comes a *pas*senger *train,*
    *Ca*sey blows the *whis*tle, tells the *Fire*man, (C) "Ring
    the *bell!"*
M   Fireman *jumps* and *says,* (F) "Good*bye,*
    Casey *Jones,* you're *bound* to *DI-I-I*-i-i-i-ie-e-e-e!"
    (Fade out)

All *(Sounds of a mighty train wreck!)*
    (Screams, roars, crashes, hissing steam!)

Solo Well, *Ca*sey *Jones* was *all-*l *right,*
    He *stuck* to his *duty day* and *night.*
    They *loved* his *whis*tle and his *ring* number *three,*
    And he *came* into *Mem*phis on the *old* I.C."

All *Head*aches and *heart*aches and *all* kinds of *pain,*
    They ain't a *part* from a *rail*road *train.*
    *Sto*ries of *brave* men, *no*ble and *grand*
    Be*long* to the *life* of a *rail*road *man.*

*This magnificent sonnet has such a vibrant spirit that it should
take the entire choir in unison to capture the flow of its thought
and emotion.*

COMPOSED UPON WESTMINSTER BRIDGE, Sept. 3, 1802
Wordsworth

All   *Earth has not anything to show more fair:*

Dull would he be of soul who could pass by   *(If you all think of the Thames River it will help you catch the rhythm and overpowering mood.)*

A sight so touching in its majesty:
This city now doth, like a garment, wear
The beauty of the morning; silent, bare
Ships, towers, domes, theaters, and temples lie.
Open unto the fields, and to the sky;
All bright and glittering in the smokeless air.
Never did sun more beautifully steep
In his first splendor, valley, rock, or hill;
Ne'er saw I, never felt, a calm so deep!
The river glideth at his own sweet will:
Dear God! the very houses seem asleep;
And all that mighty heart is lying still!

DOUBLE RAINBOW
Rachel Harris Campbell
(Published here for the first time)

Here is a deeply thoughtful poem that could well follow the Wordsworth sonnet. It will take college adults to perceive and express its subtleties. This suggested arrangement for Men and Women sections attempts to emphasize the reassuring follow-through: the "double richness"; "re-doubled hope," "second

promise." It can, and perhaps should, be done in unison to risk
no break in the "quiet but dominant" rhythm.

W   Double rainbow,
M   Double richness,
All   And the rain still falling.

Seven colors
Double arched
Against slate-blue clouds,
Above hills autumn-colored.

W   If hope, (M) redoubled hope:
W   If promise, (M) second promise.

All   And the air clean, the rain still falling thinly.

And   a   sudden,   *(There is a subtle build here to the*
unlooked-for   *key word, "Joy.")*
Known, forgotten
Joy about the heart.

Here is a poem that joins "Double Rainbow" in finding more
in the world about us than meets the eye at "first look."

MIRACLES
Walt Whitman

All   Why, who makes much of a miracle?
As to me I know of nothing else but miracles,
S   Whether I walk the streets of Manhattan,
S   Or dart my sight over the rooves of houses toward
the sky,

S   Or wade with naked feet along the beach just in the edge
          of the water,

S   Or stand under trees in the woods,

W   Or talk with any one I love,

M   Or sit at table at dinner with the rest,

S   Or look at a stranger opposite me riding in the car,

W   Or watch honey-bees bustle around the hive
          of a summer forenoon,

M   Or animals feeding in the fields,

S   Or birds, or the wonderfulness of insects in the air,

S   Or the wonderfulness of the sundown, or of stars
          shining so quiet and bright,

S   Or the exquisite delicate thin curve of the new moon
          in the spring;

W   These with the rest, *("Savoring them all together.")*
          one and all, are
          to me miracles,
    The whole referring,
    yet each distinct and
    in its
          place.

M   To me every hour of *("Captured by the wonder.")*
          the light and
          dark is a
          miracle,
    Every cubic inch of
    space is a miracle!—

All Every square yard of *(Pause—to begin from a slow*
          the surface of *thoughtful pace to an increase*
          the *of intensity to the final ques-*
    earth is spread with *tion.)*
          the same,
    Every foot of the in-
    terior swarms with
          the same,

To me the sea is a
continual miracle,
The   fishes   that
swim—the rocks—the
motion
    of the waves—the
ships with men in
them—
What stranger mira-
cles are there?

HOW DO I LOVE THEE?
Elizabeth Barrett Browning

*This is obviously a woman's poem—but since it strikes a univer-
sal chord perhaps we should consider having the men do part of
it. You choose.*

W   How do I love thee? Let me count the ways.
    I love thee to the depth and breath and height
    My soul can reach, when feeling out of sight
    For the ends of Being and ideal Grace.
S   I love thee to the level of every day's
    Most quiet need, by sun and candlelight.
S   I love thee freely, as men strive for Right;
S   I love thee purely, as they turn from Praise.
S   I love thee with the passion put to use
    In my old griefs, and with my childhood's faith.
W   I love thee with a love I seemed to lose
    With my lost saints—I love thee with the breath,
    Smiles, tears of all my life! And, if God choose,
    I shall but love thee better after death.

* * * * * * * *

Here is a poem that belongs to the college-age people
for they have seen their early classmates struggle with

limited ability do regular work, only to be joined with others in groups where goals were within reach of their aborted capability.

Thus separated, the college choir members may have lost sight of the endless patience, the intrepid striving to complete a task—or pronounce a word, the great out-pouring of love, and the gallant humor that burns through the haze that is the daily aura of these blame-less ones.

Some of these poorly endowed people miraculously find a useful place in America's fast-moving scheme of things, and they all should find the place in our hearts that this frank and sensitive poem requests. It would be well to remind the choir of these things so it can "get inside" the poem, and prepare for its reality.

LINES FROM A HOME FOR MENTALLY RE-TARDED CHILDREN
G. Lynn Nelson
In Honor of Faith Ann Vanderhyde

All   Consider my sons and
         daughters,
         America:
         They are slit-eyed
         and slobbering,
             gangling   and
         gauche;
         And their mouths
         tremble   as   they
         mumble
             the esoteric argot
             of their very pri-
         vate minds—
         While their bodies
         apologize

(This is factual, straightforward, with sympathy—but without maudlin "tears.")

for   misplaced
chromosomes
and twisted births.

Consider my sons and
daughters, America:
L   Alien   and   awful
          though they are
          to your bright
dream
You   cannot   ignore
them.
M   Though they know
          not anger,
Though they will not
arise in wrath,
Theirs is a deeper
demand:
D   They will arise
          like meek spectres
          in   your   bright
dream;
All   They   will   slink   sil-
          ently
          through the alleys
          behind your neon
hearts;

L   They will lurk in the
          shadows
          beyond your pic-
ture windows,
M   beyond your ter-
          raced lawns,
D   beyond your ter-
          raced lives;

(This begins a steady increase in intensity, caught up by each voice group, to the end of stanza three. Even this "build" is underplayed within the reality-laden mood of the poem.)

All   And they will forever
         eat with hungry
         eyes
         at the edges
         of your bright
   dream.

Consider my sons and   *(Break the climax with a pause.)*
daughters, America: *(Then be deliberate and direct to*
For that is the only   *show the mutual reward.)*
way
That they, who are
ugly,
     can be beautiful
And that you
     can be as beauti-
ful as they.

This scintillating poem presents a rare opportunity for a college verse choir. It is arranged for a four-part choir. If you have a different organization you might assign four groups temporarily to do it. It will hold an audience spellbound—and the choir will love doing it, once the intricacies are mastered.

THE BELLS
Edgar Allan Poe

Legend:
1 — Light Women
2 — Medium Women
3 — Medium Men
4 — Dark Men

I

1   Hear the sledges with   *(An octave high, Gay. Like fall-*
       the bells—Silver   *ing icicles.)*
       bells!
What a world of mer-
riment their melody
foretells!
How they tinkle,
tinkle, tinkle,
In the icy air of night!
While the stars that oversprinkle
All the heavens, seem to twinkle
With a crystalline delight;
Keeping time, time, time,
In a sort of Runic rhyme,
To the tintinnabulation that so musically wells
From the bells, bells,   *(Make them dance.)*
bells, bells, bells, bells,
bells—
From the jingling and
tinkling of the bells.

2   Hear the mellow   *(Deep-seated joy, the realization*
       wedding bells-   *of dreams.)*
       —Golden bells!
What a world of hap-
piness their harmony
fore-
      tells!
Through the balmy air of night
How they ring out their delight!—
From the molten-golden notes, and all in tune;
What a liquid ditty floats
To the turtle-dove that listens, while she gloats

On the moon!
Oh, from out the sounding cells,
What a gush of euphony voluminously wells!
How it swells!
How it dwells on the future!
How it tells of the rapture that impels
To the swinging and the ringing
Of the bells, bells,
bells, —
Of the bells, bells,   *(Keeping these bells on the same*
bells, bells,   *pitch, alternating the power,*
  bells, bells, bells, —   *will avoid a tiresome pitch*
To the rhyming and   *pattern.)*
the chiming of
  the bells!

III

3   Hear the loud alarm   *(Rude, metallic, monotonous*
      bells—Brazen   *brass bells.)*
      bells!
  What a tale of terror,
  now, their tur-
      bulency tells!
  In the startled ear of   *(Keep the "alarm" going but use*
  night   *contrasts of pitch, power and*
  How they scream out   *tempo.)*
  their
      affright!
  Too much horrified
  to speak,
  They can only shriek,
  shriek out of tune;
2   **In a clamorous ap-**   *(Begin an ominous build.)*
      pealing to the mercy
      of the fire,

In a mad expostula-
tion with the deaf
and frantic fire,

23   Leaping   higher,   *(Increase power and speed,*
     higher, higher,   *higher pitch.)*

With a desperate de-
sire, and a resolute
   endeavor

Now—now to sit, or
never,

By the side of the   *(Denoument)*
pale-faced moon.

2   Oh, the bells, bells,   *(A mother reprimanding her*
     bells!   *child.)*

What a tale their ter-
ror tells
   of despair!

3   How they clang, and   *(Skyrocket.)*
     clash, and roar!

23   What a horror they
     outpour

On the bosom of the
palpitating air!

2   Yet the ear, it fully
     knows,

By the twanging and   *(Low, slow, deliberate. Build.)*
the clanging,

How the danger ebbs
and flows;

3   Yet the ear distinctly   *(Increase build.)*
     tells

In the jangling and
the wrangling

How the danger sinks
and swells,

23   By the sinking or the
            swelling in the
            anger of the bells—
       Of the bells, —   *(All out.)*
       Of the bells, bells,   *(No variety in pitch or power to*
       bells, bells,   *end of stanza. These bells and*
            bells, bells, bells, —   *words are nonmusical, clang-*
       In the clamor and the   *ing disturbers of the peace.)*
       clangor of
            the bells!

                    IV
4   Hear the tolling of   *(Velvet melancholy.)*
            the bells—Iron
            bells!
       What a world of sol-
       emn thought their
       monody
            compels!
       In the silence of the
       night,
1   How we shiver with   *(High and scary.)*
            affright
2   At the melancholy (3)   *(Attic to cellar!)*
            menace (4) of
            their tone!
       For every sound that
       floats
       From the rust within
       their throats—is a
       groan.
12   And the people—ah,   *(Eerie)*
            the people—
       They that dwell up in
       the steeple, all alone,
4   And who tolling, toll-   *(The smooth groundswell that be-*
            ling, tolling   *gins here tops out at "glory"*

In   that   muffled
monotone,
Feel a glory in so rol-
ling
On the human heart
a stone—

12   They are neither man
      nor woman—
34   They   are   neither
          brute   nor
          human—
4   They are ghouls: —
And their king it is
who tolls: —
As he rolls, rolls,
rolls, rolls
A paean from the
bells!

34   And his merry bosom
          swells
With the paean from
the bells!
And he dances, and
he yells;
Keeping time, time,
time,
In a sort of runic
rhyme,
To the throbbing of
the bells—
Of the bells, bells,
bells—
To the tolling of the
bells—
Of   the   bells,   (12)
      bells,   (34)   bells,
      (12) bells,

*and falls off to "heart of
stone.")*

(From the bottom of the well.)

*(Faster, with poltergeist aban-
don.)*

*(Begin slower tempo at "throb-
bing." These "bells" and
words are soft and musical.)*

*(Maintain a constant pitch and
stately rhythm. Accent every-
other beat to the end.)*

> (34) bells, (12) bells,
> (34) bells —
> All   to the moaning and
>   the groaning
>   Of the bells.

This poem represents young people vividly describing the world they have inherited, with no answer in sight—until the last line.

"WHY, GOD, WHY?"

       (From FISH, a religious campus paper)
Solo I walked today through the slums of life,
     Down the dark street of wretchedness and pain
     I trod today where few have trod, and
     As I walked I challenged God —

     I saw the sots in the bar-rooms.
     I saw the prostitutes in the dance halls.
     I saw the thieves as they picked pockets.
     I saw men and women devoid of life, living
       in worlds of sin, and above the din I whis-
     pered:

Women "Why, God, Why?"   *(Low, prayerfully)*

Solo I walked today down the lanes of hate,
     Hearing the jeers of bitter men,
     Hearing the names as they cursed and spat—
     I saw the dejected men they stoned.
     I felt the anguish of their cries.
     I saw them as they slapped the lonely,
     As they turned their backs on human needs.
     Snarling, growling were the fiends of hell.

These, God called His sons?
Gasping for air, I cried:

Women "Why, God, Why?"   *(Losing patience.)*

Solo   I walked today through war's grim dregs—
Over fields of blood, over graveless men.
I saw the dead, the crucified, the headless,
The limbless, the pleading, the crying.
I saw the pain, the waste. I smelled the
Odour of rotted flesh.
I saw the children gathered 'round—
Watching, naked, hungry, weeping, diseased,
dirty—
The baby trying to nurse from a dead mother.
The ruins—the agony—the despair.
Blinded with tears, I fell down these streets.
I stumbled, then stopped, I shouted:

Women "Why, God, Why?"   *(Demanding!)*

Why do you let man sin, hate, suffer?
Unmerciful father? God, art thou blind—
Art thou wicked and cruel?
God, can'st thou watch and do naught?
Why must this be? !—

Solo   The world grew silent. —I awaited reply.
The silence was heavy—I started to tremble.
I waited long—half rebuking, half fearing.—
Then I heard from close behind me:

Men   WHY, MAN—WHY-Y-Y!!!

*This short clarion call must follow "Why, God, Why," for it
seems to say: "Look, this isn't all there is—we still have the other
side of the coin."*

SING, THEN
Rachel Harris Campbell
(Published here for the first time)

Sing, then,
In an evil time.
Let your massed chorus
Ring out proudly.

There have been other evil times;
The men of old sang then.
There will come evil times
When we are long safely dead;
The men of our race
Then will be heard singing.

Sing, then,
In the way we have sung
From oldest eld:
As wolves sing,
Lonely, signalling
Their kindred;
As swans are said to sing
Dying.

Sing, then.
It is your right
And destiny.

This dynamic poem marches through three periods of ancient history with a compelling rhythm, neatly condensing the accomplishments of the three men and somehow softening the fate of their worldly residue by the human touch the author uses in the telling.

BALLAD OF GLORY DEPARTED
Rachel Harris Campbell
(Published here for the first time)

N   Cyrus, King of Persia,
      Master of the Chaldees,
      Zoroaster's patron,
      Was a fighting man,
      Hacked him out an empire
      Half the width of Asia,
      Died at last in battle
      On the borders of Iran.

All   Then they reared a stately
      Tomb, and laid him in it,
      Paid him pomp and reverence,
      Sealed the door with tears.
      In his rich adornments,
      Gold and sard and sapphire,
      There he lay remembered
      For two hundred years.

N   Golden Alexander,
      Prince of Macedonia,
      Overlord of Hellas,
      Was a fighting man,
      Big with dreams of empire,
      Hewed his way through Asia,
      Came to Cyrus' city
      In antique Iran.

N   There he found the broken
      Tomb, the work of nomads;
      Scattered was the treasure,
      Open stood the door,

And the corse of Cyrus
In a dust of garments,
All his jewels taken,
Lay upon the floor.

All   Noble Alexander
Wept to see the ruin,
Cursed the desecration
Of the mighty dead,
Ordered reinterment
In the ancient splendor,
With the crown of Persia
On the withered head.

N   Youthful Alexander,
Burning with the fever,
Knew that he was dying
At the fall of sun;
In austere foreboding
Saw his labor ended,
Saw the empire broken
And his dream undone.

All   Then his captains, weeping,
Reared a tomb in Sidon;
Eyeing one another,
Choking down their fears,
Laid him there in splendor
For a god proved mortal.
There he lay remembered
For two hundred years.

N   Pompey, called the Fortunate,
Scourge of Mithridates,
Came to ancient Sidon
By a phantom led,

Thought of Alexander,
Learned where he was lying,
Went to pay his reverence
To the famous dead.

All   There he found the plundered
Tomb, the spoil of robbers,
Empty as the desert,
Lonely as the dawn,
Not a trace remaining
Of the hero's splendor,
All his treasure rifled
And the body gone.
Then the lordly Roman
Turned away in anguish,
Saw his own proud fortunes
Parted from his hand;
In a cruel vision
Guessed the end of Pompey—
Saw the headless body
On the bloodied sand.

FOR WHOM THE BELL TOLLS
John Donne

*This timeless poem perennially shocks new generations into an
awareness of others, and mutual responsibility. It has served
our choir well as a "signature number." Please see Chapter 13
for the full text of the poem.*

To these suggested poems you will add many more
from the list of titles, the bibliography, and your own re-

sources to challenge the varying capacities of college-adult choirs. They can be arranged as "theme programs" or simply to present a well-ordered variety of living literature. A program made up of poems from one author can make an interesting evening.

A Few Plays that Use Choral Speaking:
Auden and Isherwood, *Accent on F-6, The Skin of the Dog.*
Benét, Stephen Vincent, *Western Star.*
Corey, Orlin, *Adaptation of The Book of Job.*
Eliot, T.S., *Murder in the Cathedral, Family Reunion, The Rock.*
Frye, Christopher, *Moses, The Boy with the Cart.*
Hooper and Martin, *A Man Dies.*
Johnson, Albert, *World without End,* Adaptation of *Everyman.*
Lanier, Sidney, *The Harlequin of Dreams.*
Richardson, Howard, *Dark of the Moon.*
Stein, Joseph, *Fiddler on the Roof.*
Ward, R. H., *The Figure of the Cross.*
Willson, Meredith, *The Music Man.*

College people have limitless ability to express their still wider interests. These poems represent the many directions that may be taken:

1. "Black Misery" by Langston Hughes.
2. "The Chinese Nightingale," "Daniel," "The Santa Fe Trail," and others by Vachel Lindsay.
3. "The Creation" and others from *God's Trombones* by James Weldon Johnson.
4. "The Donkey" by G. K. Chesterton.
5. "The Elephant Song" and "Foreboding" by Don Blanding.
6. *Der Erlkönig* by Goethe (Whittier's translation).

7. "The Gettysburg Address" and "The Bear Hunt" by Abraham Lincoln. (Also the last paragraph of his first and second inaugural addresses with his farewell address to the people of Springfield make a fine unit representing his humanity and purpose.)
8. "Granite and Cypress," "Hurt Hawks," and others by Robinson Jeffers.
9. "I Hear America Singing," "There Was a Child Went Forth," and others by Walt Whitman.
10. "Lament for Ignacio Sanchez Mejias" (or "Lament for a Bullfighter") by Garcia Lorca.
11. "The Laughers" by Louis Untermeyer.
12. "Let America be America Again" by Langston Hughes.
13. "The Leaden Echo and the Golden Echo" by Gerard Manley Hopkins.
14. "Lincoln, Man of the People" by Edwin Markham.
15. "Mending Wall," "Stopping by Woods on a Winter's Evening," and others by Robert Frost.
16. "Old Tears in Galilee" by George Slartruch Galbraith.
17. "The Plot to Overthrow Christmas" by Norman Corwin.
18. "Sonnet Twenty-Nine" by William Shakespeare.
19. "Sudden Storm" and others by James Russell Lowell.
20. "The Teacher" and others by Leslie Pinkney Hill.
21. "The Thousand Years of Grace" by Alfred Lord Tennyson. (And more, and more.)
22. "Nightingales" by Robert Bridges.

15
Choral Speaking in Recreation

Three Easy First Steps

Do you want to go on a lion hunt? Well, sit down and I'll tell you how. You simply smile at your group in such a way that they will know you intend to have fun, then ask them to repeat each phrase with its action immediately after you give it to them. You might tell them, *This is for the young-in-heart and the adventuresome-of-spirit and since we're really going to be in Africa we'd better all stick together.*

Then get fixed so you can pat your knees and say, with an "of course you do" in your voice: *Do you want to go on a lion hunt?* Wait for the group to repeat this. *Allright, here we go.* Here you and the group begin patting your knees as they repeat the words. *Not so fast. After all, this is Africa.* Wait again for their response, continuing the action. *It isn't the heat, it's the humid-ITY.* Response. *Well, here's a bridge.* You thump your chests as you all walk across making a gloriously hollow sound.

Then you go through the tall grass, climb a tree, pet fuzzy baby buzzards, slosh through a swamp, swim a lake, find the lion in a cave, inspect his tonsils, realize how close you all are to the old boy—and then GET OUT!, reversing the order of travel. The full text follows immediately, but I trust you will change it according to your own imagination or to better fit the group and occasion.

"The Lion Hunt" is the first of three sure-fire numbers that should get you off to a good start and lead your group into gradually more complex responses. The mission of this first baby step is to let your people find their speaking voices, express thoughts and feelings more largely than ordinarily without embarrassment, listen to and follow directions, and have fun doing it—with others! That is the big thing. Each individual will sense the presence and reinforcement of the others as they all contribute simultaneously to the total response of the group. This feeling of belonging is the source of many more good things—as we shall see.

The Lion Hunt — An Adventure for the Young in Heart
The leader asks the group to repeat his words and actions. You all must "believe" it.
Spoken Words:

Do you want to go on a lion hunt?	*(The group repeats this, as all other words) Pat knees to create walking sensation.*
Very well, let's go!	
Not so fast; after all this is Africa.	*Pat knees again, slower.*
It isn't the heat, it's the humid-ity.	
There's a bridge.	*Beat fists on chest for hollow sound.*
This hill will slow us down.	

It's easier on the other side.	*Pat knees faster.*
Well! There's a crick.	*Stop patting knees.*
And no bridge. We'll just have to jump it.	
Back up everybody. Here we go!	*Hold hands up for the jump. Delay it.*
I thought we wouldn't make it!	
The grass is getting tall, isn't it?	*Push grass away, to make a trail.*
I can't see anything.	*Shade eyes with hand.*
Let's climb that tree.	*Climb with arms, knees and elbows.*
I still can't see anything.	*Shade eyes again.*
Well, let's go on up.	*Climb again.*
Oh, look at the buzzard's nest.	
With two little fuzzy baby buzzards in it.	*Stir them up.*
Oh; there's the mother buzzard.	*With utter disdain.*
Go away Mother Buzzard.	
Nice little fuzzy baby buzzards.	*Stir them up again.*
I said go AWAY, Mother Buzzard!	*Fighting her off.*
Help! Jump!	*Cover head.*
She wasn't so very fuzzy.	*Push grass away again.*
Say; it's getting swampy.	*Suck in breath as if walking in water.*
There's a lake. Should be a boat.	*Stop and search.*
There it is. Let's row, row, row.	*Rowing motions.*
Well, look at the Crocadaddle!	*Stop rowing.*
What's a crocadaddle?	

A crocadaddle is a hippopotamuss's pappy!

("As anyone can plainly see.")

Look at those teeth. And that grin.

Lean over the side.

Hello there you friendly crocadaddle.

OUCH!

Hold hand over nose. It's been bitten off.

Wery whunny, wery whunny!

With lower lip extended over upper lip.

Wups, the boat's leaking.

We'll just have to swim for it.

Swimming motions. (Always resourceful)

Say, this looks like lion country.

Shake off water. Begin walking softly.

Anybody scared?

I am.

(High timid voice.)

Shshshsh!

Stop everything.

There's a cave.

Let's go i-yun.

Largely, with shoulder shrug.

Careful, now.

Snap cheeks, with mouth in "OH" shape.

(Frightened gasp.)

Stop snapping cheeks, to gasp.

See those eyes? Might be the lion's eyes.

I don't ca-yer. Poke him.

Large, braggadocio.

You poke him.

See those teeth? Must be the lion's teeth.

See that tongue? Rough isn't it.

Feel the tongue.

Excuse me, Mr. Lion.

Hold his jaws wide open.

See those tonsils? Yep, they're the lion's tonsils.

Lean into the lion's mouth.

THE LION'S TONSILS! LET'S GET OUT OF HERE!!

(Run back home reversing all the motions, except rowing—the boat sank.

Repeat "Wery Whunny, Wery Whunny" and "Help, Jump" at the proper times. No other words.)

"The Lion Hunt" has never failed to capture an audience and I have seen it used successfully with people from pre-school to college age, including large high school assemblies and a "Spring Sing" crowd of four thousand college students and friends. It has been received equally well by adult groups, including church family-night crowds, luncheon clubs, a large medical convention, and notably a convention of school administrators who wanted to "do it again."

On one occasion a large group of eager boys was just ready to jump into the swimming pool at the San Diego Boys' Club when their leader was informed that the water's chlorine content was too high and a half-hour wait would be needed to make it safe. That resourceful man walked to the end of the diving board, sat down, then asked the boys to sit down—and took them on a lion hunt, for the full half-hour! The boys suggested their own variations as the safari was repeated several times.

The second "sure-fire" number is D.K. Stevens' well-known "The Musical Trust," which exacts fuller, though still easy, participation from the group. This time the leader does each stanza as a solo, from memory if possible, and asks a different third of the group to join him with the sound of the instrument that ends their stanza. A practice run-through of the sound for each group will be worth doing for the precision thus gained will enhance the fun.

This poem makes the welcome point that cooperation is necessary for success in this venture, for we see that the men with the yellow flute, the big tuba, and the drum and cymbals "couldn't make a penny" until they joined up with their respective "Tootle-Ootle-—OOmpah—Boom, Zing, Zing!"

Later, if interest warrants it, more of the poem may be assigned to each group. The full text of this delightful poem may be found in Chapter 13.

The third "no-miss" number takes a little more doing but is worth the effort for it is from the famous western poet, Lew Sarett. He titled it "The Squaw Dance" because it is one of the few Indian dances in which their women could participate. It is also known as the "good-time" dance, performed on any happy occasion; such as the Fourth of July or to end a period of mourning or to entertain visitors—or just for a good time.

The strong basic rhythm of the dance makes it easy to do in any degree of depth your group may wish to attempt. The *simplest treatment* calls for the leader to teach the group the first five lines of the poem and rehearse it several times for fun and accuracy. This gusty response occurs four times and each time the leader approaches it he raises his hand in anticipation and drops it as the signal for the group's immediate participation with the "Beat, beat, beat, beat—etc." sequence. Each time the tempo may be increased slightly according to the feeling of the poem.

In the last stanza there are three extra chances for the group to participate, first on the "Ugh" as designated. (Be sure to have them pronounce this as the "UH" in "UP" for if they try the hard "G" sound their voices

could be ruined for the rest of the evening.) The Girls'
prolonged "Yow-w-wling" and the Boys' "How-w-wling,"
which are given with the leader's lines, should bring
them back for more. (Wait until you come to this stanza
before introducing these so the group will not have too
much to learn at one time.)

THE SQUAW DANCE
Lew Sarett

From *Covenant with Earth: a Selection from the Poems of
Lew Sarett*. Edited and copyrighted, 1956, by Alma John-
son Sarett, and published, 1956, by the University of
Florida Press, Gainesville. Reprinted by permission of
Mrs. Sarett.

Legend: L — Narrator or Leader; G — Girls or Women;
B — Boys or Men; All — EVERYBODY!

All   Beat, beat, beat, beat, beat upon the drum,
      Beat, beat, beat, beat, beat upon the drum,
      And a shuffle to the left, a shuffle to the left,
      A shuffle, shuffle, shuffle to the left, to the left,
All   Hi! Hi! Hi! Hi! Hoy-eeeeeeeeeeeeeeeeee-yah!
L   Fat squaws, lean squaws, gliding in a row,
      Grunting, wheezing, laughing as they go;
      Hi! Hi! Hi! with a laugh and a shout,
All   To the beat, beat, beat, beat, beat upon the tom-
      tom,
      Beat, beat, beat, beat, beat upon the drum;
      And a shuffle to the left, a shuffle to the left,
      A shuffle, shuffle, shuffle to the left, to the left,
All   Hi! Hi! Hi! Hi! Hoy-eeeeeeeeeeeeeeeeee-yah!

L   Medicine men on the medicine drum,
      Beating out the rhythm with a steady thrum.
      Medicine gourd with its rattle, rattle, rattle,

Flinging wild with the call of battle.
Beaded drummers squatting in the ring
Leap to its challenge with a crouch and a spring;
Weathered old bucks that grunt and wheeze
As they jangle bells on their wrists and their knees—
Shining, new and olden bells,
Silver, copper, golden bells,
Cow-bells, toy bells, ringing sleigh-bells,
Beaded dance bells, "give-away" bells,
Jingling, Jangling, Jingling bells,
Set-the-toes-a-tingling bells,

All   To the beat, beat, beat, beat, beat upon the tom-tom,
Beat, beat, beat, beat, beat upon the drum;
And a shuffle to the left, a shuffle to the left,
A shuffle, shuffle, shuffle to the left, to the left,

All   Hi! Hi! Hi! Hi! Hoy-eeeeeeeeeeeeeeeeee-yah.

L   Old bucks stamping heel and toe, (All) Ugh! (L) As they snort,
And they cackle and they crow—
G   Yow-ow-ow-ow-ow-ow-ow-owl-l-l.
L   Yowling like the lynx that crouches nigh, (together)
B   How-ow-ow-ow-ow-ow-ow-owl-l-l.
L   Howling like the wolf at the prairie sky; (together)
Growling and grunting as they shift and they tramp,
Stalking, crouching—with a stamp, stamp, stamp—
Sleek limbs, lithe limbs, strong and clean limbs,
Withered limbs, bowed limbs, long and lean limbs,
Flat feet, bare feet, dancing feet,
Buckskin-moccasined prancing feet,
Eager child-feet, scuffling feet,

Feet, feet, feet, feet, shuffling feet! Hi!
All   Beat, beat, beat, beat, beat upon the tom-tom,
Beat, beat, beat, beat, beat upon the drum;
And a shuffle to the left, a shuffle to the left,
A shuffle, shuffle, shuffle to the left, to the left,
All   Hi! Hi! Hi! Hi! Hoy-eeeeeeeeeeeeeeeeee-yah.

The *second treatment* is more complex and takes more rehearsing. You simply assign more places for each group to participate and then point to them as their cue appears. This is worked out in the second stanza in Chapter 13 and could be enough "breaking up" of the poem, leaving stanzas one and three as they are in the first treatment. However, when the group is ready to do the entire poem the leader simply assigns appropriate lines to various voice groups or lets the whole group do its part in unison—and becomes the director. In this way, what started out as a recreational "fun thing" becomes a full-fledged verse-choir experience with a valued piece of Americana presenting a facet of Indian culture rarely seen by non-Indians.

The *ultimate treatment* is to have the group do the dance as near to the authentic Indian style as they can manage and to add the "give-away" feature that is a part of the dance. This brief description can serve to get you started. You would be most fortunate to have an Indian adviser at this point. (Mr. Sarett gives a full description of this dance on pp. 335-38, in his book *The Collected Poems of Lew Sarett*, New York: Henry Holt & Co. Inc., 1941.)

Both men and women dancers form a large circle and do a simple shuffle step, revolving slowly to the left to the beat of a drummer on a large tympany-sized drum, or several drummers using tom-toms, placed in the center of the circle. Then several individuals dance within the circle, using the Indian style—one basic step of which is to stomp with the ball of the foot, then tap three times with the heel while gyrating the body to express the "good time" or to dramatize the action of people and animals in the dance. Alternating the feet gets you around the area pretty well. There are many other steps.

Now for the "give-away". One of the dancers in the center approaches a chosen dancer in the ring and presents him or her with a gift. This signals that that person has been chosen to join the giver in a duo-dance in the center, and also that a gift of equal value is expected in return. This continues as long as desirable with the chosen dancers returning to the ring to make room for new ones.

Where does choral speaking come into this? In fact, the poem was written from the spectator's point of view so the amount of speaking the dancers do is optional. It could well be limited to the five lines learned in the response, with various people doing other parts of the poem in a "bouquet" of sounds and movements, relieving the formality of the occasion and doing away with the need for a director. Here your Indian adviser would be most needed to insure authentic sounds and movements.

This poem and its resulting dance is recommended for any group, young or old, that is interested in experiencing a part of authentic Indian culture. It is an especially valuable event for Y.M.C.A. and Boy Scout people, or other similar groups who are already interested in Indian lore.

Imagine an International Boy Scout Jamboree, or other large-scale function, where visitors could carry back with them this spirited and respectful representation of our American Indian! Such an event would call for full costumes with tom-toms, medicine gourds, eagle-feathered chieftain war bonnets, and other regalia. Some of the gifts the Indians exchanged were the most valued articles in their possession.

"Self-Starter Suggestions"

You will find other poems suited for particular groups in the list of titles and general bibliography in these final pages. However, here are some suggestions that may work for you:

(1) Young children love to speak or sing rhymes that accompany their games. Strangely, people with more years added enjoy returning to some of these, especially well-remembered nursery rhymes when done seriously with great gusto.

When one such number was being done by a high-school girls' camp assembly, the leader noticed the last group buzzing among themselves. It came out this way:

1 "Mary had a little lamb
2 Its fleece was whi-i-ite as snow,
3 And everywhere that Mary went—
4 SHE TOOK A BUS!"

There are many others that can stand being "fractured" in this way without undue damage.

(2) Chants and spoken rhythms will lighten the burden of calesthenics and hiking. Various branches of the

military make extensive use of this technique, especially their highly trained "Drill Units." One effective "trick" they use is to count silently for a number of beats and then shout the "ONE-TWO" that begins the chant again. John Drinkwater's "Marching Rhythm" is an excellent poem to use for hiking—or for campfire fun. Many others suitable for the campfire may be found in the list of titles or in the poems found in other chapters that have been arranged in detail.

(3) Intricate patterns of motion accompanied by speaking can be worked out to represent such things as: a circus, a complex piece of machinery, flying gliders, a parade, or the sound of animals, trees, water, and wind in a natural setting.

One drama class simulated an open-hearth furnace in a steel mill with various clanks, hisses, and roarings occuring with appropriate motions at their appointed beat of the rhythm pattern. The thrill comes after the pattern has been run a certain number of times when all the sounds join on the same beat for one gigantic, polyphonic sound!

(4) Poems, or stories, can be enlarged into creative dramatics experiences by living them out after a brief scenario has been decided upon. The values in this experience are enhanced if the individuals in the group do not try to repeat the lines of the original poem or story but rather to respond naturally to the other people as they, also naturally, live out their roles.

(5) When pent-up energy demands expression, and there is room for activity, the experience of one of our students may be re-enacted. As the leader of a

Boys' Club group that met after school in a small gym with four-tier bleachers on either side, he used Tennyson's "The Charge of the Light Brigade" in the following manner:

After reading the poem to them they engaged in an impatient chóral-speaking rendition which soon came apart at the seams due to their still-bridled energy. So the leader divided them equally as English and Russian soldiers, confining the Russians to the bleachers and giving each a soggy tennis ball. (There are many such at a recreation center.)

The game developed as the Britishers galloped the length of the gym, each being carried by a trusty "horse." They were pelted by tennis-ball "shot and shell" and their dying was both histrionic and agonizing as they were struck.

They were on their honor to fall if hit but several usually made it through the charge and retreat to shout their achievement to the accompaniment of the victorious whinnies of their mounts.

Another rich source of recreational material is found in the *ballads of the various parts of America:* the eastern mountains, the south, the northwestern, western and southwestern states; the New England states with their colonial background; in fact, each part of the country has made its particular contribution to our folk literature. Also the various national groups that have immigrated here, as well as the sailors with their sea chanteys, have further enriched this body of Americana.

These should be sung first, if the melodies are known, but may also be used as fun experiences in choral speaking by having the leader speak the verses and the group join in the choruses, with gusto.

Our older son, Harlo Kingsley, enlivened and moti-
vated a sixth-grade American History course by building
it around the ballads of the people as they explored and
settled the country. His guitar and baritone voice made
it an intriguing way to learn to appreciate and love the
country. Why not do the same in a recreational situation, and give the folks a "leetle bit more than they
expected"—in this case a great deal more.

Look Back for Fun

Finally, you may find the rhythms presented in Chapters 8 and 14 and such numbers as "Farewell to the
Steam Locomotive," and "Casey Jones," and any of the
other poems used in foregoing chapters for various ages
of value, if your group is willing to "peel off the years"
and return to earlier pleasant experiences. You could
get the group well started with the easy-to-learn ice-
breaker that introduces Chapter 1:

All   A verse choir is nothing, I guess
      But a whole lot of people who want to more or less
      Talk together—like this:
L   We have Light Voices, (M) Medium, (D) Dark Voi-
      ces, too;
All   We talk all together, (L) or sometimes just a few,
All   And we'll say a something now if we thought that
      you
      Would like to hear some things to remem-m-mber!
      (From this point on anything can happen.)

* * * * * * * *

Here is a number to break the ice for an adult group.
It is an old Scottish ballad that calls for a men-and-
women grouping.

Whistle, Whistle, Old Wife

M   Whistle, whistle, old wife and you will get a hen.
W   I wouldn't whistle, said the wife, if you could give
      me ten.

M   Whistle, whistle, old wife, and you will get a coo.
W   I wouldn't whistle, said the wife, if you could give
      me two.

M   Whistle, whistle, old wife, and you will get a gown.
W   I wouldn't whistle, said the wife, for the best one in
      the town.

M   Whistle, whistle, old wife, and you will get a man.
W   Wheeple, Whauple, said the wife, I'll whistle if I
      can!!

The best source for fun numbers would be the folk
ballads and poems that are indigenous to your community.

16
Choral Speaking In Religion

The Natural Response

The clearest example of leader-response to expression of religious feeling may be found in the early, and some present-day, black churches. The most-used form is their singing, with the song leader being as important to the service as the preacher, for he raises the emotional pitch to a high level by singing a phrase or stanza that is answered by a refrain from the congregation.

There is also a less-formalized response to the sermon that is a true example of unrehearsed choral speaking. It is made manifest in the sounds of agreement and support the members of the congregation give to the preacher. This vocal support goes well beyond the "amen corner" and often involves the entire congregation in powerful, rhythmic and immediate responses to the preacher's exhortations. He can, and often does, give himself over to a basic rhythm by phrasing the sermon to develop this antiphonal effect. This is not to say that black church services are lacking in intellectual content, but rather to recognize the deep emotional involvement of all concerned.

James Weldon Johnson treats this subject thoroughly in the preface of his masterpiece, *God's Trombones,* which is now available in a paperback edition.

A less-pronounced but just as genuine example may be found in Jewish synagogues. On one occasion when the *Book of Job* was being performed in a large synagogue on the Eastern seaboard the Coreys reported first hearing audible sighs as seeming-unconscious expressions of the deep empathy the congregation felt with the players. These were followed by an occasional distinct "Yes-s-s" and low sobbing as the people identified emotionally with the troubled Job. These sounds were interspersed with "heavy silences" that also expressed their pent-up feelings. Vocal responses by the congregation are also a part of the regular synagogue services.

There is also a freer climate in evidence in some Protestant and Catholic churches, making possible audible expressions of "emotional communion." One minister encourages this by beginning with a cordial "Good morning!" which the congregation answers in kind. Once they have found their voices, the members feel free to respond quietly as the service and sermon unfold, also giving evidence of deeper concentration and involvement.

The Structured Responses

This deeper concentration and involvement has the welcome effect of making the responses called for in the liturgy of all forms of worship more meaningful. The "sogginess" that sometimes pervades these oft-repeated passages can be dispelled with the same admonition we use in approaching the interpretation of a number by a verse choir—to think the thought and feel the emotion before expressing them. Such an approach will pay especially rich dividends when members of the congregation give voice to their responsibilities on special observances such as Holy Communion, Baptism, and the welcoming of new members.

Another refreshing tendency developing in many churches is making it easy and attractive for the worshippers to participate more vitally. This tendency is the *modernizing of the language* of the liturgy and *writing more opportunities into the orders-of-worship* for the congregation to respond to orally in unison. Young people especially are rediscovering their place in the church in this way.

Special Choral-Speaking Groups

An opportunity with great potential in attracting young people into a fuller participation in church services and activities is presented by the verse choir. The most direct procedure would be to develop a verse-speaking group and have them present an appropriate number for a worship service, or even a full program for a church family night or some other special function.

The first suggestion was followed by an Oceanside, California, church, which invited one of our students to prepare Johnson's "The Crucifixion" for their Easter morning service. He organized a group of some thirty young people, half of whom were U. S. Marines from nearby Camp Pendleton. In three weekly rehearsals they committed this major work to memory and, following their leader's directions, consumated their efforts with a soul-stirring contribution to the service.

This poem is recognized as one of the most powerful pieces of writing in American literature. Certainly it had the strongest student we could provide as a director in the person of the richly talented and dedicated young Cleavon Little—who went on to earn awards at the American Academy of Dramatic Arts and success on New York's Broadway, where he won a "Tony" award as the "Best Actor in a Musical Play" for his portrayal of the title role in *Purlie*.

A church-oriented verse choir does not need to be confined to young people. One can be recruited from any age group represented in the entire personnel. Or it can be a blend of various ages, providing a good common experience and lessening the so-called generation gap. A recently organized verse choir of 22 members in our church included teen-agers, adults and a grand old man of 86 who made good use of his well-preserved voice. Unity of spirit and mutual admiration were openly expressed.

Some years ago a downtown church in San Diego decided to introduce a verse choir into the regular morning worship services. There were more than forty in the volunteer choir, including parents and their children, which gave the scripture lesson as a memorized choral reading. They operated separately from the singing choir, though several members served in both—thanks to a behind-the-pulpit passage.

Their first offering, the *Twenty-Third Psalm*, was so well received that they were encouraged to continue with such things as: the "Love Chapter" from *Corinthians, 13; The Beatitudes; The Song of Moses; Psalms*

121, 150 and others; "The Nativity of Christ" from *Luke;* and selections from *Isaiah.* Occasionally they offered nonscriptural poems from *God's Trombones,* and other sacred literature.

At the end of the year a full evening-service was given over to a program of their selected numbers, including the *Lord's Prayer*—which took on surprising dimensions that had not been recognized in the congregation's every-Sunday praying.

Organizing any verse choir within the church "family" is made especially easy by these facts:

(1) All the prospective members are oriented by the materials they will be doing.

(2) Groups that are already organized may be selected for this new experience.

(3) Verse-choir numbers by younger groups may be enlarged into simple creative dramas for chancel presentation for the church-school assemblies.

(4) Large composite choirs may be formed by joining several smaller ones together. (If they all have been preparing the same numbers they will need few mass rehearsals.)

(5) Any such choir may become the nucleus, or integral part, of a choral-speech drama.

Chapter 5 should be especially helpful in the details of organizing these groups.

Dramatic Productions for Church-Oriented Verse Choirs

Many interesting special-day programs and plays are coming into the church and Sunday-school literature that make good use of these verse choirs in conjunction with narrators, singing choirs, pantomimes, and/or short scenes. Also, the words of songs or hymns used in these scripts could be spoken to sharpen their meaning and to vary the nature of the performance.

The richest rewards, however, would come if the opportunity were given to a budding writer, or small group of creative spirits, in the church to write such a play or program. The results of his or their work would express a personal response to a certain subject, giving it a truer pertinency than might be found in the printed script. There âre many instances in which this approach has been successful.

The Christmas, Easter, Pentacost, Passover, Hannukah, Thanksgiving, and other religious and national seasons and holidays present occasions for special observances that may be celebrated in this way.

In addition to the materials list and Bibliography you may find further help in Chapter 3 where poems, plays, and theme-programs are described—along with suggestions for their production. The six institutions with religious orientation, should be especially pertinent to your needs.

The highly developed and polished productions of Orlin Corey and of Albert Johnson should serve to inspire and guide any group that wishes to enter into serious full-theatre production of religious plays and materials.

Quality of Experience in Doing Religious Materials:

Through all of these experiences something unusual and good has been happening to each and every one of the participants. It includes a keener perception of meanings; an acute awareness of emotional essence; an arising within the speaker of a response to meet the author's inner meaning (similar to a positive and negative charge), giving the participant greater insight into deeper things.

When this happens in relation to religious material it takes on the nature of a spiritual experience, becoming a true act of worship.

The director of a teen-age verse choir asked the members to search in their own experience for what "God" meant to each of them before they again spoke the phrase, "This great God" in Johnson's "The Creation." When their thought-enriched and uninhibited expression rang out in their next performance, the composure of many of those listening was so affected that they were reduced to tears.

When such a "moment" does happen in the verse-choir experience it has the unique capacity of striking every member simultaneously, gaining momentum by their mutual reinforcement. This high-level experience is further enlarged when the *hearers add their impulse* to the circular response, as occurred in the synagogue when the congregation responded to the trials of Job. This becomes worship of a high order.

As a further enrichment, this sharpening of sensitivity has a carry-over into living by causing the person to be more aware of the now-important "little" things: such as a frantically busy humming bird; the "popped-open" eyes of a baby and the fathomless smile of a young mother; the colors of a sunset on the desert, or behind a city's skyline; the gray softness of a rainy day—or the poorly hidden hurt of a fellow human being.

This awakening to the people around us and sensitivity to their inner needs is the lasting proof and ongoing nature of the worship-quality of the experience gained by participating in a religious-oriented verse choir.

Although this awakening does not fully define the "abundant life," it is an exercise in that quality of living and can lead to its fuller realization.

All of the following materials in this chapter will not be analyzed as fully nor carry the explanations and paraphrasing that we have given the *Twenty-Third Psalm.* This seemingly simple product of the mind and heart of a young shepherd boy is so rich and deep that it must have this much, and should have more, such treatment.

Analysis of The Twenty-Third Psalm

This deeply-moving psalm is also a great poem, but it has lived through the centuries not because David set about to write a lasting piece of literature but because he was *reporting an experience* that was happening between himself and his God.

True, the writing is striking in its simplicity, beautiful in its analogies and metaphors, and powerful in its flowing rhythm—but it is striking, beautiful, and powerful because of the vital experiences it is reporting. The secret of its interpretation lies in the degree to which each individual can vicariously participate in this experience.

"The *Lord* is *my* shepherd—"
> (*"I have abiding faith in God; and therefore—"*)
"I shall not want."
> (*"Nothing that I really need will be denied me. Perhaps some whims or luxuries will not come about but those staples that fulfill the basic physical, emotional and spiritual needs will be given me."*)

"He maketh me to lie down in green pastures—"
>
> (*He provides a pleasant place of beauty; but also a field of enticing adventure to challenge and expand my whole being. For instance: a university campus, a neighborhood, an athletic field, a compatible work environment—all the enriching opportunities of life. Green pastures are also to live in.*)

"He leadeth me beside the still waters—"
>
> (*He keeps me from "going in over my head before I've learned to swim." Palestinian shepherds dug pools at the side of the swift-flowing Jordan River so the water would back up into them and provide safe drinking places, protecting their charges from undue exposure to forces beyond their ability to master.*)

"He restoreth my soul!"
>
> (*This completes the build from the two preceding lines.*)
>
> (*David's realizing this deeply satisfying state of being is the climax of this first nuance and the purpose of all that has preceded. Indeed, the depth of this realization determines the quality of all that follows in the poem. Since David's time we have tried to define this quality of existence in such terms as "inner peace," "inner awareness," "complete fulfillment," "knitting up the raveled sleeve of care," "at peace with God and man," "the whole man," "integrated personality," "feeling good clear through,"—and even the theatre bromide, "getting fat around the nerves," points in this direction. By any name, we know when it happens.*)

"He leadeth me in the paths of righteousness for His name's sake"
>
> (*"He does all this in the hope that I will follow the direction He has set and bring credit to His name."*)

"Yea, though I walk through the valley of the shadow of death, I will fear no evil — —"

> *(For Palestinian shepherds and sheep this valley was a reality where a misstep could mean a 1,500-foot fall. Today it may mean a dark alley, lying on a hospital bed with sinking strength, or engaging in combat. Ask your people to silently interject the question "WHY?" to stiffen the meaning of the next.)*

"— — for *Thou* art with me; *Thy* rod and *Thy* staff, *they* comfort me." *("It is not just any old rod and staff, for God's omnipotence renders them utterly supportive and comforting!")*

"Thou preparest a table before me in the presence of mine enemies" *(How good it is to hear someone speak well of you in a company of friends—but how ever-so-much sweeter it would be if when threatened by an antagonistic, hateful crowd to hear a brave soul shout out: "Wait just a minute; this is a friend of mine, and you've got him all wrong!")*

"Thou anointest my head with oil."

> *(A welcome creature comfort in the hot, dry desert—now raised to the level of a major, culminating spiritual blessing.)*

"My cup runneth over!"

> *(This is to be able to contain no more joy, to be satiated. In Betty Smith's warm-hearted novel,* A Tree Grows in Brooklyn, *there is a moment when little Francie's father helps her change to a better school. When the sensitive little girl asks him to "bend down" she whispers, "My cup runneth over," the only words that could describe the over-fullness of her heart.)*

"Surely—" *(This word is basic to the very heart of the experience. If the God-man relationship is solid there will be no need to say this emphatically, to*

"sell" the idea. A simple, firm, confident state-
ment will result, and will be enough.)
"—goodness and mercy shall follow me all the days of
my life— —" *(The secret here is in the word "follow."*
Perhaps David meant that these two graces
would hover over him as a bountiful bonus or
glorious aura to reward the remainder of his
days.
However, it seems more in keeping with the un-
dercurrent of the poem for him to have meant
this larger thought: that the union he felt with
God would motivate him to acts of goodness
and mercy that would "follow" after him as a
benevolent wake to benefit others his life had
touched.)
"And I will dwell, in the house of the Lord—"
(We exist in a shack, live in a decently fur-
nished house—but we dwell in an environment
of love and harmony and inspiration. How
much more and more there will be in "the
House of the Lord"!)
"Forever." *("Without end.——Without end!!")*

When the *Twenty-Third Psalm* was first presented to a
heterogeneous choir of 160 in our state-supported university it needed more than the usual explanation and
paraphrasing to gain the involvement of the entire
group.

Those students who accepted the Judeo-Christian culture experienced no problem. But there were students
embracing Oriental and Moslem religions who, even
though they tried hard, could give little more than technical accuracy, a kind of sterile lip service, to this great
statement of faith that so urgently calls for the whole
person to be involved in it.

So the director suggested, "When you say 'The Lord'

will you please hold in your mind YOUR concept of the Supreme Being of the Universe and the Guiding Principle of your life?"

This made room for the religions of the Near and Far East, for the Great Spirit of the two American Indians members, indeed for all religions with a well-defined Godhead. And it also provided a comfortable atmosphere for those philosophers and scientists who can recognize only an ambiguous Super-Intelligence. Most importantly, it challenged everyone to approach his "Lord" in an act of spoken faith.

Did you think we disregarded the agnostics, the atheists, and those who may have accepted other Gods, such as money, personal self-sufficiency, social status, or political ideologies? Not at all. We mentioned each of these in turn and recognized them as possible guiding forces that control some individuals—and suggested that they, too, be held in mind by those who may have chosen them so that they might be given a chance to prove their validity as the psalm progressed.

In addition to being central to Christ's teachings, the *Beatitudes* comprise a moving and rhythmical composition, which divides itself naturally into three distinct divisions. These include verses 1-9, 10-12, and 13-16.

In the first of these, the men's and women's sections are used, after the introduction, to bring into bolder relief the rise-and-fall aspect of the two-part verses. This antiphonal effect follows a general pattern; using the women to speak the quiet portions, and the men to give the stronger, more positive "answers."

The principal source of variety within this pattern will be the choir's responsiveness to the inner meanings, though the sheer difference in the length of the lines will add to listening interest.

THE BEATITUDES
The King James Version

All   And seeing the multitudes, He went up into a mountain: and when He was set, His disciples came unto Him; and He opened His mouth, and taught them, saying:

W   Blessed are the poor in spirit: (M) for theirs is the kingdom of heaven.

W   Blessed are they that mourn: (M) for they shall be comforted.

W   Blessed are the meek: (M) for they shall inherit the earth.

W   Blessed are they which do hunger and thirst after righteousness: (M) for they shall be filled.

W   Blessed are the merciful: (M) for they shall obtain mercy.

W   Blessed are the pure in heart: (M) for they shall see God.

W   Blessed are the peacemakers: (M) for they shall be called the children of God.

(These next three verses call for a more vigorous vocal response because they represent the dramatic struggle that ensues when one begins to live Christ's teachings, so we use the entire choir. There is also a natural build here, culminating in the phrase: "great is your reward.")

All   Blessed are they which are persecuted for righteousness' sake: for their's is the kingdom of heaven.

Blessed are ye, when men shall revile you, and persecute you, and shall say all manner of evil

against you falsely, for My sake. Rejoice and be ex-
ceeding glad: for great is your reward in heaven-
—for so persecuted they the prophets which were
before you.

*(These last four verses deal with specific analogies and gentle
importunings to remain faithful and vital. The order of the
men and women is now reversed to better express the thoughts
assigned to each.)*

M   Ye are the salt of the earth: but if the salt have lost
it's savour, wherewith shall it be salted?

W   *(As if they were "dusting off" their hands. Lightly and
faster.)*
It is henceforth good for nothing, but to be cast
out, and to be trodden under foot of men.

M   Ye are the light of the world. A city that is set on a
hill cannot be hid. Neither do men light a candle,
and put it under a bushel—

W   *(Not reproachfully, but brightly. "Getting the idea.")*
But on a candlestick; and it giveth light to all that
are in the house!

All   *(With a sense of joyous anticipation.)* Let Your light so
shine before men, that they may see your good
works, and glorify Your Father which is in heaven.

Just as the *Beatitudes* are modern in their thought, so
is Saint Francis of Assissi's prayer entitled:

ETERNAL LIFE

*(This suggested treatment gives the Women the second, or
"answering" part of each line to represent the compassionate,
healing element. The last passage is assigned to the entire choir
to demonstrate their unity resulting from the insight they all
have received.)*

All   Lord, make me an instrument of Thy peace!
      Where   there   is
      hatred—(W) let me
      sow love.   *(Emerging from the whole choir.)*

M   Where there is injury—(W) pardon.
M   Where there is doubt—(W) faith.
M   Where there is despair—(W) hope.
M   Where there is darkness—(W) light.
M   Where there is sadness—(W) joy.

All   Oh Divine Master, grant that I may not so much
      seek
      To be consoled—as to console,
      To be understood—as to understand,
      To be loved—as to love;
      For it is in giving—that we receive;
      It is in pardoning—that we are pardoned;
      It is in dying—that we are born to eternal life.

   When we were preparing our "Lincoln Record" we
searched for the poem that best represented each part
of the nation during the Civil War, and chose the lyrics
of these two songs, which we tied together with a
"bridge."
   The treatment of *Dixie* is prompted by the indomina-
ble spirit found in the Southern States and it is properly
concluded by a dignified, slow-measured singing of the
final stanza. This was inspired by the way it is sung at
the close of the recorded program that accompanies the
telling of the Battle of Atlanta at the Cyclorama in Atlanta, Georgia.

Strangely, *The Battle Hymn of the Republic* borrows its melody from the southern spiritual *Hallelujah;* and *Dixie* was written by Daniel Emmett, an Ohio entertainer. Together they make an impressive unit for any church-oriented program, or for one that commemorates Memorial Day or another national holiday. These lyrics use several new techniques, which, when mastered, will add a unique and intriguing quality to their performance.

Their arrangement is for a Men-Women organization with a guitar and/or harmonica accompaniment to set the rhythm, provide solo "spikes" and to guide the choir through the changes in spirit—and melody.

A contrapuntal Arrangement of THE BATTLE HYMN
  OF THE REPUBLIC by Julia Ward Howe
     and DIXIE by Daniel Decatur Emmett

(The guitar sets a vibrant, definite "marching" rhythm indicated in the first stanza by italics on the dominant beat. This rhythm continues, with tempo variations, under and up throughout both songs as directed. The words are given to set this rhythm. It begins on the up-beat.)

Guitar	Mine *eyes* have *seen* the *glo*ry *of* the *coming* *of* the *Lord;*
	He is *tram*pling *out* the *vin*tage *where* the *grapes* of *wrath* are *stored;*
M	*(Tramp in rhythm, continues also under stanzas 1, 2, 3, and 5. Softly at first.)*
	He hath *loosed* the *fate*ful *light*ning *of* His *terrible* swift *sword; His truth is marching on* (M) tramp, tramp, tramp *(Continuing as a transition between stanzas.)*
W Sing	Glory, glory, hallelujah; Glory, glory hallelujah

	Glory, glory, hallelujah; His truth is march-ing on. (M) tramp, tramp, tramp
W Speak	Mine eyes have seen the glory of the com-ing of the Lord;
	He is trampling out the vintage where the grapes of wrath are stored;
(Increase	He hath loosed the fateful lightning of His
the in-	terrible swift sword;
tensity	His truth is marching on. (M) tramp,
through	tramp *(only two)*
these	I have seen Him in the watch-fires of a
three	hundred circling camps;
stanzas.)	They have builded Him an altar in the evening dews and damps;
	I can read His righteous sentence by the dim and flaring lamps;
	His day is marching on. (M) tramp, tramp
	I have read a fiery gospel writ in bur-nished rows of steel;
	"As ye deal with My contemners, so with you My grace shall deal;"
	Let the hero, born of woman, crush the serpent with his heel,
	Since God is marching on. (M) tramp, tramp
W Sing	Glory, glory hallelujah—*(Begin on "sounded" and continue softly under Stanza Four.)*
M Speak	He has sounded forth the trumpet that shall never call retreat
	He is sifting out the hearts of men before His judgment seat;
	Oh, be swift, my soul, to answer Him; be jubilant, my feet,
	Our God is marching on. (M) tramp, tramp
W Speak	In the beauty of the lilies Christ was born

across
    the sea   *(Softly, then strong build.)*
With a glory in His bosom that transfigures
you and
    me;
As He died to make men holy, let us die to
make men free,
While God is marching on. (M) tramp,
tramp, tramp   *(three again)*

(This crossover will work if both groups, singing simultaneously as marked by *, will keep the same rhythm as directed.)

All	Glory, glory, hallelujah; Glory, glory, hal-lelujah
*W	Den I *wish* I *was* in *Di*xie, Hoo*ray*! Hoo*ray*!
M	*Glo*ry, *Glo*ry, *hal*le *lu*-u jah
*W	In *Di*xie *Land* I'll *take* my *stand*, to *live* and *die* in *Di*xie;
M	*His* *truth* *is* *mar* *ching* *on*-n-n-*n*-n
All	Away, away, away down south in Dixie Away, away, away down south—in Dixie!

(Legend:	*(E) Echo—"Look away" for stanzas; "Away" for choruses.* *(CC) Echo—Two sharp hand-claps.)*
W Speak	*(Fast, with high spirit.)* I wish I was in de land ob cotton, Ol' times dar am not forgotten,
M (Echo)	Look away! (E) Look away! (E) Look away! (CC) Dixie Land! In Dixie Land whar I was born in, Early on one frosty mornin' Look away! (E) Look away! (E) Look away! (CC) Dixie Land!

All sing   *(Fast, bright. Guitar full up.)*
               Den I wish I was in Dixie, Hooray!
               Hooray!
               In Dixie Land I'll take my stand to lib and
               die in Dixie;
M (Echo)   Away, (E) away, (E) away down south in
               Dixie
               Away, (E) away, (E) away down sou————th,
               —In Dixie!
M speak   *(Gusty, high-spirited outdoor voice.)*
               Dar's buckwheat cakes an' Ingen batter,
               Makes you fat, or a little fatter;
M (Speak lines)
W *(Echo)*   Look away! (E) Look away! (E) Look away!
               (CC) Dixie Land!
               Den hoe it down an' scratch your grabble,
               To Die's land I'm bound to trabble,
               Look away! (E) Look away! (E) Look away!
               (CC) Dixie Land!

*(Pause; to set new mood of slow dignity, like a hymn. Guitar
full up.)*

All Sing   Den I wish I was in Dixie, Hooray-y,
               Hooray-y
               In Dixie Land I'll take my stand to lib an'
               die in Dixie;
M (Echo)   Away, (E) away, (E) away down south in
               Dixie
               Away, (E) away, (E) away down south in
               Dixie.

                   * * * * * * * * * * * *

   Before we leave this chapter we must take a closer
look at the wealth of potential verse-choir material in

James Weldon Johnson's *God's Trombones*. These seven sermons originated with the black preachers of the Old South. Even though many were unable to read the scriptures they somehow managed to divine their meanings and to present them in cogent terms. The sermons have been faithfully reconstructed by the author, who has given us our last clear chance to read these gems of elemental faith.

Johnson has captured the essence of each sermon, without using dialect, and has adapted his own free style to bring out its special beauty. His authoritative preface gives us an understanding of and respect for these preachers and their sermons. They are preceded by "Listen, Lord—A Prayer," which brings us the faith, sorrow, and hope of the inspired "Preacher-Man" through his transparent imagery.

The first sermon, "The Creation," introduces two refreshing ideas in telling its story. The first is that the light from which the universe was created originated in God's smile; and the second that He created man as a needed counterpart—because He was lonely. "The Prodigal Son" carries us all along on an empathic journey with the impatient younger brother as he travels headlong to Babylon—and back home again.

"Go Down Death—a Funeral Sermon" must be the gentlest writing in the language as Sister Caroline is carried to her own personal reward in "the icy arms of Death—but she didn't feel no chill." "Noah" opens in the Garden of Eden and uses great imagination, and economy, as it brilliantly continues with the story of the just and righteous Noah. And "The Crucifixion" must be the most poignant telling of Jesus' agony and victory, from Gesthemene to the Cross, as it achieves emotional catharsis for both the choir and listeners.

"Let My People Go" is the longest and perhaps most colorful of the seven, as it brings to life the people and events of the Exodus story; and "The Judgement Day" allows the preacher to make the maximum use of his trombone voice as he proclaims the prophesies of Earth's last day.

The unique quality of this short book, 54 pages, is that it can so adroitly touch the extremes of power and gentleness, of expanded imagination and understatement, and of despair's lowest depth to the highest point of hope. Indeed there is so much in these sermon-poems that a multivoiced verse choir can also "pull out all the stops" at its disposal in presenting them without fear of "getting ahead" of their content.

In addition to the great wealth of choral material found in scriptural writings the following suggestions should open up the near-limitless possibilities presented by other literature with religious overtones. A few such titles are offered here. Their varied and often-unexpected sources should open the floodgates to the great body of this material that is struck off from the everyday human need to relate to God.

1. "Carol: New Style" by Stephen Vincent Benét.
2. "Desiderata" by Max Ehrmann.
3. "God's World" by Edna St. Vincent Millay.
4. "Harvest Hymn," from *The Golden Threshold* by Sarojini Naidu.
5. "The Lamb" by William Blake.
6. "A Prayer" by John Drinkwater.
7. "A Prayer of Steel" by Carl Sandburg.
8. "The Prophet" by Kahlil Gibran.
9. "Ritual" by William Rose Benét.
10. "Second Inaugural Address" by Abraham Lincoln.

11. "Simon the Cyrenian Speaks," in *Anthology of American Verse* by Countee Cullen.
12. "The Teacher" by Leslie Pinkney Hill.
13. "The Vigil of Joseph" by Elsa Barker.
14. "When Peter Johnson Preached in the Old Church" by Vachel Lindsay.
15. "Wise Men" by Myra Scovel.

17
Looking Back
— and Forward

We have seen in this brief book how choral speaking grew from a natural means of communication by primitive peoples into a refined speech art as it progressed through history. As the people of each period made their impact on it, by adding phases that were important to them and discarding others no longer needed, we see that this willing vehicle was an ever-changing, living art that "met the present need." Its vitality is attested to by its longevity and by its bending to the demands made of it, still maintaining its own innate character.

Looking forward we can already see many new functions and disciplines making use of this art, some not fully but all to their particular advantage. When it is "given its head" it will lead us into new and not-yet-dreamed-of experiences that lie over the horizon, waiting to be realized and savored by those of us who first discover them.

List of 47 Poems with Full Text Arranged for Verse Choir

"Baby Horned Toad"—Dresser (New)
"Ballad of Glory Departed"—Campbell (New)
"Battle Hymn of the Republic, The"—Howe
"Beatitudes, The"—New Testament
"Bells, The"—Poe
"Cargoes"—Masefield
"Casey Jones"—Folk
"Chicago"—Sandburg
"Composed Upon Westminster Bridge"—Wordsworth
"Dixie"—Emmett
"Double Rainbow"—Campbell (New)
"Eternal Life"—St. Francis
"Farewell to the Steam Locomotive"—Original (New)
"For Whom the Bell Tolls"—Donne
"Gift Outright, The"—Frost (Abridged)
"Horse's Version of the Ride of Paul Revere, The"—Anonymous
"How Do I Love Thee"—Browning
"I Loved You, California"—Armour
"Invasion"—Dresser (New)
"Jabberwocky"—Carroll
"Lines from a Home for the Mentally Retarded"—Nelson
"Lion Hunt, The"—Folk
"Little Boy Blue"—Field
"Miracles"—Whitman
"Musical Trust, The"—Stevens
"Negro Speaks of Rivers, The"—Hughes
"New Colossus"—Lazarus
"Non-Controversial—Peanut Butter"—Tieri (New)

"Odyssey of Runyon Jones, The"—Corwin (Abridged)
"Pledge of Allegiance, The"
"Preamble to the Constitution, The"
"Sea Fever"—Masefield
"Sing, Then"—Campbell (New)
"Singing Bushes"—Dresser (New)
"Sky Child"—Dresser (New)
"Socratic"—Doolittle
"Sounds to Remember"—Original (New)
"Squaw Dance, The"—Sarett
"Tree Toad, The"—Riley
"Twenty-Third Psalm, The"—Old Testament
"Verse Choir is Nothing, I Guess, The"—Original (New)
"Whistle, Whistle, Old Wife"—Folk
"Why, God, Why?"—From *Fish*
"Wind Talk"—Dresser
"Windy Nights"—Stevenson
"Wynken, Blynken and Nod"—Field
"Your Dream is Nearer Than You Know"—Original (New)

Glossary of Terms

(A fuller treatment of these terms will be found in the index.)

ALEATORIC MUSIC—A new use of speech by musical groups

ANALYSIS—Searching for the full meaning of materials

ANTIPHONARY OF ST. GREGORY—Authoritative standard for the true chant

ARRANGING—Adapting materials to a particular verse choir

AUTHORITY—Firm sound of speech resulting from self-confidence

CENTRAL BREATHING—Optimal breathing for speech or singing

CHORAL SPEAKING—Any group speaking together simultaneously, with unity of thought or feeling.

COGNITIVE, AFFECTIVE, PSYCHO-MOTOR—Titles given the three realms of education

COMMUNICATION—Verbal and non-verbal

CONTINUANCE—(also quantity, voice presence)—Sufficiently prolonging a sound for clarity and meaning.

358

CREATIVE DRAMATICS—"Living out" stories and poems

DEMOCRACY—Full participation of all verse choir members in planning and rehearsing materials

DISCIPLINE—Adherence to principles of group speaking for greater freedom

DRAMA CHORŌS—A special and versatile type of verse choir

EUPHONIC—Quality of beauty in the sound of speech

FOLK (also traditional)—Materials evolving from a group, not one author

GREATEST COMMON DENOMINATOR (also central core, essence)—Intellectual and emotional meaning to which the greatest number of people can respond

GROUP SPEAKING—Synonym for choral speaking

JINGLES—Elementary poetry with prominent rhyme, meter, and mental picture recall

LIVING LITERATURE—Poetry and prose that evokes strong human response

ONE-GREAT-VOICE—Total sound created by a multiple-voiced group

ORCHESTRATED VOICES—Elements of a verse choir synchronized for optimal sound and meaning

OVERDRIVE—Underlying rhythm that is smooth, unobtrusive, and effortless

PARAPHRASING—Clarifying a meaning by restating it in a well-known context

SCHOLA CANTORUM—Pope Gregory's School for Singing

SHOUTING—Disorganized loud speech unsupported by proper breathing

SING-SONG—Too-strict an adherence to rhyme and meter, overshadowing the meaning

SINGULAR VALUES—Seemingly individually held concepts that may be shared by many

SPIKES—Sharply defined increases in power, enhancing the meaning

SPOKEN MUSICALITY—Semi-musical quality resulting from orchestrated voices, enhancing the meaning

STACCATO—Noisy speech lacking in continuance and emphasizing consonant sounds

TIMING—Synchronizing rhythm, phrasing, and tempo for optimal meaning

TOLERANCE—Recognizing and accepting the contribution of others

UNIVERSALITY—Quality of materials having the broadest greatest common denominator

VARIABLES—Elements of directing, analogous to controls in music

VERSE CHOIR—Organized speaking group using disciplines of speech arts to advantage.

VOICE QUALITY—Basis for verse-choir groupings. Characteristics of an individual voice

Bibliography

Abney, Louise, and Rowe, Grace. *Choral Speaking Arrangements for the Junior High*. Boston: Expression Co., 1939.
————.*Choral Speaking Arrangements for the Lower Grades*. Boston: Expression Co., 1937.
————.*Choral Speaking Arrangements for the Upper Grades*. Boston: Expression Co., 1937.

Adams, Florence, and McCarrick, Elizabeth. *High Days and Holidays*. New York: E. P. Dutton & Co., Inc., 1927.

Aleatoric Music for Symphonic Band [Catalogue]. San Francisco: Byron Sheet Music Service, 972 Mission St. 94103.
Alexander, A. L. (Comp.) *Poems that Touch the Heart*. New York: Garden City Publishing Co., 1956.
Anderson, Charles R. (Ed.) *Sidney Lanier—Poems and Poem Outlines*. (Centennial Edition) Baltimore: Johns Hopkins Press, 1945.
Anderson, Virgil A. *Training the Speaking Voice*. New York: Oxford University Press, 1961.
Ansorge, Elizabeth F., and Lucas, H. M. (Eds.). *Prose and Poetry of America*. New York: L. W. Singer Co., 1942.
Arbuthnot, May Hall. *Children and Books*. Chicago: Scott, Foresman, Co., 1957. Third Edition, 1964.

Armour, Richard. *Light Armour.* New York: McGraw-Hill, 1954.
———. *Writing Light Verse.* Revised Edition. Boston: The Writer, Inc., 1956.
———. "I Loved You, California." *Look* Magazine, 9-25-62.

Ashton, John. *Modern Street Ballads.* London: Chatto and Windus, 1888. Also Detroit: Singing Tree Press, 1968.

Austin, Mary C., and Mills, Queenie B. *The Sound of Poetry.* Boston: Allyn and Bacon, Inc., 1964.

Bacon, Wallace A. *The Art of Oral Interpretation.* New York: Holt, Rinehart and Winston, Inc., 1972.

Bahn, Eugene C., and Bahn, Margaret L. *A History of Oral Interpretation.* Minneapolis, Minn.: Burgess Publishing Company, 1970.

Barrows, Marjorie (Ed.). *Pulitzer Prize Poems.* New York: Random House, 1941.
———. *Read Aloud Poems Every Child Should Know.* Chicago: Rand McNally and Co., 1957.

Barrows, Sarah Tracy, and Hall, Katherine H. *Games and Jingles for Speech Development with Suggestions for Teachers.* Boston: Expression Co., 1936.

Barton, Clifford E. *Verse Choir in the Elementary School.* Darien, Conn.: Educational Publishing Corp., 1958.

Benét, Rosemary, and Stephen Vincent. *A Book of Americans.* New York: Holt, Rinehart and Winston, Inc., 1933.

Bible, The, Authorized Version

Boyd, L. M. "Personal Glimpses" (Pasternak incident quoted in Introduction). *Readers' Digest,* July, 1971.

Brown-Azarowicz, Marjory Frances. *A Handbook of Creative*

Choral Speaking. Minneapolis, Minn.: Burgess Publishing Co., 1970.

Brown, Helen A., and Heltman, Harry J. *Read Together Poems.* Vols. 1-6. New York: Harper and Row Publisher, Inc., 1950-51.
————. *Choral Readings for Fun and Recreation.* Philadelter Press, 1955.
————. *Choral Readings from the Bible.* Philadelphia: Westminster Press, 1956. Same author.)

Campbell, Rachel Harris. *Ballad of Glory Departed and Other Poems.* Fayetteville, Arkansas: Rose Dragon Press, 1972.

Carmer, Carl Lamson. *Deep South.* New York: Farrar and Rinehart Inc., 1930.

Chamberlain and Winn. *Tales and Trails.* Syracuse, New York: Iroquois Publishing Co., 1949.

Cheney, Sheldon. *The Theatre: 3000 Years of Drama, Acting and Stagecraft.* New York: Longman's, Green & Co., 1929.

Child, F. J. *The English and Scottish Popular Ballads.* Boston: Houghton, Mifflin Co., 1932.

Ciardi, John. *How Does a Poem Mean?* Boston: Houghton, Mifflin Co., 1959.

Coger, Leslie, and White, Melvin R. *Readers Theatre Handbook.* Glenview, Illinois: Scott, Foresman, Co., 1967.

Coleman, Alice, and Theobald, John R. *Introducing Poetry.* New York: Holt, Rinehart and Winston, 1964.

Corey, Orlin. *The Book of Job Arranged for Stage.* Cloverlot, Anchorage, Kentucky: The Children's Theatre Press, 1960.

Corwin, Norman. *Thirteen by Corwin*. New York: Holt, Rinehart and Winston, Inc., 1942.

Cox, John H. *Folk-Songs of the South*. Cambridge, Mass.: Harvard University Press, 1925.

Cullen, Countee. *On These I stand*. New York: Harper and Row, 1947.

Cummings, Edward Estlin. *Fifty Poems*. New York: Grossett and Dunlap, 1940.

Cunningham, Cornelius Carman. *Making Words Come Alive*. Dubuque, Iowa: William C. Brown Co., 1951.

————. *Literature as a Fine Art*. New York: Nelson and Son, 1941.

Dawson, Mildred A., and Choate, Alberta Mary. *How to Help a Child Appreciate Poetry*. Belmont, California: Fearon Publishers (Educ. Div. of Lear Siegler, Inc.), 1960.

Dickinson, Edward. *Music in the History of the Western Church*. New York: Charles Scribner & Sons, 1902.

Dr. Seuss. (Please see Geisel, Theodore Seuss.)

Dresser, Elizabeth T. Unpublished: "Singing Bushes," "Baby Horned Toad," "Wind Talk," "Invasion," "Sky Child," San Diego, California.

Drew, Elizabeth A. *Poetry–A Modern Guide to Its Understanding and Enjoyment*. New York: W. W. Norton & Co., Inc., 1959.

Dunning, Stephen; Leuders, Edward; and Smith, Hugh (compilers). *Reflections on a Gift of Watermelon Pickle and Other Modern Verse*. New York: Lothrop, Lee & Shepard Co., 1969.

Ehrmann, Max. *Poems of Max Ehrmann*. Boston: Crescendo Publishers, 1966.
———. "Desiderata." *New York Times,* 8-11-71.

Enfield, Gertrude. *Verse Choir Values and Techniques*. Boston, Mass.: Expression Co., 1937.

———. *Holiday Book for Verse Choirs*. Boston, Mass.: Expression Co., 1937.

Evans, Patricia. *Rimbles*. Garden City, New York: Doubleday and Co., Inc., 1961.

Field, Eugene. *Collected Poems*. New York: Charles Scribner's Sons, 1907.

Finley, Grace S. *Speech and Play*. Boston: Expression Co., 1940.

Frost, Robert. *Complete Poems of Robert Frost*. New York: Holt, Rinehart and Winston, 1962.

Frostic, Gwenn. *These Things are Ours*. Benzonia, Michigan: The Presscraft Papers, 1960.

Geiger, Don. *The Sound, Sense and Performance of Literature*. Chicago: Scott, Foresman Co., 1963.

Geisel, Theodore Seuss. *And To Think That I Saw It On Mulberry Street*. New York: The Vanguard Press, 1937.
———. *Horton Hatches the Egg*. New York: Random House, 1940.
———. *Yertle the Turtle*. New York: Random House, 1950.
———. *How the Grinch Stole Christmas*. New York: Random House, 1957.
———. *Beginner Books*. New York: Random House, 1957.
———. *Ten Apples Up On Top*. New York: Random House, 1961.
———. *Hop On Pop*. New York: Random House, 1963.

Gibran, Kahlil. *The Prophet.* New York: A. A. Knopf, 1923.
———. *Thoughts and Meditations.* New York: Bantam Books, 1968.

Gray, Poland P. *Songs and Ballads of the Maine Lumber Jacks.* Cambridge, Mass.: Harvard University Press, 1925.

Gullan, Marjorie. *Choral Speaking.* London, Methuen & Co., 1931.
———. *Spoken Poetry in the Schools.* London: Evans Bros., 1926.
———. *The Speech Choir: with American Poetry and English Ballads for Choral Reading.* New York: Harper and Bros., 1937.

Gullan, Marjorie, and Gurrey, Purcival. *Poetry Speaking for Children.* London: Methuen & Co., 1950.

Gullan, Marjorie, and Sansom, Clive. *The Poet Speaks.* London: Methuen & Co., Ltd., 1955.

Gummere, Francis B. *Old English Ballads.* New York: Russell and Russell, 1967.

Hamm, Agnes Curran. *Selections for Choral Speech.* Boston: Expression Co., 1935.

Harrington, Mildred P. *Our Holidays in Poetry.* New York: The H. W. Wilson Co., 1929.

Hazeltine, Alice I. *Year Around Poems for Children.* Nashville, Tenn.: Abingdon Press, 1956.

Heltman, Harry J., and Brown, Helen A. (Eds.). *Choral Readings for Teenage Worship and Inspiration.* Philadelphia: Westminster, 1959.

Hicks, Helen Gertrude. *The Reading Chorus.* New York: Noble and Noble, Inc., 1939.

Housman, Alfred Edward. *The Name and Nature of Poetry.* New York: McMillan Co., 1933.

Huffard, Grace. *My Poetry Book.* New York: Holt, Rinehart and Winston, 1956.

Hughes, Langston. *Selected Poems.* New York: Alfred A. Knopf, Inc., 1959.
———. *Poems from Black Africa.* Bloomington, Indiana: University Press, 1963.

Hughes, Rosalind. *Let's Enjoy Poetry.* Vol. 1. (grades K-3). Boston: Houghton Mifflin, Co., 1958.
———. *Let's Enjoy Poetry.* Vol. 2 (grades 4-6). Houghton Mifflin Co., 1961.

Johnson, Albert. *World Without End* [a play]. Boston: Walter Baker, 1935.
———. *Church Plays and How to Stage Them.* (This book includes Prof. Johnson's treatment of *Everyman.*) Philadelphia: United Church Press, 1966.

Johnson, James Weldon. *God's Trombones.* New York: The Viking Press, 1927.

Keefe, Mildred Jones, A.M. *Choric Interludes.* Boston, Mass.: Books for Libraries Press, 1942.

Keppie, Elizabeth. *The Teaching of Choric Speech.* Boston, Mass.: Expression Co., 1932.
———. *Choral Verse Speaking.* Boston: Expression Co., 1939.
———. *Speech Improvement through Choral Speaking.* Boston: Expression Co., 1942.

Kipling, Rudyard. *Rudyard Kipling's Verse* (Definitive Ed.). New York: Doubleday, Doran & Co., 1940.

Lanier, Sidney, *Poems of Sidney Lanier.* New York: Charles Scribner's Sons, 1929.

Lewis, Richard. *Miracles.* (Poems by Children of the English-Speaking World). New York: Simon and Schuster, 1966.

Liggett, Clayton E. *The Theatre Student—Concert Theatre.* New York: Richard Rosen Press, Inc., 1970.

McKuen, Rod. *Listen to the Warm.* New York: Random House, 1967.

MacLeish, Archibald. *The Collected Poems.* Cambridge, Mass.: The Riverside Press, 1962.

Mary Dorothy, Sister. *Choral Speaking.* New York: Educator's Washington Dispatch, 1950.

Masefield, John. *Salt Water Poems and Ballads.* New York: Macmillan Co., 1936. Copyright 1916.

———. *Poems.* (complete edition with recent poems). New York: Macmillan Co., 1941.

Masters, Edgar Lee. *Spoon River Anthology.* New York: Macmillan Co., 1914. Thirty-fourth printing—1971).

Matthews, Brander. *Poems of American Patriotism.* Freeport, New York: Books for Libraries Press, 1970.

Nelson, G. Lynn. *Lines from a Home for Mentally Retarded Children.* Lincoln, Nebraska: Capitol Association of Retarded Children Newsletter, July, 1972.

Noyes, Alfred. *Collected Poems.* New York: Frederick Stokes, 1913.
———. *Forty Singing Seamen and Other Poems.* New York: Frederick Stokes, 1930.

Peace, James R. *The Verse Choir in Secondary Schools.* M.A. Thesis on loan at San Diego State University Library.

Pieric, Marie. *Dramatic and Symbolic Elements in Gregorian Chant.* New York: Desclee Co., 1963.

Poe, Edgar Allan. *Collected Works.* New York: Charles Scribner's Sons: 1910.

Prather, Hugh. *I Touch the Earth, The Earth Touches Me.* Garden City, New York: Doubleday & Co. 1972.

Quiller-Couch, Sir Arthur Thomas. *The Oxford Book of English Verse.* New York: Oxford University Press, 1940.

Rasmussen, Carrie. *Choral Speaking for Speech Improvement* (elementary school). Boston, Mass.: Expression Co., 1939.
———. *Let's Say Poetry Together and Have Fun.* Vol. 1, Grades 1-3. Vol. 2, Grades 4-6. Minneapolis, Minn.: Burgess, 1963.

Raubicheck, Letitia. *Choral Speaking is Fun.* New York: Noble and Noble Publishers, Inc., 1955.

Rehner, Herbert Adrian. *The Dramatic Use of Choral Interpretation and Choral Speaking.* Chicago, Illinois: Bruce Howard Publishing House, 1951.

Robinson, Marion Parsons, and Thurston, Rozetta Lura. *Poetry Arranged for the Speaking Choir.* Boston: Expression Co., 1936.
———. *Poetry for Men to Speak Chorally.* Boston: Expression Co., 1939.

Roethke, Theodore. *The Collected Poems of Theodore Roethke.* Garden City, New York: Doubleday, Doran & Co., Inc., 1966.

Rosetti, Christina. *Poetical Works of Christina Georgina Rosetti.* New York: Macmillan Co., 1904.

Rumpf, Oscar J. *Cries from the Hurting Edges of the World; Choric Readings by Oscar J. Rumpf.* Richmond, Virginia: The John Knox Press, 1970.

Sarett, Alma J. (Ed.). *Covenant With Earth, A Selection from the Poems of Lew Sarett.* Copyrighted 1956 by Alma J. Sarett. Gainseville, Florida: University of Florida Press, 1956.

Sarett, Lew. *The Collected Poems of Lew Sarett.* New York: Henry Holt and Co., Inc., 1941.

Schauffler, Robert Haven. *The Days We Celebrate* (4 volumes). New York: Dodd, Mead & Co., 1940.

Schory, Harold F. *America Speaks.* Danville, Illinois: The Interstate Printers and Publishers, 1944.

Sechrist, Elizabeth Hough. *Christmas Everywhere* (Rev.) Boston: Books for Libraries Press, 1970.
———. *Poems for Red Letter Days.* Philadelphia: Macrae Smith, 1951.

Seuss, Dr. Please see Geisel, Theodore Seuss.

Shapiro, Karl Jay. *Selected Poems.* New York: Random House, 1968.

Sheldon, William D.; Lyons, Nellie; and Rouault, Polly. *The Reading of Poetry.* Boston, Rockleigh, New Jersey, Atlanta, Dallas and Belmont, California: Allyn & Bacon, Inc., 1966.

Smith, Marguerite. *Wings to Fly* (A Handbook of Choral Reading for English Teachers). Boston: Expression Co., 1938.

Stern, Philip Van Doren (Ed.). *The Life and Writings of Abraham Lincoln.* New York: The Modern Library, 1939. ("The Bear Hunt," page 289).

Stevenson, Burton (Ed.). *Poems of American History* (Rev. Ed.). New York: Books for Libraries Press, 1970, 1922.

Stevenson, Robert L. *Poems and Ballads by Robert Louis Stevenson.* New York: Charles Scribner's Sons, 1903.

Stuart, Jesse. *Man with a Bull-Tongue Plow.* New York: E. P. Dutton & Co., Inc., 1959.
———. *Jesse Stuart Reader.* New York: McGraw-Hill Book Co., Inc., 1963.

Sutton, Vida Ravenscroft. *Seeing and Hearing America; Studies in Spoken English and Group Speaking.* Boston: Expression Co., 1936.

Swann, Mona. *Many Voices* Book 1 for 8-12 yrs. Book II for older children. London, England: Harold Howe, Ltd., 1934.
———. *Wonderful World.* London: Macmillan Co., Ltd., 1955.
———. *An Approach to Choral Speech.* New York: St. Martin's Press, 1964.

Swenson, May. *To Mix with Time: New and Selected Poems.* New York: Charles Scribner's Sons, 1963.
———. *Poems to Solve.* New York: Scribner's, 1966.
———. *Half Sun, Half Sleep* (new poems). New York: Charles Scribner's Sons, 1967.
———. *Iconographs: Poems.* New York: Charles Scribner's Sons, 1970.

Switz, Theodore Maclean, and Johnston, Robert A. *Great Christian Plays and Selected Choral Readings.* Greenwich, Conn.: Seabury Press, 1956.

Taylor, Loren E. *Choral Drama* (children). Minneapolis: Burgess Publishing Co., 1965.

Teasdale, Sara. *The Collected Poems of Sara Teasdale.* New York: Macmillan Co., 1966.

Tieri, Sadie Lou. *Non-Controversial—Peanut Butter* (unpublished). Encinitas, California.

The Torah. (Coupled with the Prophets and Writings make up the Tanach that is the Hebrew Scriptures, commonly known as The Old Testament.)

Tower, Donald Maclean (Ed.); Russell, C. J.; and West, C. W. *The Prose and Poetry Series.* Syracuse, New York: W.L. Singer Co., 1941-45.

Untermeyer, Louis (Ed.). *Modern American and Modern British Poetry.* New York: Harcourt, Brace, Jovanovich, Inc., 1955.

Updike, John. *Verse.* Greenwich, Conn.: Fawcett Publishers Inc., 1965.

Van Doren, Mark (Ed.). *An Anthology of World Poetry.* New York: Albert and Charles Boni, 1928.

Van Riper, Charles, and Irwin, John V. *Voice and Articulation.* Englewood Cliffs, New Jersey: Prentice-Hall, Inc., 1958.

Wagenknecht, Edward (Ed.). *The Story of Jesus in the World's Literature.* New York: Creative Age Press, Inc., 1946.

Waring, Fred. *God's Trombones,* Poems by James Weldon Johnson, Music by Roy Ringwald. A Fred Waring Presentation. Delaware Water Gap, Pennsylvania: Shawnee Press, Inc..

White, A. M. G. (Ed.). *Anthology of Choral Readings.* New York: Girl Scouts, Inc., 1944.

Wynne, Annette. *All Through the Year.* New York: Frederick A. Stokes, 1932.

Three Choral-Speaking Records:

"The Book of Job." The Everyman Players. An Orlin and Irene Corey Production. Waco, Texas. Word Records, Inc.

"Heartbeats of a Nation." Poems By and About Lincoln. The San Diego State Verse Choir. Four historical ballads. The Sinnerman Trio. Available at the Aztec Shops, San Diego State University, San Diego, California.

"Speak Four Trio." Scriptural Speech-Drama. Presented by Paul Baker. Waco, Texas. Word Records, Inc.

Index